The Architectural History of Venice

Deborah Howard

B.T. Batsford Ltd, London

for Malcolm Longair

By the same author:
Jacopo Sansovino: Architecture and
Patronage in Renaissance Venice

First published 1980

First paperback edition 1987

© Deborah Howard 1980

ISBN 0 7134 1189 9

Filmset in 'Monophoto' Bembo by
Servis Filmsetting Ltd., Manchester
Printed in Great Britain by
The Bath Press, Avon
for the publishers, B. T. Batsford Ltd.
4 Fitzhardinge Street, London W1H 0AH

HALF TITLE
1 Land reclamation on
the northern fringes of
the city. Detail from
Jacopo de' Barbari's
bird's-eye-view map of
Venice, 1500

FRONTISPIECE
Palazzo Dolfin, later
Manin, by Sansovino,
begun 1538
(A.F.Kersting)

Contents

List of Illustrations and Plans   PAGE 7

Preface   PAGE 9

**Glossary of architectural terms and
    Venetian words**   PAGE 11

CHAPTER I   **Introduction**   PAGE 14
The origins of the city

CHAPTER II   **Byzantine**   PAGE 19
Byzantine religious architecture on the islands of Torcello and
Murano — Byzantine religious architecture in Venice itself —
Byzantine domestic architecture — Veneto-Byzantine
Palaces — Thirteenth-century transformations

CHAPTER III   **The Mediaeval City**   PAGE 46
Venice as an urban environment — Building materials and
techniques — Essential services and other amenities

CHAPTER IV   **Gothic**   PAGE 67
Gothic ecclesiastical architecture: the Mendicant orders —
Some smaller Gothic churches — Gothic secular
architecture — The Palazzo Ducale — The interior planning
of Venetian Gothic palaces — Stylistic transformations — The
first Gothic palaces — Gothic palaces in the fourteenth
century — Fifteenth-century Gothic palaces — The Venetian
Scuole

CHAPTER V   **Early Renaissance**   PAGE 102
The beginnings of the Renaissance in Venetian architecture —
Religious architecture in Early Renaissance Venice — Mauro
Codussi — Architecture during the Wars of the League of
Cambrai

CHAPTER VI   **'Roman' Renaissance**   PAGE 136

Sebastiano Serlio — Sansovino and Sanmicheli — Andrea
Palladio

CHAPTER VII   **Baroque**   PAGE 174

The beginnings of the Venetian Baroque — Baldassare
Longhena — Giuseppe Sardi

CHAPTER VIII   **Palladianism and Neoclassicism**   PAGE 193

Rossi and Tirali — Scalfarotto and Massari — Visentini and
Temanza — Giannantonio Selva

CHAPTER IX   **Venice since the Fall of the Republic**   PAGE 213

The Napoleonic Kingdom 1805–14 — The second and third
periods of Austrian rule (1814–48 and 1849–66) — Venice as
part of Italy: 1866–World War I — The rise of Fascism:
World War I–World War II — The post-War years

Notes to Chapters I–IX   PAGE 238

Bibliography   PAGE 249

Index   PAGE 256

List of Illustrations
and Plans

Note
All buildings illustrated are in Venice unless otherwise stated.

1   Land reclamation on the northern fringes of the city. Detail from Jacopo de' Barbari's bird's-eye-view map of Venice, 1500
2   Torcello Cathedral and church of Santa Fosca
3   Torcello Cathedral, interior
4   Santi Maria e Donato, Murano
5   San Giacomo di Rialto
6   Basilica of San Marco, interior
7   'The arrival of the body of Saint Mark in A.D. 829' thirteenth-century mosaic above the Porta Sant'Alippio, Basilica of San Marco
8   North-south cross section of the Basilica of San Marco
9   Basilica of San Marco, view from the Piazzetta
10 Gentile Bellini: 'Procession in Piazza San Marco', Accademia Gallery, Venice
11 Remains of house belonging to Marco Polo's family, Corte Seconda del Milion
12 Palazzo Loredan and Palazzo Farsetti
13 Fondaco dei Turchi; appearance before nineteenth-century restoration
14 Fondaco dei Turchi, present state
15 Thirteenth-century house in Salizzada San Lio
16 Palazzo Donà
17 Ca' da Mosto, later Osteria del Leon Bianco
18 Plan of Venice, *c*.1346, from the *Cronaca Magna*
19 Vittore Carpaccio: 'Miracle of the True Cross', Accademia Gallery, Venice
20 Stone bridge near San Felice
21 Campo San Polo, with former canal along the east side. Detail from Jacopo de' Barbari's bird's-eye-view map of Venice, 1500
22 View of the Ghetto from outside
23 Calle del Paradiso
24 Suburban villas on the Giudecca. Detail from Jacopo de' Barbari's bird's-eye-view map of Venice, 1500
25 Antonio da Canal, called Canaletto: 'The Stonemason's Yard', National Gallery, London
26 Vittore Carpaccio: 'The Dream of Saint Ursula', Accademia Gallery, Venice
27 Scala del Bovolo, Palazzo Contarini, San Luca
28 Palazzo Centani, San Tomà, courtyard
29 Vittore Carpaccio, 'The Courtesans', Museo Correr, Venice
30 The Scuola Grande di San Marco and Santi Giovanni e Paolo
31 Santi Giovanni e Paolo, interior
32 Santa Maria Gloriosa dei Frari
33 Santa Maria Gloriosa dei Frari, interior
34 Santo Stefano, interior
35 San Giovanni in Bragora
36 Madonna dell'Orto
37 Palazzo Ducale
38 Ruskin's 'orders' of Venetian-Gothic arches, from *The Stones of Venice*
39 Palazzo Ducale, Sala del Maggior Consiglio
40 Palazzo Priuli-Bon, San Stae
41 Palazzo Priuli, San Severo
42 Ca' d'Oro
43 The two Giustiniani palaces and Ca' Foscari
44 Palazzo Contarini-Fasan
45 Palazzo Pisani-Moretta
46 Scuola Vecchia della Misericordia
47 Scuola dei Calegheri
48 Porta dell'Arsenale
49 Ca' del Duca, San Samuele
50 'House in a Marshy Place', from Filarete's treatise on architecture
51 Palazzo Dario
52 Palazzo Ducale, courtyard
53 Palazzo Ducale, Scala dei Giganti
54 San Giobbe, interior
55 Santa Maria dei Miracoli
56 San Michele in Isola
57 San Pietro di Castello
58 Santa Maria Formosa
59 Santa Maria Formosa, interior
60 San Giovanni Crisostomo, interior
61 Scuola Grande di San Giovanni Evangelista, staircase
62 Palazzo Vendramin-Calergi, formerly Loredan
63 Piazza San Marco. Detail from Jacopo de' Barbari's bird's-eye-view map of Venice, 1500
64 Torre dell'Orologio, Piazza San Marco
65 Procuratie Vecchie, Piazza San Marco
66 Rialto market, before the fire of 1514. Detail from Jacopo de' Barbari's bird's-eye-view map of Venice, 1500

67   Scuola Grande di San Rocco
68   Scuola Grande di San Rocco, Sala del Capitolo
69   Venetian palace façade, from Serlio's treatise on architecture
70   Fortezza di Sant'Andrea
71   The Venetian Zecca, or mint
72   'Il Volo del Turco', anonymous woodcut
73   The Zecca and the Library of Saint Mark's
74   Jost Amman: 'The Procession for the Doge's Marriage with the Sea', woodcut
75   Piazza San Marco, view towards the Basilica
76   Library of Saint Mark's
77   Loggetta at the foot of the Campanile
78   Fabbriche Nuove di Rialto
79   Palazzo Dolfin, later Manin (frontispiece)
80   Palazzo Corner, San Maurizio
81   Palazzo Grimani, San Luca
82   San Francesco della Vigna, interior
83   Section of the church of the Incurabili
84   Andrea Palladio's project for the Convento della Carità
85   East wing of the cloister of the Convento della Carità
86   San Francesco della Vigna, façade
87   San Giorgio Maggiore
88   San Giorgio Maggiore, interior
89   Church of the Redentore
90   Redentore, façade
91   Redentore, interior
92   Palazzo Balbi
93   Santa Maria della Salute
94   Santa Maria della Salute, interior
95   Monastery of San Giorgio Maggiore, staircase
96   Palazzo Pesaro
97   Ca' Rezzonico, formerly Bon
98   San Salvatore and Scuola Grande di San Teodoro, engraving by Carlevaris
99   Santa Maria degli Scalzi, façade
100   Santa Maria del Giglio, façade
101   San Moisè, façade
102   San Stae, façade project by Giacomo Gaspari
103   San Stae, façade
104   Palazzo Corner della Regina
105   San Nicolò da Tolentino
106   San Simeon Piccolo
107   Santa Maria del Rosario, called the Gesuati
108   Gesuati, interior
109   Massari's design for the new church and hospital of the Pietà
110   Santa Maria della Pietà, interior
111   Palazzo Grassi
112   Palazzo Grassi, courtyard
113   Palazzo Civran
114   Church of the Maddalena
115   Gardener's house in the garden of Palazzo Zenobio
116   Teatro la Fenice

117   Teatro la Fenice, auditorium
118   Ala Napoleonica, Piazza San Marco
119   San Maurizio
120   Lighthouse tower at San Giorgio Maggiore
121   Caffè Florian, Piazza San Marco
122   Corpo di Guardia, Arsenal
123   Coffee-house in the Giardini Reali
124   Rio Terà di Sant'Agnese
125   Ponte di Ghetto Nuovo
126   Via 22 Marzo
127   Mulino Stucky
128   Albergo Excelsior, Lido
129   'Casa de Maria', Giudecca
130   Palace in the Bacino Orseolo
131   Casa Salviati
132   Casa del Farmacista, Lido
133   Fire Station on the Rio di Ca' Foscari
134   Palazzo del Casinò, Lido
135   'Masieri Memorial House', unexecuted project by Frank Lloyd Wright
136   Stazione di Santa Lucia
137   Headquarters of the Società Adriatica di Elettricità
138   Cassa di Risparmio di Venezia, Campo Manin
139   Model for the civic hospital at Cannaregio, by Le Corbusier

Plans and maps

Map of upper Adriatic region   *page 10*
Map of Venice   *page 18*
Torcello Cathedral, and remains of baptistery   *page 21*
Santa Fosca, Torcello   *page 23*
San Giacomo di Rialto   *page 26*
Basilica of San Marco   *page 28*
Ca' Loredan and Ca' Farsetti   *page 41*
Santi Giovanni e Paolo   *page 71*
Palazzo Ducale   *page 80*
Ca' Foscari and Palazzi Giustiniani   *page 86*
Santa Maria Formosa   *page 119*
San Salvatore   *page 130*
Scuola Grande di San Rocco   *page 135*
Fortezza di Sant'Andrea   *page 142*
Library of Saint Mark   *page 147*
Piazza San Marco   *page 148*
Palazzo Grimani   *page 156*
San Francesco della Vigna   *page 159*
Church of the Incurabili hospital   *page 160*
San Giorgio Maggiore   *page 166*
Church of the Redentore   *page 171*
Hospital of the Mendicanti   *page 175*
Santa Maria della Salute   *page 183*
Ca' Rezzonico   *page 187*
Palazzo Corner della Regina   *page 197*
Santa Maria della Pietà   *page 202*
Teatro la Fenice   *page 210*

Preface

Most writers on Venetian art fall into one of two categories – those who appear seldom to have been to Venice, and those who seem never to have been anywhere else. I have tried to avoid both these pitfalls, but I admit that I would never have undertaken to write this book but for my own great affection for the city. Indeed, I like to think of Venice as my second home. The scope of this book has been restricted to Venice itself, rather than the whole of the Veneto, in order to keep the book to a manageable length.

I am grateful to Michael Stephenson who first had the idea for this book, and to his successor as Editor, Paula Shea, whose excellent combination of toughness and understanding has sustained me through the various stages of preparation.

I should like to thank the directors and staff of the following archives and libraries for their assistance and co-operation during the preparation of the manuscript: Biblioteca Marciana, Venice; Biblioteca Correr, Venice; Biblioteca della Fondazione Cini, Venice; Archivio di Stato, Venice; University Library, Cambridge; library of the Department of Architecture and History of Art, Cambridge; Marquand Library, Princeton; library of the Institute for Advanced Study, Princeton; and the libraries of the Warburg and Courtauld Institutes, London.

Among the friends and colleagues who have generously shared their ideas and helped me to sort out individual problems I should mention in particular Adolfo Bernardello, Miklos and Serena Boskovits, Bruce Boucher, Susan Connell, Jane Glover, Professor Michelangelo Muraro, David and Ellen Rosand, and Juergen and Anne Schulz. I owe a continuing debt to Howard Burns, who first introduced me to Italian architecture as an undergraduate, and who has provided inspiration and guidance ever since. Warm thanks are due to Francesco and Maria Grazia Bertola for their generous hospitality in Venice.

I should like to express my deep gratitude to A.F. Kersting and Sarah Quill, who have taken most of the photographs for this book, and who have both gone to great lengths to satisfy the most awkward requirements. Bertl Gaye took the photograph of me on the backflap of the jacket. I am grateful to Linda Auerbach, Paula Bozzay, Louise Cooper, Molly Jones and Denise Newman, who have helped with typing the manuscript at various times.

My two children, Mark and Sarah, have been far more tolerant and co-operative than one could possibly expect of them at such a young age (the book was started on Mark's first birthday and completed shortly before

Sarah's first birthday). I owe a great deal to Janet Titley and the Ladybird Day Nursery at Fenstanton for providing such happy, homely environments for them while much of the work was done. My husband, Malcolm Longair, has given up countless days of his very precious time to babysitting, reading the various drafts of the text, listening to my ideas, and helping to prepare maps and plans. Without his unwavering support and encouragement this book would never have been started, let alone completed. My debt to him is immeasurable.

Note

Unless otherwise stated, all plans are taken from L. Cicognara, A. Diedo and G. Selva, 'Le fabbriche e i monumenti cospicue di Venezia', 2 vols., Venice 1838–40.

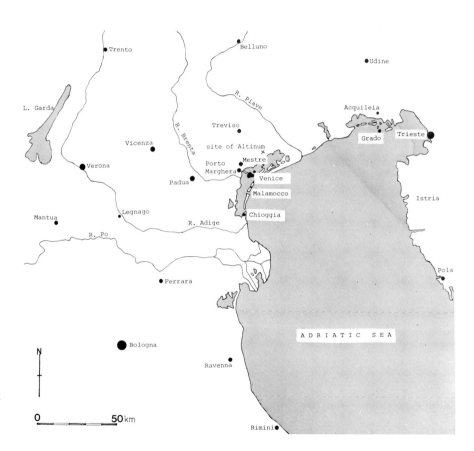

Map of the Upper Adriatic region showing places mentioned in the text

Glossary of architectural terms and Venetian words

Aedicule   the framing of a door, window or other opening with columns supporting an **Entablature** or **Pediment**

Albergo   originally the whole building of a Venetian *Scuola*; later restricted to the small meeting room on the upper floor

Altana   wooden platform on the roof of a Venetian house

Androne   large hall on the ground floor of a Venetian palace or *Scuola*

Apse   a vaulted semi-circular or polygonal recess, usually at the end of a **Chancel** or chapel

Atrium   originally the inner, open-air court of a Roman house; later a covered entrance hall

Balustrade   a row of short pillars topped by a railing, e.g. surrounding a balcony

Baptistery   a chapel in or near a church, where baptisms are carried out

Barrel Vault   (also called tunnel vault) a continuous semi-circular vaulted roof

Basket Capital   a **Capital** decorated with carving made to resemble a wicker basket

Bastion   a projection at the angle of a fortification, from which the adjoining walls can be defended by covering fire

Bay   the division of a wall between two columns, piers or buttresses

Biforate Window   a window divided vertically by a column to form two separate, arched openings

Blind Arcade   a purely decorative arcade attached to a wall surface

Calle   in Venice, a narrow street or alley

Campanile   a bell tower

Capital   the head of a column or pillar

Casa Fondaco   a characteristic type of early Veneto-Byzantine merchant's family-palace, with two superimposed waterfront arcades flanked by corner towers

Casemate   a vaulted room within the walls of a fortress, with openings for firing and lookout

Chancel   section at the east end of a church containing the main altar and reserved for the clergy and choir

Clerestory   the upper walls of the nave of a church, pierced by windows

Composite   one of the **Orders** of classical architecture, combining features of the **Ionic** and **Corinthian** orders

Corbel   a block projecting from a wall and supporting a beam or the base of an arch

Corinthian   one of the five **Orders** of classical architecture, characterized by a **Capital** decorated with leafy ornament

Cornice   the projecting section at the top of an **Entablature**

Crenellation   defensive rooftop parapet with alternating raised elements and spaces

Crocket   carved ornament, usually leaf shaped, projecting from the sides of a Gothic pinnacle

Cupola   a dome, usually fairly small in size

Cusp   the point at the meeting of two curves, especially in Gothic tracery

Dentilled Moulding   a row of small square blocks decorating the underside of a **Cornice**

Diaper Pattern   type of wall decoration composed of adjoining diamond shapes

Dog-toothed Moulding   a type of zigzag carved stone ornament found in Byzantine and Romanesque architecture

Doric   one of the classical **Orders**, characterized by a simple **Capital** without leafy ornament or **Volutes**, its **Frieze** generally decorated with **Triglyphs** and **Metopes**

Entablature   the uppermost part of a classical **Order**, consisting of the whole horizontal section supported by the columns or pillars

Exedra   a curved or rectangular recess in a wall surface

Extrados   the upper curve of an arch

Faubourg   a suburb or quarter outside the walls of a mediaeval city

Fondaco   in Venice a trading post or foreign merchants' centre; see also *Casa Fondaco*

Fondamenta   a waterside street in Venice

Four-light Window   a window consisting of four adjoining upright arched sections

Frieze   horizontal band, either plain or decorated, along the centre of an **Entablature**

Greek Cross   a cross with all four arms of equal length

Iconostasis   a screen in Byzantine churches, separating the **Chancel** from the nave

Intrados   the inner rim of an arch

Ionic   one of the classical **Orders**, with its **Capital** decorated by **Volutes**

Lancet   a slender, pointed-arched window

Lantern   a small rooftop turret with windows all around it

Lintel   a horizontal beam or stone bridging the top of a door or window opening

Lunette   a semi-circular window or area of wall surface

Machicolation   a projecting gallery round the top of a mediaeval fortification, from which missiles etc. could be dropped on invaders

Metope   the square space between two **Triglyphs** in a **Doric Frieze**

Mezzanine   a low storey between two higher ones

Narthex   separate section at the west end of the nave of a Byzantine church

Oculus   a circular window

(the) Orders   the classical 'language' of architecture. The five main orders are the **Doric**, **Ionic** and **Corinthian** orders, all of Greek origin, and the Tuscan and **Composite**, of Roman origin. Each of these has its own characteristic proportions and decorative details. When the orders are superimposed, the Doric or Tuscan is normally the lowest in the sequence, followed by the Ionic, Corinthian and Composite. The columns or pillars of each order are slightly shorter and narrower than the one below.

Ogee Arch   a type of Gothic arch in which the convex curves become concave towards the apex of the arch

Paston   a kind of Venetian flooring, composed of ground terracotta bricks and tiles set in cement and then polished

Pediment   a classical low-pitched gable over a door, window or façade, either triangular or **Segmental** in shape

Pendentive   the curved triangular area of wall surface above each pair of the arches supporting a dome

Piano Nobile   the principal living storey of an Italian palace, usually the first floor (in the English sense)

Pianterreno   the ground floor of an Italian building

Pier   a solid support or pillar, square or rectangular in section

Pilaster   a shallow **Pier** projecting only slightly from the wall

Piscina   an open space or street in Venice formerly occupied by water

Portego   the Venetian word for a **Portico**, also used to refer to the large central halls on the living storeys of Venetian palaces

Portico   an open colonnade, usually attached to a building on one side

Proto   the architect in charge of the upkeep or construction of the buildings and other real estate property belonging to a Venetian institution or public body

Quatrefoil   a type of Gothic tracery in the form of a four-lobed leaf or flower

Retrochoir   choir placed behind the high altar of a church

Rio   a Venetian canal

Rio Terà   a street in Venice formed by the infilling or covering of a canal

Riva   quayside street in Venice, literally the 'bank' of a waterway

Rustication   masonry made of stone blocks, often roughly hewn, or stucco decoration with the same appearance; because of its defensive connotations, normally found on the lower floors of buildings

Salizzada   a paved street in Venice

Salone   a large room in one of the main living storeys of an Italian building

Scuola   Venetian guild

Segmental Pediment   a **Pediment** with a curved upper edge

Serliana   a three-bay window with the central **Bay** arched and the two lower side portions topped by straight **Entablatures**; so called because of its use by Serlio; also known as a 'Palladian window'

Ship's-Keel Ceiling (or 'soffitto a carena di nave')   in the upper Adriatic region the wooden ceiling of a church or large meeting hall which in form and construction resembles an upturned ship

Six-Light Window   window consisting of six adjoining upright arched sections

Sottoportego   in Venice a portion of a street, usually arcaded on one side, passing underneath a building

Spandrel   the section of wall directly over the curve of an arch

Stilted Arch   an arch with vertical extensions ('stilts') between the **Capitals** and the springing of the arch

String Course   a continuous narrow horizontal band on a wall surface

Terrazzo   a type of Venetian flooring consisting of small coloured stones set in cement, with a highly polished surface

Thermal Window   a large **Lunette**-shaped window divided into three sections by two vertical supports

Tondo   a circular window or decorative panel

Traghetto   gondola ferry in Venice

Transepts   the arms of the cross in a **Cruciform** church

Trefoil   a type of Gothic tracery in the form of a three-lobed leaf or flower

Triglyphs   blocks with vertical grooves, alternating with the **Metopes** in a **Doric Frieze**

Volute   a scroll-like form in classical architecture, especially in the **Ionic Capital**

Zattere   literally 'rafts', the name given to one of the shores of Venice where many rafts were moored (*see map of the city*)

CHAPTER 1

Introduction

The long and eventful history of Venice is vividly depicted in documents and diaries, books and paintings. But most evocatively of all it is preserved in the fabric of the city itself. Like animal fossils petrified in layers of rock, so the life of the Venetian people through the ages is recorded in the architecture of the archipelago on which the city was founded.

From the beginning Venetians, on their malarial, swampy islands, lived differently from the inhabitants of mainland Italy. The individuality of their way of life was partly a response to the unusual physical environment, but this in turn moulded the Venetian character. On the Italian journey which he made only a decade before the Fall of the Venetian Republic in 1797, Goethe still sensed the special resilience of the Venetian people:

> This race did not seek refuge in these islands for fun, nor were those who joined later moved by chance; necessity taught them to find safety in the most unfavourable location. Later, however, this turned out to their greatest advantage and made them wise at a time when the whole northern world still lay in darkness; their increasing population and wealth were a logical consequence. Houses were crowded closer and closer together, sand and swamp transformed into solid pavement. . . . The place of street and square and promenade was taken by water. In consequence, the Venetian was bound to develop into a new kind of creature, and that is why, too, Venice can only be compared to itself.[1]★

The architecture of Venice is remarkable not only for its ingenious solutions to the technical problems of building in amphibious surroundings. It also embodies artistic achievements of the highest level. This book will con-centrate on the finest, most influential buildings, those which, most of all, reward one's attention with their subtlety and inventiveness, and offer the most lasting satisfaction. It is not a guide book, because excellent guide books to the city have been produced since the sixteenth century. Nor is it a description of what one might be tempted to call the typical buildings of each age, for these are, by definition, distinguished by their ordinariness. It is, rather, an attempt to pinpoint the highlights of artistic achievement, to explain how their designs evolved through the centuries, and to show how ideas brought in from outside Venice were transformed and incorporated into a peculiarly Venetian style of architecture. Conventional style labels – Byzantine, Gothic, Baroque and so on – will be used with their generally

★ Superscript numerals refer to the notes at the end of the book.

accepted, relatively loose meanings, since the exact definition of any artistic style is a controversial matter which would only distract attention from the main arguments of the book.

Because of our ignorance of the identity of most mediaeval architects, the early chapters will dwell on the actual monuments and the visual and historical changes of which they are evidence. It was in the Middle Ages that the characteristic Venetian building types evolved, to suit each particular function required by the city's way of life. From the Renaissance onwards, the emphasis of the book changes. The leaders of artistic innovation emerge as real people, their personalities recorded by their contemporaries, and their individuality enshrined in their buildings. It would obviously be impossible, in a book of this size, to include every architect who is known to have worked in Venice, or even all the buildings of the most outstanding architects, for a work of such comprehensiveness would need the labours of a lifetime and at least ten volumes, and might well lose sight of the summits of achievement. The author hopes, simply, that the supreme quality of the buildings themselves will justify this attempt to chronicle their evolution.

The origins of the city

The name *Venezia* was inherited from a province of the Roman Empire, called Venetia, which bordered the northern part of the Adriatic Sea. According to Francesco Sansovino, the author of the first full-scale printed guide book to Venice, published in 1581, *Venetia* was believed to derive from the Latin phrase *Veni etiam*; 'that is to say', he wrote, 'come back again, and again, for however many times you come you will always see new and beautiful things.'[2] It would be futile to quarrel with this engaging definition, for one could hardly object to its sentiment, however dubious the etymology.

Despite the Roman origin of the city's name, the islands on which Venice was to be founded were inhabited in Roman times only by small groups of fishermen, who supplemented their living producing salt by the evaporation of sea water. The nearest Roman town was the mainland settlement of Altinum. With the break up of the Roman Empire, the province of Venetia became part of the Eastern, or Byzantine, Empire, ruled from Constantinople. At this time the principal cities in the area were the ports of Aquileia and Ravenna.

The legendary date for the founding of the city of Venice is 25 March A.D. 421, at the time of the invasions of Attila the Hun. There seems to be little evidence to substantiate the myth of the foundation of Venice, dramatically commemorated in Verdi's early opera *Attila*. It was towards the end of the sixth century that the Barbarian or Lombard invasions on the mainland began to force the wealthier inhabitants of the province of Venetia to take refuge on the lagoon islands. There the refugees joined the native fishermen, preferring to remain under Byzantine domination rather than to submit to Barbarian rule. For the next two centuries the island of Rivo Alto, or Rialto, literally meaning high bank, which was eventually to form the nucleus of the city of

2 Torcello Cathedral, founded A.D. 639, and church of Santa Fosca, eleventh to twelfth centuries (*Sarah Quill*)

Venice itself, remained a centre of little significance.

In A.D. 697 the lagoon settlements were made an independent military unit under a *dux*, or doge. The local administrative centre was at first Ravenna, soon to be captured by the Lombard invaders. The Doge then moved to Malamocco, situated on one of the *lidi*, the long sandy islands which enclose the lagoon. The chief threat to the existence of the Venetian state at the outset was the invasion by Charlemagne's son Pépin in A.D. 810. Malamocco was captured, and the Doge fled to Rivo Alto. The bishopric of Rialto (also called Olivolo-Castello) had already been established on a nearby island, and from this time onwards the importance of the lagoon archipelago centred on the Rialto increased steadily. It was this small settlement which was to become the capital of the independent Venetian Republic, which emerged as the power of the Byzantine Empire gradually declined.[3]

Rising from the inimical wastes of the lagoon, Venice was like an oasis in a desert – except that the shifting sands all around were largely submerged in shallow water. Like a desert city, Venice had no farmland round about to feed her inhabitants or to provide goods for export. Local agriculture was confined to gardens and vineyards on the archipelago itself, while the lagoon waters yielded nothing but fish and salt. Like an oasis town Venice depended for survival on long-distance trade routes, dealing in goods such as oriental silks and spices that were precious rather than bulky. It was not until the expansion on to the Terraferma in the fifteenth century that the Republic acquired a hinterland.

The harsh physical environment contributed a very special quality to the visual surroundings in which the city's architecture evolved. Venice has a magical air which has more in common with the world of the *Arabian Nights* than with the bustling cities of the Italian mainland. The expanse of nothingness all around suggests the ephemeral nature of a desert mirage. From the waters of the lagoon the outline of the city is blurred by ever-changing reflections, and a strange luminosity is created by the huge expanses of sky stretching from one horizon to the other. Whereas Rome has her Seven Hills, and a backcloth of green Tuscan hills rises at the end of every Florentine street, Venice seems to lie in an infinity of sky and water. Even when the mountains of the mainland emerge from the haze on clear winter days, they seem ethereal and insubstantial. The buildings of the city are framed only by each other, and their profiles are silhouetted against nothing but sky. This was the context in which the architecture of Venice developed, and without which it could never have evolved as it did.

Of the appearance of the early lagoon settlements little is known. A splendid pre-Roman lagoon boat, preserved in the Natural History Museum in Venice, is a forceful reminder of the fine seamanship of the first settlers. The romanticized description written by the Roman official Cassiodorus in A.D. 537 compares the fishermen's houses to 'aquatic birds, now on sea, now on land.' The Venetians, he writes, 'have abundance only of fish; rich and poor live together in equality. The same food and similar houses are shared by all; wherefore they cannot envy each other's hearths and so they are free from the vices that rule the world.'[4] The first houses of the lagoon boatmen were wooden huts, raised on stilts to protect them from high tides and floods. On some of the higher islands houses could be built directly on patches of gravel topping the sandy soil, but elsewhere land had to be reclaimed little by little. Areas to be drained were enclosed with basket work dykes, navigation channels were excavated, and the mud dredged from the canals was used to raise the level of the reclaimed land (*Fig. 1*).

After Rivo Alto became capital of the Venetian state in 810, the city must have grown rapidly, but most of the inhabitants then lived in wooden houses roofed with thatch, which have perished in fires long ago. Even the first churches were of wood, and it is recorded that the church of San Salvatore had a thatched roof until as late as 1365.[5] Only the most important public buildings such as the Doge's Palace and the ducal chapel, the church of San Marco, were built of brick and stone. The earliest permanent structures on these sites, too, have virtually disappeared, though as we shall see later archaeological investigations have revealed something of their original form.

For the most vivid impression of an early lagoon settlement we must go instead to the island of Torcello. It was here that the Bishop of Altino transferred his seat in 638 when forced to flee from the mainland in the Barbarian invasions. The oldest buildings on the island, the Cathedral and Baptistery, date originally from that time (*Fig. 2*). Torcello later became a flourishing centre of wool manufacture as well as an important episcopal centre. Then, from the fourteenth century onwards, the island declined as Venice prospered, and was eventually devastated by malaria and abandoned. It now has only a small number of inhabitants, and most of the domestic buildings from its more prosperous days have perished. Nevertheless, it is not inconceivable that the small two storey houses which still stand on the island, with their big oven-houses attached at the side, may be survivals of a more ancient type of lagoon dwelling. Most important, in its present lonely, desolate state (except when overrun by tourists on a summer Sunday), Torcello reminds us of the bleak, hostile nature of the terrain on which the city of Venice was founded.

Map of Venice. Buildings are marked by the numbers of the black and white illustrations (or the principal exterior view if illustrated several times)

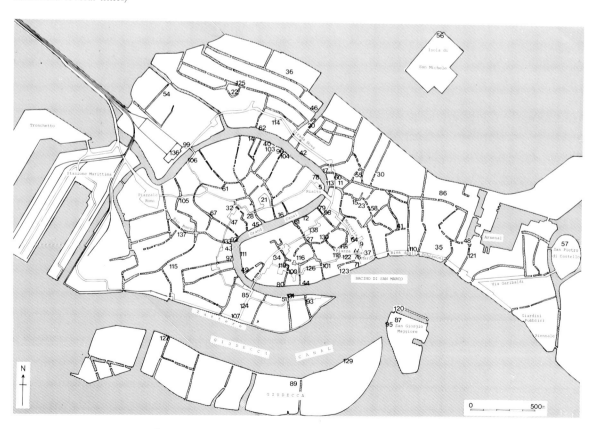

CHAPTER II

Byzantine

It was in the Byzantine period that the foundations of Venetian architecture were laid, both literally and conceptually. The Byzantine style lasted longer in Venice than in any other city of western Europe. The earliest surviving monuments of the Venetian archipelago date from the seventh century, and the style persisted until the thirteenth century when the Gothic pointed arch finally began to oust Byzantine forms. During these six centuries many changes occurred in the political and commercial affiliations of the state, and these in turn led to transformations in the nature of Venetian Byzantine architecture.

The origins of the Byzantine style are rooted in the traditions of the Roman Empire. When Emperor Constantine set up his capital in Byzantium in A.D. 330, after his conversion to Christianity, the centre of gravity of his Empire moved from West to East. But it was in the heritage of the classical Roman world that the Early Christians found the models for their first churches. Two types, in particular, seemed best suited to their needs – the Roman basilica, or secular meeting hall, for accommodating large congregations, and the centralized tomb structure, which was adapted for shrines and baptisteries.

In the centuries following the fall of the Roman Empire Early Christian churches of both these types sprang up in the Byzantine provinces of the Adriatic, in towns like Ravenna and Aquileia. As these cities were overrun by Barbarian invaders, their architectural traditions were preserved on island refuges, such as Torcello, Murano and Rivo Alto. In 811, the *Pax Nicephori* between Charlemagne and the Eastern Empire confirmed the existence of Venice as a semi-independent province of Byzantium, the only Italian city to retain an affiliation with the East. From this time on, while her merchants took advantage of trading privileges with the Byzantine Empire, Venice began to look eastward for cultural inspiration. The direct influence of classical prototypes began to recede, and the ancient Roman sense of order and clarity was lost in an aura of oriental mystery as the huge vaulted spaces of the great churches of Byzantium began to make their impact.

Gradually, however, the autonomy of Venice became greater, while the power of the Byzantine Empire waned; and the increasing commercial and political power of the Republic brought a new independence of spirit. The start of this trend was boldly symbolized in 829 when the Greek soldier-saint, Saint Theodore, was replaced as the patron saint of Venice by Saint Mark, whose body had been audaciously captured from Alexandria. Now commercial horizons started to widen dramatically. By the tenth century Venetians were trading extensively with the Islamic world as well as with Byzantium, and were beginning to renew contacts with the mainland of Western Europe. The Venetian visual imagination was captured by the colourful, cosmopolitan crowds which thronged the city, and by the exotic stories told by sailors and merchants. This brought a growing desire to decorate the stark exteriors and cavernous spaces of the great Byzantine monuments such as the Basilica of San Marco with mosaics, inlaid marbles and carvings. Because of the strong oriental influence this new decorative idiom was essentially two dimensional, far removed from the high relief and rudimentary perspective of classical Roman ornament. This enabled the bold forms of the city's Byzantine buildings to be preserved intact.

The period of the Crusades, which began at the end of the eleventh century to protect pilgrims to the Holy Land from the Turks, brought an increasing flow of travellers through Venice. These returned with a fuller knowledge of the world of Islam, often bearing with them rare oriental marbles, precious works of art and military trophies looted from the Turks and from the weakening Byzantine Empire. Tinged with its exotic eastern flavour and embellished with spoils from the Crusades, the late Byzantine architecture of Venice reveals a new self confidence and individuality. Whereas in mainland Europe the stark Romanesque style was emerging from the remnants of Early Christian and Carolingian traditions, Venice had her own personal equivalent in her Veneto-Byzantine architecture. Through the whole spectrum of its evolution, the Byzantine legacy provided Venice with the basic building types and techniques as well as decorative traditions, which were to influence and guide Venetian builders of the future.

Byzantine religious architecture on the islands of Torcello and Murano

Splendid examples of early Veneto-Byzantine churches, little altered or embellished during later centuries, are still to be found on the islands of Torcello and Murano. These once thriving island communities were later eclipsed as the city of Venice grew in importance, with the result that the inhabitants had neither the funds nor the stimulus to modernize or replace their buildings.

The churches of Torcello are among the oldest examples of Byzantine architecture in the Venetian archipelago. The seventh-century Baptistery, of which little survives other than the foundations of the perimeter wall and the bases of the columns, is an important relic of this very early period. At this stage Rome rather than Byzantium was still the dominant influence, and indeed the Baptistery, with its inner ring of eight columns which presumably once supported a dome, follows in the tradition of Early Christian centrally-planned baptismal chapels such as Constantine's Lateran Baptistery in Rome.

In its essential elements the Cathedral, which stands behind the remains of the Baptistery, also preserves its seventh-century form, although it was substantially rebuilt in the ninth and eleventh centuries. An inscription

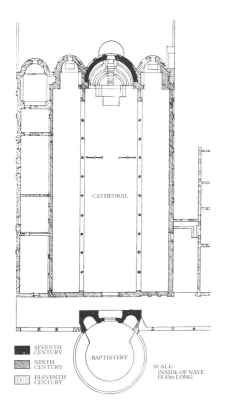

SEVENTH CENTURY
NINTH CENTURY
ELEVENTH CENTURY

CATHEDRAL

BAPTISTERY

SCALE:
INSIDE OF NAVE
IS 43m LONG

ABOVE, LEFT
Torcello Cathedral,
founded A.D. 639, and
remains of seventh-
century Baptistery,
ground plan. After Niero

ABOVE
3 Torcello Cathedral,
interior (*A.F.Kersting*)

discovered during excavations in 1895 records that the church, dedicated to the Virgin, was founded under Emperor Heraclius by order of Isaac, exarch of Ravenna in 639. It is now assumed that the seventh-century church was a simple triple-naved rectangular space with a single apse at the east end, in other words a typical Early Christian basilica of the form inherited from Roman secular architecture. Basilicas of this type already existed in the upper Adriatic region – fine sixth-century examples survive at Grado and Ravenna – and it was surely Ravenna that provided the artistic inspiration as well as the directive. Although the plan has survived with only minor alterations, little of the actual fabric of the seventh-century Cathedral is still visible. The wall of the central apse and perhaps the lower part of the entrance wall date from that time, and excavations have uncovered some of the original mosaic floor, in a black and white squared pattern, under the present pavement. In 1929 the original seventh-century altar, unearthed during archaeological investig-ations, was re-erected in the chancel.

A second phase of building, begun in 864 under Bishop Adeodato, is recorded in the chronicle of Johannes Diaconus. To this period the two smaller side apses and the crypt beneath the central apse are usually attributed. It is possible that the present perimeter walls date from the same time. The traces of frescoed draperies on the chancel wall are also thought to be ninth-century fragments.

However, the present aspect of the Cathedral owes most of all to the final building campaign launched by Bishop (later Doge) Orso Orseolo in 1008

(*Fig. 2*). At this stage the floor was raised and a new mosaic pavement begun. The sturdy upper walls of the nave, with clerestory windows on the south side which still preserve their ancient stone shutters hung on stone hinges, seem to belong, too, to this final phase of building. The interior colonnades with their stilted brick arches are of the same period, although two of the capitals on the right side of the nave, earlier in style, were presumably re-used from the previous structure. And finally, the present square campanile was erected at the back of the Cathedral.[1]

Despite these transformations the Cathedral retains much of the character of its sixth-century Early Christian prototypes, Sant'Apollinare in Classe and Sant'Apollinare Nuovo in Ravenna, and the Basilica of Grado. The massive brick exterior is decorated only by concentric layers of brickwork around the windows and blind arches. Inside the Cathedral the fine marble columns, the delicately carved capitals and the exquisite mosaics, contrasting sharply with the rugged exterior, are again reminiscent of the Ravennan antecedents (*Fig. 3*). The semi-circular row of steps in the apse, mounting to the bishop's throne in the centre, is typical of early episcopal churches in the area. However, the heightened profile of the stilted arches shows that contacts with the eastern Byzantine Empire were beginning to leave their mark on the architecture of the Venetian lagoon. Similarly, the four beautiful marble *plutei* (panels decorated with Byzantine-style relief carving) beneath the eleventh-century *iconostasis* show how far local craftsmen were becoming influenced by more eastern styles of decoration. The most impressive quality of the interior of Torcello Cathedral is one of calm and extraordinary dignity. The decorative elements, though of high quality, are in a sense subordinated in scale and feeling to the overriding simplicity of the great, solemn space. The stately colonnades of the nave lead one with a slow, measured pace across the cold mosaic floor towards the eventual climax, the bishop's throne and the imposing mosaic figure, Mary mother of Christ, presiding majestically above.

Beside the Cathedral of Torcello stands the little church of Santa Fosca, which was built to house the body of the Early Christian martyr of the same name, brought to the island before 1011 (*Fig. 2*). There is no convincing reason to doubt that the nucleus of the present church still preserves its eleventh-century form.[2] The church of Santa Fosca had a very different function from that of the Basilica alongside it. Built as a martyrium, it had no need to serve as a setting for processions in great episcopal ceremonies, but was essentially a place for more secluded worship and meditation. Thus the church was not modelled on the great classical basilicas with their spacious naves and side aisles, but on a different type of architecture more suited to the needs of shrines and sepulchral buildings. It was the Romans who promoted the tradition for small centralized tomb structures in Italy. The form adopted at Santa Fosca, however, also reflects the influence of later Byzantine models. Like the fourth-century Mausoleum of Galla Placida in Ravenna, the plan of the church (*p. 23*) is a Greek cross, that is, a cross with all four arms of equal length, although it is transformed, by means of curved pendentives supported on free-standing columns, to a circular drum above. The elegant simplicity of this arrangement is one of the church's most impressive features. The theme of the Greek-cross structure supporting a great central dome was one which long preoccupied Byzantine architects. The great church of Hagia Sophia in Constantinople, erected by Emperor Justinian in the sixth century, is one of the most famous early examples. And it was also to become a central theme in the history of religious architecture in Venice. The builders of Santa Fosca probably intended their church to be roofed by a dome, but the construction must have proved too great a challenge. The existing wooden conical roof, tiled on the outside, was a cheaper, safer solution, and one which in no way detracts from the overall effect.

The portico that completely surrounds the church, except on the apsed east side, is probably a twelfth-century addition. Here the Greek-cross plan is ingeniously transmuted into an octagon, with five bays along each of the sides of the arms of the cross and three bays on the shorter diagonals between. The combination of round and polygonal columns adds an element of variety to the colonnade, while the distinctive stilted arches, considerably more elongated than the earlier arches inside the church, punctuate the dark shadows of the arcade with repeated vertical accents and lead the eye up to the imposing accumulation of masses on the roofline, intriguingly complicated yet perfectly harmonized. This array of protrusions of different shapes, rising to a climax in the centre, already seen in Italy in the sixth-century church of San Vitale in Ravenna, is typical of Byzantine churches of the Near East.

The eastern apse at the back of the church is decorated on the outside with elaborate patterns in the brickwork, which constitute the only external adornment, apart from the columns of the portico and the white crosses, each containing the Hand of God, on the end wall of each transept. The dog-tooth

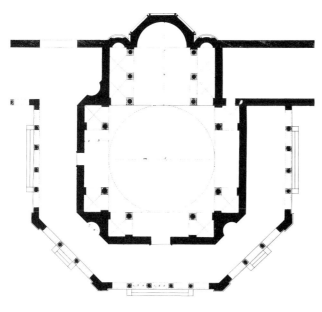

Pianta del Tempietto di Fosca nell'Isola di Torcello

Santa Fosca, Torcello, eleventh to twelfth centuries, plan

23

4 Santi Maria e Donato, Murano, seventh to twelfth centuries. View of rear apse (*A.F.Kersting*)

pattern which is the characteristic motif of the apse decoration was a common ornament on early Veneto-Byzantine churches, otherwise so bare on the outside. The combination of the rich red colour of the brickwork and the crisp white marble detailing must have provided an element of warmth for the early Venetians in their bleak, inhospitable environment. Fostered by the local availability of building materials, this combination of red and white was long to be a favourite colour theme in Venetian architecture. For all its individuality, the church of Santa Fosca is an important example of early Byzantine religious buildings in the Venetian lagoon; like the Cathedral beside it, it still preserves the characteristic contrast between the starkness of its external aspect and the solemn gravity of its beautifully proportioned interior.

A third fine representative of the sacred architecture of the period is the church of Santi Maria e Donato on the island of Murano (*Fig. 4*). Like the churches of Torcello, Santi Maria e Donato was probably founded in the seventh century. As early as 999 it was mentioned in contemporary records as a church dedicated to the Virgin. The dedication to San Donato was added in 1125 when the relics of the saint's body were brought to Murano from the Greek island of Cephalonia. The magnificent mosaics on the floor are dated 1140, by which time the church must have been substantially completed.[3] Originally built in honour of the Virgin, like the Cathedral of Torcello, it only became a shrine once the main layout of the building was already established. Thus the simple basilical plan with a single apse at the east end, like the first Cathedral at Torcello, was chosen in preference to the more intimate, centralized martyrium type, represented by Santa Fosca. The separate centralized Baptistery, which once stood in front of the entrance façade, was demolished in 1719. Unlike Torcello this was not an episcopal centre, so that the apse has no flight of steps leading up to a bishop's throne. Instead the choir serves as the reliquary chapel for the saint's remains.

The main part of the exterior of San Donato reveals its naked brickwork decorated with simple concentric brick arches in the typical Veneto–Byzantine manner. However, the apse, the section which contains the saint's relics, is exceptionally ornate for the period. Here again we find the zig zag terracotta patterns and dog-tooth mouldings which appear on the apse of Santa Fosca, but the articulation is far more elaborate, with two tiers of blind arcades, their paired marble columns flanking brick niches below and enclosing a gallery above. Some fragments of earlier Byzantine carving are also incorporated into the decoration.

Unlike Torcello Cathedral, San Donato has definite transepts. Although these do not project on the plan, they are prominent on the exterior, being higher than the side aisles. In the nave the two rows of stilted arches, supported on marble columns with fine Veneto–Byzantine capitals, are replaced at the crossing by four huge square piers which may possibly have been intended to support a dome. In the event, as at Santa Fosca, this was never done. The present wooden 'ship's-keel' ceiling dates from the fifteenth century. Now that the flamboyant Baroque altars in the transepts have been removed in the course of recent restoration work, the spacious, lucid interior recalls its twelfth-century state to a remarkable extent, as does the distinctive brick and terracotta exterior.

Byzantine religious architecture in Venice itself

In these island churches we have seen evidence of Byzantine ecclesiastical architecture in the lagoon at various stages between the seventh and twelfth centuries, little altered since then. In Venice itself the situation is rather different. The two most important surviving Byzantine churches, San Giacomo di Rialto and San Marco, one founded on each of the two principal islands of the city, have both been substantially transformed since the early period. As we shall see, San Giacomo was completely rebuilt in later restorations, while the core of San Marco is virtually hidden by lavish mosaic and sculptural decoration. Yet both are more important in the development of religious architecture in Venice than any of the more remote island churches, for they were constantly seen and visited by both Venetians and travellers. Both are variations on the Byzantine theme of the Greek cross supporting a central dome, one church being in a sense a miniature and much simplified version of the other.

The legendary date for the founding of the church of San Giacomo di Rialto, affectionately known to Venetians as San Giacometto, is A.D. 421, the very year that the city of Venice itself was supposedly founded. Francesco Sansovino's sixteenth-century guide to Venice even names the four bishops who consecrated the church in the following year.[4] Substantial restorations were carried out in 1071, and it is likely that the present configuration dates

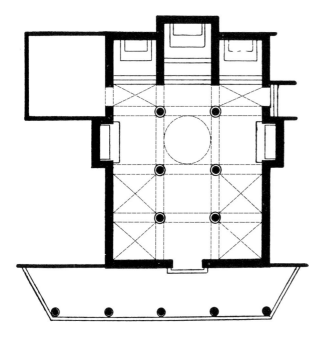

ABOVE
San Giacomo di Rialto,
plan. After Lorenzetti

ABOVE, RIGHT
5 San Giacomo di
Rialto, known as San
Giacometto, eleventh
century, completely
restored in the
seventeenth century
(*A.F.Kersting*)

essentially from that time. The fine Gothic entrance portico, added subsequently, and the great clock built in 1410, give the façade its distinctive character (*Fig. 5*).

A further attempt at restoration in 1531 failed to secure the ancient structure, which had miraculously escaped the great fire that devastated the Rialto market in 1513. Finally in 1601 a decree of the Senate authorised the complete rebuilding of the church.[5] So great was Venetian reverence for this historic building that its original form and even its tiny size were preserved. The only significant alteration was the raising of the church on to a higher base to reduce the risk of flooding. In addition, three large semi-circular windows were opened up beneath the barrel vaults to improve the lighting, and rich Baroque altars – oppressively heavy in such a small space – were erected in the chancel and the two side chapels. Together with the loss of the old mosaics, which were still visible in the later sixteenth century, these changes must have considerably changed the character of the interior, once bare and dimly lit with flickering mosaics. However, the simple Greek-cross structure (*above*), with its central dome supported on free-standing columns, reproduces faithfully that of the original Byzantine church. The six Greek marble columns with their beautifully carved eleventh-century capitals (which, again, seem enormous in such a restricted space) were preserved in the rebuilding.

On the entrance side the area is slightly extended with an extra pair of columns to suggest a rudimentary nave. However, the dominating effect of the central dome, with its high drum and lantern, serves to draw one's attention to the centralized ground plan. Small, centrally-planned Byzantine churches of this type probably once existed in most of the parishes of the city, but no others commanded such respect and affection that they have survived to this day. Nevertheless, the centralized parish church had considerable advantages, for a small compact space was ideal for the parochial services. The administration of the sacraments and preaching to the local residents were the main functions of these churches, which had no need of huge processional naves or secluded chapels for private worship. It was an old tradition in Venice that the parish priests were elected by the parishioners themselves, or rather, by the householders of the parish. No monastic communities were attached, only small bodies of secular clergy. And it was the residents of the parishes who were responsible for financing the building and maintenance of their churches. San Giacometto itself is a slightly unusual parish church, being a national monument as much as a local landmark, but it is still important as the only remaining example of these small Byzantine parish churches in the city of Venice.

'The composition of the dome is so well assembled and so well supported by the arches which sustain the vaults', wrote Francesco Sansovino of San Giacomo di Rialto, 'that it is a marvellous thing to see, and one might say that it was the model for the Church of San Marco.'[6] In reality the two monuments create very different effects, one so small, the other so huge, one so modest, the other so richly decorated. Yet Francesco's observation was a perceptive one, since both are variations on the great Byzantine theme of the Greek cross supporting a large central dome.

The Basilica of San Marco has the aura of a great cathedral; but in reality it did not become the Cathedral of Venice until as late as 1807. Before then the seat of the Patriarch of Venice was the church of San Pietro di Castello, founded at the time of the establishment of the Bishopric of Rialto in 774/5 on the island of Olivolo (also called Castello) on the eastern margins of the city. In the mid-fifteenth century the office of Bishop was merged with that of Patriarch of Grado to become the Patriarchate of Venice, with its seat at San Pietro.[7]

San Marco, on the other hand, was the private chapel of the Doge, and above all, it was a great shrine which housed the body of Saint Mark. The legend recounting the acquisition of this relic – the most precious in the city – is complex and colourful. Briefly, two Venetian merchants, accompanied by two monks, skilfully removed the body of Saint Mark from its tomb in Alexandria (where the saint is said to have been martyred), substituting in its place the body of Saint Claudia. The relics were exported in a basket of pork, to deter prying Moslem customs officials, and brought back to Venice in 828/9. This momentous event, known as the *traslatio*, is commemorated in the famous thirteenth-century mosaic on the façade of the Basilica, over the Porta Sant'Alippio, in which the body of Saint Mark is shown being carried into the church built in his honour, portrayed in its thirteenth-century state (*Fig.* 7).

After the *traslatio* Saint Mark quickly displaced the eastern soldier-saint, Saint Theodore, as the patron saint of the city, as it were symbolizing the Venetian State's gradual break-away from Byzantine rule. The mythology associated with the Marcian relics continued to grow – including, for instance, the dramatic story of the loss of the Saint's body and its miraculous reappearance in the burial vault of the Basilica. As the popularity of the Saint

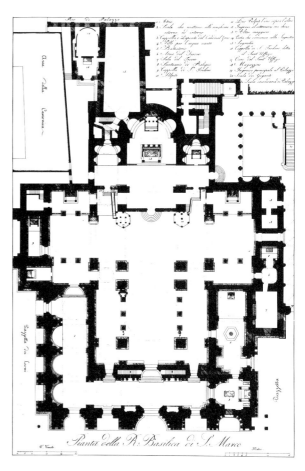

grew, so too did the wealth of the Procurators of Saint Mark, who were in charge of the building and upkeep of the Basilica. Whereas in most of the great cities of feudal Europe bequests and tithes flowed into the episcopal treasuries to finance the building of fine cathedrals, many Venetians made their pious donations not to the remotely situated Cathedral of San Pietro di Castello, but to the Ducal Chapel, the Basilica of Saint Mark. Thus the Basilica became a potent symbol of Venetian religious devotion and civic pride; and as such it played the same role in Venice as the great mediaeval cathedrals in other European cities.

Of the original church, begun soon after the arrival of the body of Saint Mark in Venice in 829, very little is now visible. Modern excavations have, however, shown that the ninth-century church was in fact broadly similar in plan to the core of the present structure (*above*). It was in the form of a simple Greek cross with a single apse at the east end. The wall which now separates the atrium from the nave is essentially the west wall of the ninth-century structure, including its great entrance niche. The walls were built of stone left over from the construction of a nearby abbey, as well as some second-hand building stone from Torcello, and probably also from Roman remains on the mainland. The five domes, one over the crossing and one above each of the arms of the cross, seem to have been roofed in wood, like the dome of Santa Fosca in Torcello.[8]

As at Santa Fosca, which was also built as a reliquary chapel, the Byzantine cruciform plan was chosen for the great shrine to house the Saint's body. The choice of the Greek cross places San Marco firmly in the tradition of apostles' churches. The plan is indeed very similar to the church of the Holy Apostles in Constantinople, built by Emperor Justinian in the sixth century. This famous Byzantine monument no longer exists, but it is known from written descriptions and from its supposed likeness to the contemporary apostle's church of Saint John at Ephesus. Even in parts of Italy which were affiliated with the western church, and were thus divorced from Byzantine traditions, cruciform plans were traditionally chosen for apostles' churches, such as the church of Sant'Ambrogio in Milan. That the Venetians thought of their patron saint specifically as one of the apostles is attested by their avid collecting of holy relics of other apostles, many of which are still preserved at San Marco.

Early chronicles record that the ninth-century church was badly damaged in the great fire of 976. However, the fact that the repairs, carried out by Doge Pietro Orseolo, were completed within the space of only two years, indicates that the building cannot have been totally destroyed. The restoration seems to have been a makeshift affair, for already in the mid-eleventh century, less than 100 years later, it was decided to rebuild the church yet again, this time on a more radical scale. This final reconstruction, which continued through the reigns of three Doges, was begun under Doge Domenico Contarini (1042–71) and finished under Doge Vitale Falier (1086–96).[9]

To envisage San Marco as it appeared in the ninth century, the architectural historian has to depend on the archaeologist. The aspect of the eleventh-

7 'The arrival of the body of Saint Mark in A.D. 829', thirteenth-century mosaic above the Porta Sant'Alippio, Basilica of San Marco, showing the Basilica in its thirteenth-century state *(Osvaldo Böhm)*

century Basilica can, however, be relatively easily reconstructed from the evidence of the present building. What is needed, above all, is a great effort of imagination, to erase from one's mind the profusion of mosaics, fine marbles, and florid rooftop sculpture, which now adorn – and largely conceal – this great Veneto-Byzantine monument.

It was in the eleventh century that the wooden domes were replaced by brick vaults, a daring undertaking in view of the unstable nature of the Venetian subsoil, and one which has led to structural problems ever since. (The Florentine architect Jacopo Sansovino first made his reputation in Venice when he successfully repaired the domes by encircling them with iron rings in 1527.)[10] The only other brick dome erected in the Venetian lagoon in the Byzantine period was that of the little church of San Giacomo di Rialto. To picture the effect of the new brick domes, we must try to imagine San Marco without one of its most memorable features, that is, the five lofty domes roofed with lead and topped by onion-shaped lanterns which now surmount the church (*Fig. 8*). These flamboyant cupolas are simply outer shells, added in the thirteenth century to make the skyline of the church more prominent. The exterior would originally have had the same profile as the lower, inner domes which we see inside the church.[11] This flatter type of cupola is more typical of the Byzantine churches of Constantinople and Greece, from which the builders of San Marco drew their inspiration.

In order to support the extra weight of the brick domes the walls had to be considerably thickened. The church was also enlarged on both the north and south sides: on the north to embrace the remains of the chapel of San Teodoro which was finally demolished at this time, on the south to include what was probably a corner tower of the old Ducal Palace and which now forms part of the Treasury of San Marco. At the west end a narthex was added, and at the east two smaller apses were built on either side of the main presbytery. (The Baptistery on the south side, and the corresponding extension to the atrium on the north, are thirteenth-century additions.) Despite these extensions, the Greek-cross configuration was retained, thus preserving the link between San Marco and the Apostoleion in Constantinople.

Each domed space forms, in effect, a separate, smaller-scale Greek cross, with four barrel-vaulted spaces to buttress the lateral thrust of the dome. The predominance of the overall Greek-cross plan is stressed by screening off the subsidiary barrel-vaulted spaces behind arcades, which also serve to support the galleries. The present raised 'cat walks' are the somewhat vertiginous remains of the original galleries. It seems that they were once much wider, like those which survive at the ends of both transepts and at the west end of the nave, but that they were subsequently narrowed to allow more light into the aisle-like spaces beneath. The existing galleries show clear evidence of this change, for the outer balustrades are of the solid Byzantine type with carved *plutei* (relief panels) while the inner ones are typically Gothic in style with their rows of slender colonnettes. The reason for this change must have been the blocking-up of many of the upper windows to provide extra wall space for the mosaic decoration, which would have made the interior too dark.[12]

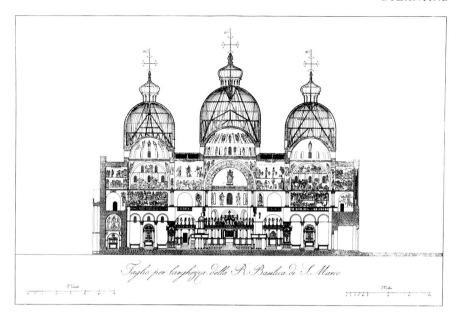

Taglio per larghezza della R Basilica di S. Marco

The spaces of the interior are not neatly compartmentalized, but are interconnected by means of colonnades and arched openings (*Fig. 6*). For example, the four huge piers which support the central dome are penetrated by great archways, with the weight redistributed on four smaller piers in each case. This lightens the visual effect considerably, and enables air to flow more freely between one domed space and another. It even allows a continuous vista down each side of the nave to suggest side aisles. The apparent lightness of the structure is also conveyed by the way in which the cupolas seem not to rest directly on the great arched barrel vaults, but to hover effortlessly just above them. The transition from the square spaces below to the circular domes above, a problem which preoccupied many mediaeval builders, is here accomplished skilfully and smoothly by means of curved pendentives.

That the resemblance between San Marco and the Apostoleion in Constantinople was recognized from the start is clear from an early twelfth-century manuscript, written by a monk at San Nicolò di Lido, which states that the new Basilica was built 'in a construction similar to that of the Twelve Apostles in Constantinople'. However, if we study the plan of San Marco carefully (*p. 28*), we can see how the Byzantine model was subtly transformed to suit the rather different liturgical function of the Venetian church.[13] For instance, it becomes clear that the four domes over the arms of the Greek cross in San Marco are not in fact equal in size; those over the transepts and the east end are smaller, while the cupola above the western arm of the crossing is not only wider but is also slightly elongated to extend the nave space. As a result, the colonnades which support the galleries have only three bays in each transept, but four on either side of the nave. This subtle extension of the nave recalls the similar arrangement at San Giacomo di Rialto. The longitudinal axis is further emphasized by the blocking-off of the ends of the transepts, and by the three apses at the east end, which suggest a directional force that has pushed

8 North-south cross-section of the Basilica of San Marco (From L.CICOGNARA, A.DIEDO, and G. SELVA, *Le Fabbriche e i monumenti cospicue di Venezia*, vol.I, Venice, 1838)

out the far wall. Whereas the plan of the Apostoleion was perfectly symmetrical on all four axes, with the high altar beneath the central dome, in San Marco, on the other hand, the form of service called for a secluded presbytery for the clergy at the east end. The tomb of Saint Mark was placed in the crypt under the chancel, directly beneath the high altar. The Doge and other high State officials sat on special seats in the choir, which was also at the eastern end of the church. The directional emphasis of the space, aligned towards the chancel, not only suited the liturgy, but also made the Basilica a more appropriate setting for the great processions which accompanied all the principal Ducal ceremonies.

The eleventh-century Basilica with its new brick domes would have made a powerful but stark impression. Brick was in fact the chief building material, and the typical terracotta dog-tooth mouldings were used to decorate the Byzantine arches, both inside and out. Only the lunette-shaped south wall of the nave and the apsed east end of the chancel preserve their naked brickwork to this day. Like the other Byzantine churches in the lagoon, the windows were framed by concentric brick arches, as if to reveal the successive layers of the massive brick walls. The lower walls were articulated mainly by a series of niches, some curved, some rectangular, an Italian decorative tradition probably derived from Roman tomb architecture. Stone was used for the columns, capitals, horizontal mouldings and balustrades inside the church, and for some of the details of the exterior, such as the engaged columns of the eastern apse.

By the time of the execution of the thirteenth-century mosaic on the façade, showing the *traslatio* of the body of Saint Mark, the Basilica had completely changed its outward appearance (*Fig.* 7). This mosaic, the only one of the original series in the arches of the portico to survive, must date from before 1267 when it was mentioned in Martino da Canal's famous chronicle. It decorates the lunette on the northernmost bay of the façade, over the Porta Sant'Alippio.[14]

No longer do we see the heavy brick structure with its low domes and its niches, but instead a façade bedecked with fine marbles and mosaic decoration, crowned by soaring domes. It would be hardly an exaggeration to claim that this transformation could not have been possible but for the Venetian triumphs in the Fourth Crusade in 1202–04. For this expedition Venice supplied a magnificent fleet of warships, in return for a large cash payment and an equal share of all spoils and territorial conquests. Brilliantly led by the blind and aged Doge Enrico Dandolo, the Venetian fleet was instrumental in the capture of Constantinople, and also took possession of much of the Dalmatian coast.[15] In the looting which followed the fall of Constantinople, the Venetians seized whatever they could transport home, including precious holy relics, and the four bronze horses which were placed over the entrance to San Marco. The wealth of oriental marble columns on the façade of the Basilica must also have been imported to Venice from 1204 onwards. The favourite place for displaying looted sculpture was the south wall of the church, facing the Doge's Palace, which was the first façade to be

seen by visitors arriving by sea (*Fig. 9*). The south wall of the Treasury, in particular, is inlaid with pieces of Byzantine relief carving, with the delightful porphyry group of the four Tetrarchs huddled together on the corner.

    The arrival of such splendid trophies as these from the Fourth Crusade, and later from the Genoese wars, encouraged other embellishments to the Basilica. We have already seen how the cupolas were raised, and the Baptistery and the north wing of the atrium added. It seems also to have been in the thirteenth century that some of the Gothic details, which had been inserted into the Byzantine structure, were hidden beneath more classical rounded arches, to unify the style in what has been identified as a kind of Venetian 'proto-Renaissance'.[16]

    This is not the place to discuss in detail the mosaics, the inlaid marble floors, and the sculptural decoration of the interior. What is important is to realize how the eleventh-century architecture was gradually transformed during the long process of decoration. Both the marble pavements and the mosaics are symptomatic of the archaizing tendency which runs through the whole history of Venetian art. The beautiful geometric patterns which decorate the floors, like the pavements of San Donato di Murano and the Cathedral of

9 Basilica of San Marco, founded ninth century; view from the Piazzetta *(A.F. Kersting)*

Torcello, recall Roman and Early Christian traditions, revived on a scale which is unusual in mediaeval architecture. These pavements were apparently begun soon after the completion of the eleventh-century Basilica. A few fragments of mosaics from this early period have been uncovered on the façade, contemporary with those of Torcello, but mosaic decoration on a more expansive scale began in earnest in the twelfth century. Whereas in most Italian churches the mosaic technique was superseded by fresco painting from about the thirteenth century, the mosaic decoration of San Marco did not cease until the nineteenth century. It is true that the local glass-making industry on the island of Murano fostered the existence of a Venetian school of mosaicists; but this industry would never have flourished for so long, had not Venetian taste continued to appreciate this archaic medium.

The Venetian fondness for archaism is also apparent in the sculptural decoration. As workshops of Lombard and local craftsmen produced a blend of Italian and Byzantine motifs, so ancient and modern decorative traditions were retained side by side, and spoils were juxtaposed with custom-made pieces.[17] So closely could the Italian stone-carvers imitate the style and technique of Byzantine sculptors that it is often difficult to distinguish between the oriental originals and the locally produced versions. The plain marble panels which cover many of the lower wall surfaces, like hangings of moiré silk, were put in position from the late eleventh century onwards. Each marble surface was laid alongside its mirror image, to create the shimmering effect so characteristic of the lagoon churches of the Veneto-Byzantine period.

The result of these decorations was to transform the solid brick wall-surfaces of the interior into brilliant aethereal visions above, and undulating watery patterns below (*Fig. 6*). Light flickering on the mosaics and reflected from the polished marble surfaces dances about in the huge vaulted spaces, dissolving the once clearly separated pools of light and shade. There can be no

10 Gentile Bellini: 'Procession in Piazza San Marco', signed and dated 1496. Accademia Gallery, Venice (*Osvaldo Bohm*)

doubt that the clarity and apparent solidity of the eleventh-century building was sacrificed. However, we must not forget that the mosaics, the floor patterns, and the marble facings on the walls, were all begun soon after the completion of the new church. This suggests that its builders always intended the heavy architectural framework to be adorned with rich surface decoration. While it must be admitted that the quality of the mosaic designs varies greatly, the general conception cannot be seen as a betrayal of the intentions of the founders of the church. Indeed it is characteristic of Byzantine architecture in the lagoon that most of the interior decoration is in two dimensions, or in very low relief, so that the integrity of the architectonic elements is not undermined.

By the end of the fifteenth century, the exterior of the Basilica of San Marco had reached more or less its final form (except for the later renewal of some of the façade mosaics). The evidence for this is the painting of the 'Procession in Piazza San Marco' by Gentile Bellini, signed and dated 1496, which gives a precise and detailed view of the Basilica at that time (*Fig. 10*). From this picture we can deduce that the gothic cusps over the upper lunettes, the skyline pinnacles and statues, and the roof-top crockets like white-hot flames licking the bases of the domes, were fourteenth and fifteenth century additions, since none of these features appears in the Porta Sant'Alippio mosaic. The least fortunate alteration is surely the opening-up of the central lunette to make a huge blank window, presumably to admit more light into the church after other windows had been blocked up to make way for the mosaics.

To the western eye, San Marco has a distinctly oriental air. Certainly it is far more eastern in feeling than the Byzantine churches of Torcello and Murano, where little decoration was added after the time of the Fourth Crusade. Spoils plundered from Constantinople give an eastern aspect to the outer walls, while inside the church the dramatic shafts of light and pools of shadow, softened by reflections from the vast expanses of glittering mosaics, make the interior more magical, less static in character than the other Byzantine churches of the lagoon.

Yet San Marco is not simply a Byzantine monument transplanted to Venetian soil. To a visitor from the Near East it would seem equally foreign, for the building was largely erected and decorated by Italian craftsmen, whose stamp is imprinted in every part of the building. Not only Lombard stonemasons, but also, in later centuries, such famous Tuscan artists as Paolo Uccello and Jacopo Sansovino had a hand in the decoration. At San Marco a remarkable blend is achieved between Italian and Byzantine influences, although more than in any other Venetian building it is the oriental flavour which is the dominant one.

Byzantine domestic architecture

The few surviving Byzantine churches of the Venetian archipelago have their secular equivalent in a small number of fine Veneto-Byzantine palaces. Precise dating of the oldest extant Venetian palaces is impossible, as there is little documentation from this early period. We can, however, be fairly sure that almost nothing remains of the domestic architecture of the city before the twelfth century. Only a few fragments seem to be older than this. A small Byzantine window with its delicate stone tracery – reminiscent of those on the façade of San Marco – is set into a garden wall near San Tomà, but it is certainly not *in situ* and may well have come from a church. Remains of three great round-headed arches in the courtyard known as the Corte Seconda del Milion, behind the church of San Giovanni Crisostomo, may possibly date from as early as the twelfth century (*Fig. 11*). These arches, one of which preserves its carved Byzantine-style marble decoration, are believed to have once formed part of the nearby palace belonging to Marco Polo's family.

The only known secular buildings which can be securely dated to the twelfth century are those erected for the Procuracy of Saint Mark on either side of Piazza San Marco when the Piazza was enlarged by Doge Sebastiano Ziani (1172-78).[18] Both wings were rebuilt in the sixteenth century, but their original appearance is faithfully recorded in Gentile Bellini's painting, the 'Corpus Domini Procession' of 1496 (*Fig. 10*). From this picture we know that the buildings were long two-storey wings with ground floor porticoes containing shops, and arcaded balconies on the *piano nobile*. The round-headed openings of the lower storey are twice as wide as those above. The roofline is crenellated, more for decorative effect than for defence purposes. This type of

11 Remains of house belonging to Marco Polo's family, Corte Seconda del Milion, early twelfth century? (*A.F.Kersting*)

building, which could be extended to any length simply by the addition of extra bays, was to have an important influence on later constructions in the Piazza; and as we shall see, it shares its two-storey arcades with some of the early Veneto-Byzantine palaces.

There is a curious time lag between religious and secular architecture in mediaeval Venice. The scarcity of surviving domestic buildings from the period of the final rebuilding of San Marco in the later eleventh century can be partly explained by the fact that the early lagoon houses were built not of brick or stone – or even ancient spoils – but of wood; and a series of terrible fires in the eleventh century ravaged almost every part of the city, and obliterated many of the early wooden dwellings. The more modest houses were, out of economic necessity, rebuilt in wood over and over again, despite the constant danger of fire; but from about the twelfth century onwards the wealthier families began to erect more durable palaces of brick with stone detailing.

Another important explanation is the economic one. It was in the thirteenth century, the period of the Fourth Crusade and the Venetian victories over the Genoese (at Acre in 1258, Settepozzi in 1263, and Trapani in 1266) that Venetian maritime supremacy in the Adriatic became firmly established (although the Genoese still remained potentially dangerous rivals). By this stage Venetian merchants dominated trade in grain and salt in the Adriatic. They also had important entrepôt trade in silks and spices from the east, and textiles and metals from Northern Europe. The Venetian government exerted strict controls over shipping and trade, organizing convoys of armed galleys to protect the fleets of merchant vessels, usually round ships powered by sail. However, each merchant ship was financed not by the state but by a private individual, or by a patrician family acting in a partnership of brothers known as a *fraterna*.[19] The merchants could, if necessary, raise the money to finance a voyage by borrowing from other individuals, a system which allowed the owners of capital to spread their resources, to protect themselves against the loss of a ship through piracy, storms or war. The result of this efficiently run system of mercantile activity was that, by the thirteenth century, the more fortunate Venetians were becoming rather wealthy. It was these rich patrician merchants who now found themselves with the resources to build family palaces.

Veneto-Byzantine palaces

The exact form of the earliest Venetian palaces is debatable, for those that survive have undergone centuries of alterations and embellishments. However, it will become clear that they had little in common with the tall stone towers which the Italian nobility were erecting in other Italian cities. The construction of high buildings was hazardous in Venice because of the soft and constantly shifting nature of the terrain. The loss of a large number of the church *campanili* through the centuries is evidence for this, the collapse of the Campanile of San Marco in 1902 being certainly the most dramatic example.

Whereas early views of many Italian cities (Siena, Perugia, Florence and Bologna are good examples) show skylines thick with great stone towers erected by the most powerful families in the twelfth and thirteenth centuries, in mediaeval Venice only the *campanili* were prominent landmarks on the horizon. True, some later secular buildings in Venice reached to a great height, but this occurred only where there was an acute shortage of land (for example, in the Jewish ghetto), or when a particularly rich family wished to display its wealth by building a palace which towered above all its neighbours (such as the two huge palaces built by the Corner family in the sixteenth century) (*Figs. 22 & 80*).

Early Venetian palace builders lacked supplies of local stone with which to erect lofty towers, as well as firm foundations on which to build them. More important, the structure of their society did not create any need – physical or psychological – for such strongholds. The main function of the tall towers elsewhere in Italy seems to have been defensive rather than offensive. Although the twelfth-century traveller Benjamin of Tudela spoke of rival families fighting each other from the tops of their towers in both Pisa and Genoa, this probably happened rarely.[20] The towers did, however, give the nobility a sense of security in the frequent feuds which occurred between families.

In Venice things were different. In an attempt to prevent power struggles between individual families, the Dogado was not made a hereditary office. Instead, a constitution was evolved which, though excluding virtually all but the aristocracy from the administration, allowed a remarkably democratic system of government within the nobility itself. This unique system, which survived almost unchanged until the Fall of the Republic in 1797, naturally discouraged internal rivalry and hostility among the upper classes. What is more, there can be no doubt that the constant fight against nature helped to unite the Venetian people, and gave them a sense of common pride in their city.

The practical function of Venetian palaces was also different. The nobility earned their living not from landowning, as in other Italian city states at this period, but from seafaring and trade. As a result, their homes had to serve not only as residences but also as the headquarters for their trading ventures. Although many of them invested profits in property in the city and on the mainland, this was not at first their chief source of income. The very way in which Venice was settled obviously meant that at the outset land was extremely scarce. The feudal system and its aftermaths passed the city by.

One type of palace which evolved to suit the special needs of the Venetian patrician can be loosely defined on the basis of a few surviving Veneto-Byzantine palaces. The most impressive examples are the neighbouring Palazzi Loredan and Farsetti (now the municipal offices), and the Fondaco dei Turchi (now the Natural History Museum) (*Figs. 12 & 14*). None of these palaces appears to date from before the thirteenth century; in the case of the Palazzo Farsetti it is recorded that Enrico Dandolo, who built the palace, brought back some oriental marbles for the building after the Fall of

OPPOSITE, TOP

12 Palazzo Loredan and Palazzo Farsetti, probably thirteenth century, with later additions (*Sarah Quill*)

OPPOSITE, BELOW

13 Fondaco dei Turchi, probably thirteenth century. Appearance before nineteenth-century restoration

Constantinople in 1204. The Fondaco dei Turchi is so-called because in 1621 it became the trading centre and residence for Turkish merchants in the city. It was completely refaced in the nineteenth century, although its previous appearance is recorded in old views and photographs (*Fig. 13*). The façade of the Palazzo Farsetti, too, was remade in the last century; and the two upper floors of both this palace and the Palazzo Loredan are additions to the original Veneto-Byzantine structure. Nevertheless, a general idea of the type can be identified from examples such as these.[21]

The main feature of these early palaces was the two-storey arcade along the waterfront, with the ground-floor portico for loading and unloading merchandise (*p. 41*). The portico led into a great hall, called the *androne*, used for displaying armour and for business negotiations, with storerooms and offices on either side and a kitchen at the back. The living quarters were upstairs, with the rooms leading off a great T-shaped central room, known as the *salone* or *portego*, over the *androne*. At the back was a courtyard with a well and an open staircase. It is not improbable that there were low towers at each end of the façade, but these would have had no defensive function. Early views of Venice, such as the depiction by an English artist in a manuscript of Marco Polo's writings in Oxford, show ornate little turrets on many of the buildings. Some early dwellings, such as the house on the Riva degli Schiavoni where

14 Fondaco dei Turchi, present state (*A.F.Kersting*)

Petrarch stayed and the previous palace on the site of Ca' Pesaro, are definitely known to have had corner towers.[22] There were, of course, many variations on the general theme, depending on the size of the palace and the shape of the site. The position of the nearby canals was also important, since every house of any significance had to have both land and water entrances.[23]

As we have seen, such defenceless, outward-looking palaces, with their porticoed façades, had little in common with domestic architecture in other mediaeval Italian cities. Several scholars have, however, made much of the curious affinity between early Venetian palaces and the smaller country villas of the late Roman Empire, with their two storey arcades and projecting tower blocks on each side.[24] This classical building-type seems to have disappeared from the Italian countryside after the Barbarian invasions, although we cannot be certain since most mediaeval farm buildings have now vanished. The type did, however, survive in the eastern Mediterranean after the division of the Empire, and it was surely in the east that Venetian merchants found the inspiration for their early palaces. The question of the precise directions of influence in this case is still unclear, for building traditions that were widely diffused over the eastern Empire cannot be easily distinguished from those that were later transmitted across the eastern Mediterranean by Venetian colonisers. The fact that the Venetian word *fondaco*, the name used for the earliest

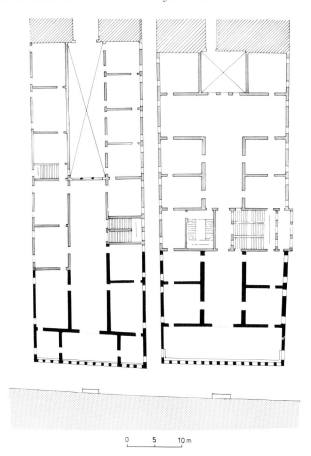

Ca' Loredan and Ca' Farsetti, probably thirteenth century. *Piano nobile* of each. After Maretto. (Heavy shading indicates the earliest portions of the buildings)

merchants' palaces, derives from the Arabic *fondouk*, or trading post, is evidence for the link with Islamic traditions. It is notable how well this type of palace suited the needs of the Venetian merchant, and how easily it could be adapted to the peculiar physical conditions of Venice and varied to suit individual circumstances. Indeed, so adaptable was the scheme that it was even revived in the Veneto countryside in the Renaissance.

We should not be too surprised to discover that away from the main canals domestic architecture took a somewhat different form. There are two fairly well preserved thirteenth-century façades in the Salizzada San Lio, which show that in relatively normal urban locations the architecture had much in common with buildings of the same period in nearby mainland cities such as Padua (*Fig. 15*).[25] Both houses have shops on the ground floor opening directly on to the street, with the shop windows and doors framed by great stone piers and wooden lintels in the characteristic Venetian fashion. Each building preserves a fine thirteenth-century biforate window on the first floor, presumably once belonging to the main living rooms. One house has two high wings flanking a huge central archway; the other probably had the same form originally, although one of the side blocks has now vanished. Both have been so completely rebuilt inside that one cannot reconstruct the original plans, but obviously houses such as these had a far more modest function than the larger palaces. They had no facilities for loading or unloading merchandise from boats, nor huge central halls which would have occupied valuable space rather uselessly, while the shops were probably for letting, as a source of income.

In mainland Italy the protective character of domestic buildings precluded elaborate decoration on the outer walls. In Venice, by contrast, an arcaded water frontage was a splendid vehicle for architectural expression. In the thirteenth century the Romanesque round-headed arches, like those which characterized Doge Ziani's Procuratie Vecchie, were superseded in secular buildings by the Byzantine stilted arches which had been prominent in religious architecture since the eleventh century. The large scale importation of sculptural fragments and precious marbles into Venice after the Fourth Crusade is reflected in the inlaid medallions and Byzantine reliefs which adorn many thirteenth-century palaces. Meanwhile stonemasons from Lombardy and the Veneto were employed to carve exquisite capitals and cornices, which harmonized effortlessly with the eastern elements to produce a characteristically Venetian synthesis, well illustrated in the façade of the Palazzo Loredan.

The rapid vertical accents of the porticoed Veneto-Byzantine façades – with their narrow bays, slender columns, and tall stilted arches – allowed an effect of lightness to be achieved without weakening the structure. Only the main water entrance usually had a wider archway, for emphasis and convenience. The openness of the façade walls was not only decorative, but also had an important practical advantage in Venice, allowing as much light as possible into the buildings. This was especially significant in the case of the great central halls, which stretched far back from the façades. Because of the shortage of land in the city, the buildings were so closely spaced that relatively little light could enter from the sides and the rear.

Thirteenth-century transformations

During the thirteenth century a gradual change towards a less 'transparent' type of palace façade took place. In buildings such as the Palazzo Loredan and the Fondaco dei Turchi the side blocks were only subtly differentiated on the façade, by partly closing the porticoes on the ground floor and placing *caesurae* – solid piers or paired columns – in the upper colonnades. Later, however, it became more common to restrict the *piano nobile* arcade to the centre of the palace, indicating the position of the huge *portego* inside, the room which needed the most illumination. A fine example of this arrangement, and one which nevertheless retains the typically Veneto-Byzantine stilted arches, inlaid Byzantine reliefs, basket capitals, and finely carved string course, is the much restored Palazzo Donà (*Fig. 16*). (The balustrade, as in the case of virtually all thirteenth-century palaces, is a later addition.) The ground-floor portico has here been abandoned, to be replaced by a single large water gate in the centre, leading straight into the *androne*. This more solid type of façade, in which the wall surfaces are visible, not concealed behind screening porticoes, must have been considerably cheaper and simpler to build. It was to become the most common arrangement (again with many variations on the theme) for waterfront Gothic palaces of the fourteenth and fifteenth centuries.

Naturally, the transition to the Gothic style also involved a transformation of architectural language. Ruskin has identified a series of stages or 'orders' by which the Veneto-Byzantine arch evolved into the Gothic arch (*Fig. 38*). To begin with, a small point or cusp appears on the outer rim, or extrados, of the stilted, round-headed arch. Then the inner rim, or intrados, also becomes pointed, to form a stilted ogee arch with a slight inflection in the crown. This stage can be seen as preparing the way for the introduction of the true Gothic arch, already widespread on the mainland in the thirteenth century.[26]

Unfortunately, as Ruskin himself was aware, a Darwinian view of evolution, however elegant the scheme may be, cannot always be easily applied to architecture, for there is no direct, hereditary process by which 'genes' are passed from one palace to another. Furthermore, the relative age of thirteenth-century palaces is uncertain, and only a small fraction of those built survive today, most of them radically altered since that time. It would be a great over-simplification to place them in chronological sequence to fit Ruskin's evolutionary stages. The coexistence of different 'orders' in individual buildings adds to the difficulties. For example, in the Ca' da Mosto (later the home of the great fifteenth-century Venetian explorer, and subsequently a famous inn, the Osteria del Leon Bianco), the now fragmentary Veneto-Byzantine arcade on the ground floor is surmounted by a *piano nobile* which corresponds with Ruskin's second stage, that is to say, with a slight inflection on the outer crown of the arch (*Fig. 17*). In this case one could suggest that the building was rebuilt preserving the older Byzantine waterfront portico, or completed very slowly – or even that these lower portions were brought from another building, since they fit together somewhat awkwardly. Other examples, however, are more complicated. For instance, in the Palazzo Leon in the Corte del Remer, a wide Byzantine archway on the *piano nobile* adjoins a biforate window of Ruskin's third stage which was apparently constructed at the same time. (The more mature Gothic arches of the staircase below were probably added later.) A glance at the religious architecture of the thirteenth century gives a further indication of the complexity of the subject. Gothic windows had already begun to appear in the fabric of San Marco in the twelfth century, whilst in the thirteenth century, as we have seen, there were attempts to conceal Gothic forms behind conventional Romanesque arches. Meanwhile the great new churches built by the Mendicant orders in the thirteenth century, which will be discussed in a later chapter, were probably being constructed in a plain, early Gothic style.

We should perhaps see the thirteenth century as a period in which Ruskin's various 'orders' coexisted. The style of each building would have depended to a great extent on the tastes of the individual patron. Throughout the history of Venetian architecture, as elsewhere, there have been a few enlightened or *avant garde* patrons, while the rest have been more conservative. At the same

time conscious archaizing was probably always more prevalent in Venice than in other Italian cities. The fact that Venetian merchants travelled widely in the east must account for the appearance of the stilted ogee arch in the city, for this has a distinctly Oriental flavour and is surely of Islamic origin. It did not appear widely elsewhere in Europe, and thus cannot be seen as an essential stage in the transition from the Romanesque to the Gothic style.

17 Ca' da Mosto, later Osteria del Leon Bianco, thirteenth century onwards *(Sarah Quill)*

CHAPTER III

The Mediaeval City

Venice as an urban environment

By the end of the thirteenth century the city of Venice was a true metropolis. The 70 or so principal islands of the archipelago, each one a separate parish, had been enlarged by drainage and reclamation until they coalesced to form a coherent urban organism, separated only by canals. The population in 1300 had probably grown to nearly 120,000 inhabitants, about the same figure as that recorded in 1969. Venice was then one of the largest cities in Western Europe. It seems that only Florence, Milan, Naples, Palermo and, outside Italy, Paris were of comparable size.[1]

At this point we should therefore pause to examine the urban structure of the city, its peculiar problems and its unusual features. The earliest known plan of Venice, datable to about 1346, shows clearly that the city was already a compact 'land-mass', although the representation is extremely schematic (*Fig. 18*). (The plan seems to be based on a twelfth-century prototype, partly updated by the copyist.)[2] The only buildings shown are the more prominent churches and the crenellated enclosures of the Arsenal and Piazza San Marco. There are also some fortifications indicated on the landward side of the city. By this time there must already have been a comprehensive system of streets (though these do not appear on the map) as well as canals. To a great extent the network still survives today, but one can gain an even better idea of the character of Venice in the Gothic period from the wonderfully detailed and reliable bird's eye view of the city by Jacopo de'Barbari which is dated 1500.

Like other major European cities – London, Florence, Paris and Rome are familiar examples – the city of Venice is traversed by a principal waterway, in this case the Grand Canal, which winds in an inverted S-shape through the city. One could safely say that all important cities in mediaeval Europe had water access, since water transport was the cheapest method for conveying supplies and merchandise. However, in most cases there was a clear demarcation between land and water, whereas in Venice – as in some towns in the Low Countries such as Amsterdam – the whole city was obviously crisscrossed by canals. A number of the original canals have now been filled in to make streets, but their presence is usually recorded in the street names by words like *rio terà* or *piscina*.

Like London, Venice had only one bridge across the main waterway. This was the Rialto Bridge, situated at that most significant geographical landmark, the lowest bridging point – that is to say, the most seaward point at which a bridge could easily be built. It was also the uppermost point to which sea-going vessels could navigate. The original pontoon bridge was replaced at

OPPOSITE
18 Plan of Venice, *c.*1346, from the *Cronaca Magna* (*Biblioteca Marciana, Venice*)

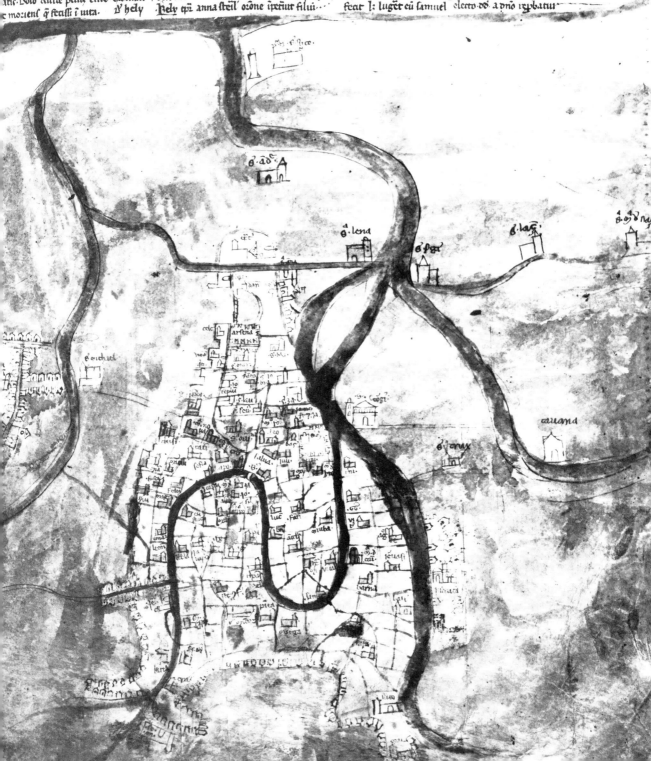

the end of the fourteenth century by a permanent wooden structure. This bridge came to a dramatic end in 1450 when it collapsed under the weight of crowds of spectators during the visit of Emperor Frederick III of Austria.[3] The bridge was rebuilt, once again in wood, with a drawbridge in the centre, this time lined with shops like the Ponte Vecchio in Florence. This picturesque structure is vividly depicted in Carpaccio's famous painting of the 'Miracle of the True Cross' dated 1494 (*Fig. 19*). The present stone bridge, built by an architect named (most appropriately!) Antonio da Ponte, dates from the end of the sixteenth century. The importance of the Rialto Bridge to the Venetians is indicated by the fact that the State had commissioned designs from architects as renowned as Michelangelo, Sansovino, Palladio and Vignola. Even da Ponte's relatively sober project cost the huge sum of 250,000 ducats.

The first bridges over the smaller canals were also built of wood. Even today wooden bridges are still common in the city, although nowadays the walking surfaces are usually asphalted. Later, stone bridges were also erected, built in a characteristic low arc, with broad, shallow steps. These early stone bridges – surviving examples can still be seen near the church of San Felice (*Fig. 20*) and on the island of Torcello – had no railings at the sides. Until the eighteenth century, rival factions from neighbouring parishes used to have spectacular fist-fights on the tops of these bridges, with many of the less fortunate assailants toppling into the water.

The Rialto Bridge continued to be the only fixed crossing point on the Grand Canal until the 1850s, when bridges were erected at the Accademia and the railway station. Anyone wishing to cross the Grand Canal at another point could avoid the detour to the Rialto Bridge by taking a *traghetto* or gondola ferry. These *traghetti* (most of which have only recently disappeared and a few

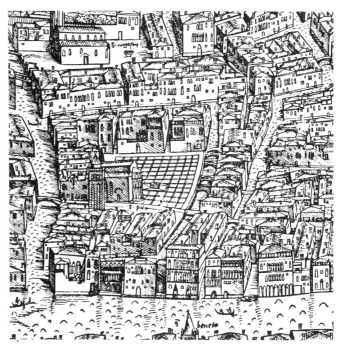

ABOVE
21 Campo San Polo,
with former canal along
the east side. Detail from
Jacopo de' Barbari's
bird's-eye-view map of
Venice, 1500

of which still function today) were operated at 13 different points along the Grand Canal. One of the *traghetti* even crossed beneath the Rialto Bridge, to save people the trouble of climbing the steps of the bridge. The English traveller Thomas Coryate, writing in 1611, warned visitors against this particular crossing, claiming that:

> '. . . the boatmen that attend this ferry are the most vicious and licentious varlets about all the City. For if a stranger entreth into one of their Gondoloas, and doth not presently tell them whither he will goe, they will incontinently carry him of their owne accord to a religious house forsooth, where his plumes shall be well pulled before he commeth forth againe.'[4]

The *traghetto* jetties can be recognized by their water-side platforms decorated with trellises of vines and lamps. Until they were largely superseded by the *vaporetto* service (which receives a heavier public subsidy), the positions of the *traghetti* remained unchanged. It would be no exaggeration to say that the layout of streets, houses and shops was therefore just as much affected by their presence as by the positions of the city's bridges.

Again like London, mediaeval Venice had two important centres – the commercial centre on the island of Rialto and the political centre at Piazza San Marco. The episcopal centre at San Pietro di Castello never had the significance of, for instance, the Piazza del Duomo in Florence, or those of Milan or Pisa. San Marco and Rialto were the highest and driest of the marshy islands, and therefore provided the firmest building sites for the early settlers. Unlike the Cities of London and Westminster, however, the commercial and political centres of Venice lay not on the same bank, but on opposite sides of the principal waterway. This gave even greater importance to the link provided by the Rialto Bridge. The street connecting Rialto with Piazza San Marco, known as the Merceria, was the most frequented thoroughfare in the city. As a result, there was a heavy concentration of shops in and around the Merceria.[5] Nevertheless, in spite of the great importance of the route, it never became a broad, stately highway, since no wheeled traffic apart from hand carts used it. To this day it is narrow, crooked, and often badly congested.

This observation leads us to consider the very distinctive transportation system within Venice itself, and its effects on the planning of the city. To a modern planner Venice has certain utopian features. In particular, pedestrian traffic in the city has never been seriously threatened by wheeled vehicles other than barrows. Even before the days of the motor car, Venice was far quieter than other cities. Henry James remarked in 1882:

> 'There is no noise there save distinctly human noise; no rumbling, no vague uproar, nor rattle of wheels and hoofs. It is all articulate and vocal and personal. One may say indeed that Venice is emphatically the city of conversation; people talk all over the place because there is nothing to interfere with its being caught by the ear. . . . The still water carries the voice, and good Venetians exchange confidences at a distance of half a mile.'[6]

In Venice pedestrians and goods traffic are conveyed on completely separate, overlapping systems. The two superimposed communication patterns did not, however, evolve completely independently. Every market had to have both land and water access. We see from Barbari's map that Campo San Polo, which was the site of one of the two principal weekly markets in the city (the other was in Piazza San Marco), originally had a canal along its curved side to transport goods to the stalls (*Fig. 21*). Similarly, every important palace had to have water access as well as a street entrance. A canal mooring was needed to bring in supplies of food and fuel, and for loading and unloading merchandise when the owner was involved in trade. Until the present century, wealthy families would have owned at least one private gondola for their own use, as well as small flat-bottomed boats for carrying goods. These were tied up at the characteristic decorated wooden mooring posts in front of the palaces. Although there were a few horses in Venice, the Venetian palace obviously had no need for extensive stables; and in Venice, boatyards, or *squeri*, took the place of coach-builders in mainland cities. Horse-riding in the Merceria was forbidden in 1297; after that time riders used to tie their horses to a leafy fig-tree at the Rialto end of the street.[7]

The layout of the canals was determined by the natural position of the lagoon channels. Although these were altered slightly in the process of drainage and land reclamation, it was essential not to impede the natural flow of the tides, which was vital for the removal of sewage and debris from the canals. Regular dredging has always been necessary to prevent the silting up of the navigational channels, both in the city and in the shallow waters of the lagoon. For the earlier settlers water was the only important means of transport, since the individual islands were too small for streets to have much significance.

In contrast to the canals, the layout of the pedestrian walkways seems incoherent. Venice is one of the few important mediaeval cities which had no previous Roman settlement on the site. Most Italian cities still preserve traces of the regular Roman grid pattern in their street plans, but Venice has few straight streets of any length. As every lost tourist becomes only too well aware, many of the streets come to a dead end on the bank of a canal or in a small courtyard. Each parish was built up street by street around its own church and *campo* (literally a field, though by the time of Barbari's map most *campi* were paved) in the centre of each island.

A series of studies of the urban fabric of Venice, organized by Saverio Muratori in the 1950s, identified a possible pattern of evolution in the structure of the city. In the most ancient parishes, established before the transfer of the Dogeship to the Rialto in 812, the society was almost totally dependent on water transport. The most powerful families apparently lived around small enclosed courtyards, forming a cellular pattern, traces of which still remain – for instance in the area around San Giovanni Cristostomo. The studies suggest that about 14 of the 70 parishes of the city date from this very early 'pre-Dogal' period. From the ninth century onwards the more open mercantile society which was evolving began to need land as well as water transport, to provide quick internal communication. Settlements of this period grew up in a linear pattern along the new streets, such as the Salizzada San Lio (*Fig. 15*), while the existing closed courtyards were linked by connecting passages. According to Muratori's scheme the large communal *campi* which are now such a prominent feature of the townscape first became widespread in the tenth century. The typical parish *campo* is rectangular in shape, with the church on one side, and with residential developments taking place along transverse streets.[8]

The streets of one parish met those of another almost accidentally when, in the process of land reclamation, the islands joined up. In consequence, though the principal thoroughfares were linked by bridges over the canals, the other streets did not fit together easily. Even the bridges often crossed the canals at an angle because the streets were out of alignment. It is still possible in a map of modern Venice to detect discord in the street patterns at parish boundaries. Because of the absence of fast wheeled traffic there was little need to eliminate kinks in the street network. The person on foot could easily scuttle round corners that a horse-drawn coach could not possibly have negotiated. Some of the streets of Venice are less than one metre wide. In Goethe's words:

'As a rule one can measure the width of an alley with one's outstretched arms; in the narrowest one even scrapes one's elbows if one holds them akimbo.'[9]

The narrower alleys cause particular problems to pedestrians carrying umbrellas!

Other mediaeval cities had their share of higgledy-piggledy, narrow, winding streets, but few such labyrinths have survived because of the danger of fire and the problems of traffic congestion and overcrowding.

All these difficulties struck Venice, too, but it was harder to eliminate them.

Fires were an ever-present hazard in the city, and because of the closely spaced buildings they spread rapidly, especially in windy conditions. Venice was to some extent fortunate, in that most parts of the city had nearby canals to supply water for fire fighting, but this did not prevent numerous, terrible conflagrations. Possibly the most traumatic of all was the fire which devastated virtually the whole of the island of Rialto in 1514, but the chronicles and histories of Venice record many other major fire disasters.

Traffic congestion on both streets and canals was a perpetual worry, and was controlled by strict government legislation. Special magistracies were responsible for keeping the streets and canals free of obstruction. All private individuals had to apply to these magistracies for planning permission to build in the city. Careful measurements were then taken of the widths of the neighbouring streets or canals, to ensure that any new buildings would not encroach on public property. There was a constant struggle to regulate the number of stalls obstructing the streets, porticoes and public open spaces of the Rialto and Piazza San Marco. Heavy fines and even short terms of imprisonment failed to deter the illegal stallholders, eager for custom in the most frequented parts of the city. A resolution was even passed in 1548 ordering pig owners to ensure that their animals did not run loose in the streets.[10]

Keeping the streets clean was not easy. Even today they are swept daily, in the early hours of the morning. The English visitor, James Howell, who wrote in 1651 that the streets of Venice were:

> '. . . so neat and eevenly pavd, that in the dead of Winter one may walk up and down in a pair of Sattin Pantables and Crimson Silk Stockins and not be dirtied.'[11]

must have been exceptionally lucky with the weather. Goethe had a lower opinion of Venetian streets.

'If only they would keep their city cleaner!' he wrote in Venice in 1786.

> '. . . On rainy days a disgusting sludge collects underfoot; the coats and *tabarros*, which are worn all year round, are bespattered whenever you cross a bridge, and since everybody goes about in shoes and stockings – nobody wears boots – these get soiled, not with plain mud, but with a vile-smelling muck.'[12]

Overcrowding was a problem that Venice could do little to remedy, for there was not much scope for expansion on the margins of the city. Whereas in a mainland city like Florence a series of new walls enclosed progressively larger areas as the city grew, Venice could only grow by the painful process of draining land from the lagoon. The shortage of land was most acute in the quarters around the Rialto and Piazza San Marco. The demand for property in these central zones made the price of land tremendously high. Sites on the Grand Canal, which had the advantage of prestige as well as a fine view, were also much sought after. The high land values led to certain characteristic features in the city's architecture. A house owner could more cheaply extend

his accommodation by adding an extra storey on top of his own building, than by acquiring a neighbouring site. One can often see the various floors of a palace built in progressively later styles towards the top – conspicuous examples include the Ca' da Mosto, and the Palazzo Priuli-Bon at San Stae (*Figs. 17 & 40*). As Goethe put it:

> 'The houses grew upward like closely planted trees, and were forced to make up in height what they were denied in width.'[13]

The most extreme example of this process of upward growth can be seen in the former Ghetto (called by the Venetian word for iron foundry, since there was once a foundry on the site) where all Jewish residents were forced to live (*Fig 22*).

A house owner could also enlarge his living accommodation by building out his house over a public street, so that the street passed through a short arcade known as a *sottoportego*. Except in Piazza San Marco and the Rialto market, continuous shopping arcades like those of mainland cities such as Padua and Bologna are not found in Venice, where the streets are too narrow, but these space-saving *sottoporteghi* are very common.

Another means of expanding the interior space in a dwelling was to project the upper storeys a short distance over the street, supported on wooden or stone corbels. One of the most interesting examples is the street picturesquely named the Calle del Paradiso, adjoining the Salizzada San Lio (*Fig. 23*). The narrow street is flanked by shops and workshops on each side, with staircases leading to the living apartments above. (This layout is typical of Venetian small

ABOVE, LEFT
22   View of the Ghetto from outside
(*A.F.Kersting*)

ABOVE
23   Calle del Paradiso, thirteenth to sixteenth centuries (*A.F.Kersting*)

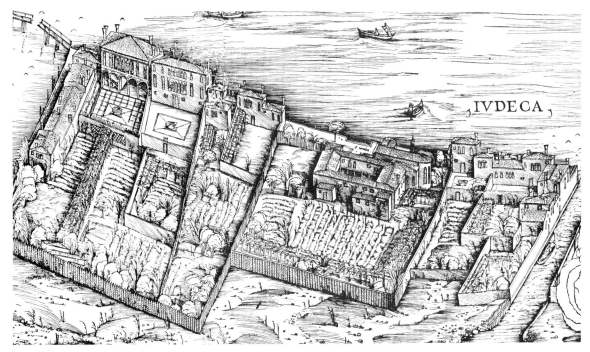

IVDECA

24 Suburban villas on the Giudecca. Detail from Jacopo de' Barbari's bird's-eye-view map of Venice, 1500

scale property developments.) The upper floors project on either side almost to within arm's reach of each other. At each end of the street they are joined by decorative Gothic arches – a device commonly used in Venice to indicate property ownership. The arch at the canal end is decorated with a relief of the Madonna della Misericordia and dated 1407, but the buildings themselves have probably been replaced in piecemeal fashion, for the dates of the various parts range from the thirteenth to the sixteenth centuries.

Despite the serious shortage of land, there are open spaces in Venice. Francesco Sansovino claimed that all the parish *campi* place side by side would make an area large enough for the site of a whole city.[14] There have always been plenty of private gardens, even in the more central parts of Venice. The visitor on foot is hardly aware of the gardens, which are concealed behind high walls, but seen from the top of the Campanile of San Marco, the city does not in fact lack greenery. Sansovino mentioned all the most famous gardens in his guidebook in 1580, admiring their fountains, rare plants, sculpture, and even paintings.[15] According to Barbari's map of 1500, the island of Giudecca was then occupied by pleasant suburban villas with extensive gardens (*Fig. 24*). At that time the peripheral quarters, which are now mostly built up, were gardens, orchards and vineyards. Just as any walled city in the later Middle Ages had cultivated areas, chiefly market gardens, inside the fortifications, so Venice had semi-rural areas within the boundaries of the city, to provide fresh fruit, vegetables and dairy produce.

Before the twentieth-century wave of emigration, with large numbers of the inhabitants moving to the neighbouring mainland town of Mestre, the population pressure in Venice was only alleviated by natural causes, in the form of high mortality rates and outbreaks of plague. Epidemics spread easily

in the overcrowded conditions, especially since no one realised that bubonic plague was carried by rats, and typhus by lice. By far the most terrible pestilence was the Black Death, which killed 50 or 60% of the population of the city between 1347 and 1349. A series of lesser epidemics struck the city at intervals during the next two centuries, but these did not have a significant effect on the population. For instance, after the severe famine of 1527, serious outbreaks of typhus and bubonic plague occurred, but so many of the victims were starving peasants from the mainland, who had migrated to Venice in search of food, that the resident population was reduced by only about 4%. During the sixteenth century the population rose rapidly, to reach its all-time peak of 190,000 before the next great plague of 1575–77, when one third of the inhabitants of Venice perished. Another outbreak of similar magnitude occurred in 1630–31. On each occasion there was a rapid, partial recovery in population, as immigrants from the mainland flocked into the city to take up the vacant jobs. In general the population of Venice since about 1300 has remained remarkably stable, fluctuating between about 100,000 and 140,000 for most of this period. The figures refer to the city itself, which has no sprawling suburbs on account of its restricted site. This fact obviously distinguishes Venice from other important European cities; but we must not forget that the city did develop its own suburbs on the nearby mainland and on the Lido.

25 Antonio da Canal, called Canaletto: 'The Stonemason's Yard', c.1726–1727, showing the preparation of stone for the new façade of San Vidal. The church, convent and Scuola of the Carità can be seen on the opposite bank of the Grand Canal (*National Gallery, London*)

Building materials and techniques

Venice is founded on sand, silt and clay, topped by gravel in the higher spots such as Piazza San Marco and the Rialto. Most visitors think of Venice as flat, but anyone who lives in the city for some length of time soon learns that there are minor variations in elevation, for the lower parts are more likely to be flooded in the high tides. In reality Piazza San Marco is no longer one of the highest points; its level has sunk, not only because of the subsidence resulting from the removal of Artesian water from the bedrock of the lagoon, which has affected the whole city, but also on account of the great weight of buildings around the Piazza, which has compressed the subsoil over the centuries.

In the streets, the paving stones are laid directly on to the sand, as one can clearly see when repairs are carried out. Before the fifteenth century few streets were even paved – they were merely paths of beaten earth. The streets of Venice do not need to support heavy weights; buildings, on the other hand, naturally need a more elaborate substructure. Only in the first areas to be settled was the ground firm enough to proceed without special foundations. In these parts, alder stakes about one metre long support a base of elm and larch and foundation walls of large stone blocks. Elsewhere every building had to be supported on wood piles, driven deep into the alluvial clay by teams of labourers with heavy wooden hammers, cheered on by rhythmic beating songs. These piles were at least four or five metres long. Most of the piles were sunk underneath the outside walls of a building, those which had to carry the greatest load. Interior dividing walls had less substantial foundations, a fact which has led to subsidence in many cases. Clay was excavated from within the solid line of piles marking the perimeter walls. Along the edge of a canal a stockade of piles lined with wooden planks served to keep water out of the foundations, and a moat was dug around the building before the site was drained. More piles were sunk in the central space, and the ground was built up with layers of crushed brick and stone, and larch rafts set in cement. The tops of the piles were smoothed off about three metres below the high tide level, to serve as a base for the brick foundation walls. Layers of larch planks, each layer arranged at right angles to the one below, helped to spread the load on the soft ground. The walls were very wide at their base, but narrowed gradually towards the water level.[16]

Brick was the most common building material in Venetian architecture, for it was the only one produced locally. The bricks made of clay from the nearby mainland have a rich red–brown colour, which gives a characteristic element of warmth to the townscape. Roof tiles came from the same source. The simplest finish for brick walls is pointing, that is, sealing the mortar joints with a lime solution and a light stucco. However, many of the brick walls which are now exposed were once completely covered with stucco. The typical Venetian stucco was made of powdered brick and grains of marble in a lime base, producing a warm red colour and a glistening finish. Examples are still visible, though modern stucco work is coloured artificially. Some of the stuccoed walls were covered with a light grey plaster and then frescoed, but the wall paintings soon perished in the saline atmosphere. Fragments of frescoed figures by Giorgione and Titian, rescued from the Fondaco dei Tedeschi, can be seen in the Accademia Gallery.

There is no local stone in the immediate vicinity of the lagoon. The soft yellowish limestone quarried near Padua weathers so easily that it could not be used in Venice. The building stone most widely used in the city is the brilliant white, marble-like limestone from Istria, which could be cheaply transported from the quarries by sea.[17] Istrian stone is very easy to carve, yet it is remarkably resistant to weathering, even in the humid, saline, and now badly polluted atmosphere of Venice. (Canaletto's evocative painting in the National Gallery, known as the 'Stonemasons' Yard', shows stonecutters preparing huge blocks of white Istrian stone for the new façade of the nearby church of San Vidal (*Fig. 25*). Details such as window frames, capitals and bases, cornices, balustrades and doorways, are usually of Istrian stone. A layer of the same stone at the high water mark of a building helped to impede rising damp in the walls, although now that the land is sinking these damp courses are no longer effective. From the Renaissance onwards the grander buildings were faced entirely in white Istrian stone. These façades radiate a dazzling brightness in sunlight, especially where they are exposed to the rain that washes away accumulations of grime and soot.

Red marble from Verona was also used for carved details such as portals and fireplaces in the more expensive buildings. This stone has a glowing rust-red colour when polished, although it weathers to a rougher whitish surface. The weathering process is well demonstrated by the two red marble lions in the Piazzetta dei Leoncini behind San Marco, whose backs are polished to a shiny red by many generations of Venetian children riding them, while the rest of their bodies have turned a dull pink. The recent restoration of the Loggetta at the foot of the Campanile of San Marco has revived the red polished surface of the Verona marble, which had faded through the same weathering effect (*Fig. 77*). A checked pattern of red marble from Cattraro and white Istrian stone was popular for the paving of ground floor rooms such as *androni*, as the colours were only intensified when the floor was wet.

Other precious marbles added to the prestige value of a building. As we have seen, San Marco is adorned with pieces of oriental marble looted from Constantinople (*Fig. 9*). The façade of the Palazzo Vendramin-Calergi (now the winter Casinò), built at the beginning of the sixteenth century, is adorned with carved porphyry, serpentine, and veined oriental marble (*Fig. 62*). The Loggetta, built by Jacopo Sansovino in 1537–45, has carved details of white Carrara marble and the dark-green stone known as *verde antica*, as well as red Verona marble and Istrian stone, while the columns are of various rare oriental marbles (*Fig. 77*). The same architect, sent to restore the church at Pola in Istria, removed the priceless marble columns for use in his own buildings, chiefly the Library. (He replaced them by brick piers, but within a decade the 'restored' church at Pola was a total ruin.)[18] One of the most remarkable instances of the ostentatious use of costly materials was the Ca' d'Oro, built by Marin Contarini in the early fifteenth century (*Fig. 42*). As we shall see, the building accounts show that the façade was not only decorated with precious marbles, but was once also painted in ultramarine (the most expensive colour pigment of all, made from ground lapis lazuli) and gold.

Wood was the indispensable raw material for the Venetian building industry.[19] It was needed not only for piles but also for ceiling timbers and roof beams. Dalmatian oak, imported by sea, was the most resilient wood for piles, though it was restricted in length. Oak supplies were also floated by river to Venice from Friuli and from the area around Treviso. By the early thirteenth century coniferous wood, chiefly larch or spruce, was already being floated down to Venice along the rivers from the forests of Cadore and the Dolomites. This softer type of wood was especially useful for ceiling beams, not only because of the length of the timbers but also on account of their light weight and their elasticity. On the unstable Venetian soil the greatest possible flexibility was needed in a building to absorb minor shifts in the foundations. For this reason vaulted ceilings are rarely found in Venice, except in churches where they are usually supported by wooden cross beams. Ceiling beams were closely spaced to provide the maximum support, and topped by one or two layers of wooden planks. Resin in the fir wood gave a degree of natural protection against damp. The visible timbers were often richly decorated with painted or carved designs. With the huge demand for wood – especially oak – for the Venetian shipbuilding industry, the mainland forests were becoming badly depleted by the end of the fifteenth century. As a result the price of wood rose sharply, but there was no possible substitute in the building trade. The foundations alone might cost as much as a third of the total cost of a building.[20] Building accounts preserved from the restoration and extension of Ca'Giustinian in the 1470s show that wood accounted for 43% of the total cost of materials.

The need for flexibility also fostered the development in Venice of special types of flooring. In the simplest houses, the floors were merely bare wooden boards or sometimes brick tiles, with beaten earth in the ground-floor rooms. A more elegant surface, known as *paston*, was composed of ground tiles and bricks set in cement and polished to bring out the red terracotta colour, which was intensified by the addition of the pigment cinnabar in the top layer. From the fifteenth century onwards, *paston* was largely superseded by a more decorative version called *terrazzo*.[21] In living apartments this surface, like *paston*, was laid on top of the boards covering the ceiling of the floor below. It was made up of two layers of crushed brick and stone set in cement, each layer well beaten down with battering rams for several days. About a year had to elapse between the laying of the two layers. The top layer also contained chips of coloured marble, so that when it was smoothed off with mill stones and oiled with linseed oil the effect was like a random mosaic. As in the case of *paston*, the cement base and tiny stones gave a certain elasticity to the floor surface, so that it could resist minor stresses and strains without cracking. If cracks did appear, it was a fairly simple matter to lay another thin layer of *terrazzo* on top. According to Francesco Sansovino, *terrazzo* floors were so highly polished that one could see one's own reflection in them, and carpets were even put down to prevent footprints marking the floors.[22]

The other Venetian building practice which greatly impressed foreigners was the extensive use of glass in the windows. The glass industry on the island of Murano, and even Venice itself, was flourishing by the end of the twelfth century.[23] Glass furnaces were finally banned from Venice in 1291 because of the risk of fire, and the industry became concentrated in Murano. Sansovino, writing in 1580, claimed that even the humblest buildings in Venice at that time had glass windows, whereas in other cities they had to make do with oiled canvas or parchment.[24] The round discs of clear bottle glass were held in place by lead and iron, in wooden window frames, as one can clearly see in Carpaccio's painting of the 'Dream of St Ursula' in the Accademia Gallery (*Fig. 26*). (This picture gives a vivid impression of a Venetian bedroom in the late fifteenth century.) Some bottle glass windows still exist in Venice, though most have been replaced by plate glass. As we have seen, Venetian buildings needed the largest possible windows to admit light in the cramped surroundings, but without the local supply of glass large windows would have been unthinkable in the Venetian climate.

Iron was not used very extensively in Venice, for it tends to corrode in the damp climate, but small quantities of iron were needed in every building for door locks, window fittings, hinges, railings and other such details. From the nineteenth century onwards it became common practice to secure leaning structures with iron tie beams. Earlier, iron chains had been used for the same purpose. Neither method proved very satisfactory in the long run, since iron is too rigid to accommodate minor movements in the structure. Buildings restored in this way have tended to develop serious cracks in the walls. Furthermore, the effect of the iron rusting where it comes in contact with the atmosphere has caused corrosion in the walls around the points of insertion of the tie rods or chains.

Each building technique was carried out by specialist craftsmen belonging

26 Vittore Carpaccio: 'The Dream of Saint Ursula', signed and dated 1495, showing a fifteenth-century Venetian bedroom. Accademia Gallery, Venice *(Osvaldo Böhm)*

to separate artisans' guilds.[25] There were bricklayers, stonemasons, *terrazzeri*, carpenters, glaziers and iron workers. These craftsmen had to serve an apprenticeship of five to seven years, usually starting at between 12 and 15 years of age, followed by a period of two or three years as assistant to a guild member. At the end of the training they had to take a test to prove their competence, before they were admitted as *capomaestri* or master craftsmen. Sons of guild members, if apprenticed to their fathers, were exempted from the final examination. The successful candidates in the *terrazzo*-makers' test, which involved making a floor of 50 Venetian square *passi* (paces), not only had to pay a fee but also had to invite the examiners to dinner. The labourers who assisted the *maestri* were not guild members, except in the stonemasons' yards, but were casual employees paid by the day. Each workshop had one *capomaestro*, who employed two or three assistants in addition to his own sons and his apprentices. The patrons, or groups of individuals, wishing to erect a building usually did their own subcontracting. They invited estimates from various craftsmen for each job, and awarded the contracts to the *maestri* offering the most favourable terms. Only the stonemasons supplied their own raw materials, for they had to choose the most suitable stone for each job. Otherwise a patron had to arrange separate contracts with the suppliers of bricks, lime, sand, wood and iron, as well as with boatmen to transport heavy cargoes, such as mud excavated from the canals or rubble for the foundations. By this system each artisan needed very little capital. He merely had to own or rent a workshop and provide his own tools. And indeed he had little opportunity to accumulate capital. Both the practice of subcontracting by the patron, which prevented the growth of larger scale firms of all round building contractors, and the statutes of the individual guilds, discouraged the acquisition of wealth or power by a single craftsman. The skilled artisan was a respected member of Venetian society, but he was kept firmly in his place.

As elsewhere in mediaeval Europe the designers of buildings, like other artists, were rarely named or recorded in documents, and few of their works of art were signed. It should not, however, be assumed that in the Middle Ages buildings grew almost organically, fed by a kind of communal urge to build. Most architectural designs were probably the product of close collaboration between the patron and the chief artisan, usually a stonemason, and it is the identities of the patrons rather than the architects that have survived to posterity. Before the Renaissance, when the value of creative genius at last began to command as much respect as the wealth and enterprise of the patron, it is rarely possible to identify the artistic personalities of individual architects. The fact that the title *architectus* was not used in Venice until as late as the 1470s, apart from one known isolated example in 1455, is symbolic of the change in attitude which came about at this time.[26]

OPPOSITE
27 Scala del Bovolo, Palazzo Contarini, San Luca, *c.* 1499 *(Sarah Quill)*

Essential services and other amenities

The peculiar physical environment of Venice, the building techniques adopted, and the particular functions of the buildings have all contributed to

the special character of Venetian architecture. The provision of essential commodities such as heat, light, water supply and sewage disposal also led to solutions which have left their imprint on the urban landscape. Certain distinguishing features are immediately obvious to the visitor, others are less easily recognized, but all show a high degree of adaptation to the surroundings.

Every dwelling in the city needed efficient heating. Venetian winters can be bitterly cold, especially when the piercing wind called the *bora* blows from the north-east. Snow is not uncommon, though it rarely lies for long because of the proximity of the Adriatic Sea. The most famous frost was probably that of 1788, recorded in an anonymous painting in the Museo del Settecento at Ca' Rezzonico. But in spite of the fact that the temperature rarely falls below freezing point, the constant dampness gives a raw chill to the winter air.

Renaissance portraits show that it was fashionable for those who could afford it to dress in furs and heavy velvet cloaks – and with reason. As late as 1849, in a letter of 3 December, Effie Ruskin complained of the cold in Venetian palaces:

> '. . . We went today and looked over several Palaces but although the outsides are splendid Venetian Gothic I cannot fancy how the Italians live, for the insides although perfectly clean have such a want of comfort about them . . . and no fire places, even in this cold weather. Each member of the family carries about on their arm an earthen basket or pot with hot charcoal in it . . . The tesselated floors, although very smooth and glittering, are extremely cold and all their arrangements seem made for heat and not cold.'[27]

The great central halls, or *porteghi*, of Venetian palaces were usually unheated, and with their huge expanses of window at either end they must have been extremely draughty. We read in Francesco Sansovino's guide of 1581 that:

> 'All the bedrooms have fireplaces, but not the living-rooms. This is certainly wise, because when one gets out of bed, the fire is nearby, not only to dry the humidity which one gathers around oneself when sleeping, but also to heat the rooms and to purge the evil vapours which rise from the air or other sources.'[28]

(Sansovino also believed that centuries of burning fires had in some way purified the unhealthy air which the first settlers encountered in Venice.)[29]

Fireplaces were normally on the outside walls, arranged one above the other and connected to the same chimney. The disposition of windows in pairs, with a space between, commonly seen on the exteriors of buildings such as the façade of the Fondaco dei Tedeschi, indicates a sequence of rooms in the living apartments inside, each with one window on either side of the fireplace. In the more modest buildings the chimneys were often projected outwards from the side of the building, supported at the base on a stone shelf, in order to save valuable space in the interior. The smaller dwellings were obviously easier to heat than the great palaces, so that the poorer people could at least survive without fine furs and rich materials.

The remarkable chimney pots, which appear in views of Venice from Carpaccio to Canaletto, and a few of which still survive today, were one of the most curious features of the Venetian townscape. Of unusually large size, they were generally in the form of truncated, upturned cones, although there were many other variations. It is revealing that this was also the characteristic shape of the funnels of early American wood-burning steam trains, wood being the fuel normally used in Venice. The main function of the chimney-pots was to prevent sparks from escaping from the flues, for the risk of fire in the city was always a problem. They served not only as cinder traps, but also, of course, to keep out the rain and perhaps to improve the drawing power of the fires by impeding down draughts in the chimneys. Whatever the precise technical explanation, the Venetians evidently took pride in embellishing these conspicuous terracotta chimney pots with painted or relief decoration, as one can see, for example, on the left side of Carpaccio's painting of the 'Miracle of the True Cross' (*Fig. 19*).

The small enclosed courtyards, which punctuate the dense urban fabric of Venice, were important for the provision of both natural light and fresh water. Some were private courts inside palaces, usually placed at the back or on one side, others gave access to a number of more humble houses, generally the property of a single landlord. Until the sixteenth century, staircases were generally accommodated in the courtyards, to save space inside the buildings. The poorer dwellings had simple wooden ramps, while palaces were provided with elaborate stone staircases with carved balustrades, some originally roofed with wooden canopies. The most flamboyant external stairway in the city is the splendid spiral staircase known as the Scala del Bovolo (*bovolo* is the Venetian dialect word for a snail shell), built for a branch of the Contarini family in about 1499 (*Fig. 27*).

The provision of an adequate supply of fresh water has always raised problems in Venice, for the canal water is strongly saline, and is polluted by the discharge from the city's sewers. Some wells supplied saline lagoon water for ordinary domestic use, but rain water normally provided all the water for drinking. Public wells in the parish *campi* yielded enough water except in times of drought, when unscrupulous profiteers sold fresh water brought from the mainland in barges at exorbitant prices. The occupants of private palaces relied on rain water collected from their rooftops, funnelled through Istrian-stone gutters and drainpipes to the well in the courtyard (*Fig. 28*). There it was collected underground, filtered through sand, and stored beneath the well.[30] The fine Istrian-stone or Verona marble well heads, called *pozzi*, are a notable component of the Venetian scene. Their simple, solid, squat, cylindrical shape is characteristic, and a number of them are extremely ancient, to judge by their Byzantine-style carved decoration. It is typical of Venetian visual sensibilities that such a basic functional necessity should have become the excuse for decorative expression.

Sewage disposal was less of a problem in Venice than the water supply, for the ebb and flow of the tides removed the effluent with great efficiency. Even today the city relies on natural drainage. Except in high summer the canals do

not smell offensive, and then only in the most sluggish corners. Until this century the drains discharged their effluent at mid-tide level, so that the outlets were actually exposed at low tide, but now they are out of sight. Houses with no direct access to a canal were connected with covered drains leading to the nearest waterway. Only those houses that were furthest from the canals had to be content with cesspits. In this respect Venice had a great advantage over mainland cities – at least until the era of mains drainage. Solid refuse was collected in boats and carried to dumps on the mainland, or used to build up land for reclamation. In the mid-sixteenth century there were complaints that

28 Palazzo Centani, San Tomà, house of Carlo Goldoni; courtyard with exterior staircase and well, fifteenth century (*A.F.Kersting*)

64

mud, rubble and other rubbish supposed to be deposited at Marghera was being dumped in the lagoon, because the boatmen did not take the trouble to complete the long journey.[31]

Finally we should mention the profusion of balconies on Venetian buildings, and the curious sun terraces, called *altane*, on many of the rooftops. Balconies at *piano nobile* windows were not unknown in the grander town palaces in other parts of Italy, especially after they were introduced by Bramante in his famous House of Raphael in Rome in the early sixteenth century. Open *loggie* under the huge overhanging eaves of Florentine palaces served a similar purpose (though in the hotter climate of Florence shade was preferred to sun). But in Venice, because of the shortage of space for gardens and the poor light inside the buildings in congested areas, balconies are far more numerous than elsewhere, especially where the windows offer expansive views of the city.

Early examples took the form of simple Istrian-stone ledges supported on stone brackets and provided with plain iron railings for safety. Frequently the balconies are not coeval with the houses, having been added or replaced at a later date. Very broadly, one can date Venetian balconies (though not the buildings behind) to within a hundred years or so by the form of the balustrade. The typical Quattrocento baluster was a slender classical colonnette, while the stone hand rails often had seated seated lions or small stone busts at the corners. In the sixteenth century Sansovino introduced a new type of baluster borrowed from Michelangelo in Florence, which became extremely popular (*Figs. 76 & 80*). This was broadest in the middle, with a cubic block at the centre. Sanmicheli at the same period also used balusters which were broader in the middle, but with a 'waist' at the centre (*Fig. 81*). In the seventeenth century a more Baroque type of baluster, broader at the bottom, was adopted, sometimes alternating with uprights broader at the top, as in Longhena's Ca' Pesaro (*Fig. 96*). The eighteenth century's Rococo taste favoured little curved balconies with wrought-iron railings. Naturally this generalized outline does not accommodate all possible forms of balustrade, for the Venetian decorative imagination ranged far and wide, as we can see in the marvellous balconies of the Palazzo Contarini-Fasan (traditionally known as the House of Desdemona) which are like petrified Burano lace (*Fig. 44*).

The rooftop *altane* were in the form of wooden platforms supported on brick piers and reached by way of a staircase from a dormer window. A good example appears on the skyline of Carpaccio's 'Miracle of the True Cross'. The *altana* was used for drying washing, beating carpets, and for taking the sun. We must not forget that Venetian noble ladies were strictly chaperoned, and were only allowed out in the streets veiled and accompanied by their maids. Instead, they spent much of their time on the *altane*, bleaching their hair to the fashionable Titian-blonde colour. For this purpose they wore special straw hats without crowns, draping their long hair – anointed with a special preparation called *acqua di gioventù* – over the broad brims. Carpaccio's enigmatic painting in the Museo Correr, misleadingly known as 'The Courtesans', shows two noble ladies idling away their time on balcony or *altana*, with the help of a child, two dogs, a peacock, and some other tame birds (*Fig. 29*). In the corner of the picture one can see the absurdly high platform-soled shoes which restricted their movements yet further, for they could hardly walk unsupported. Coryate saw a lady fall on a stone bridge in her platform shoes, 'but I did nothing pitty her, because shee wore such frivolous and (as I may truely terme them) ridiculous instruments.'[32]

Though a number of examples have been drawn from later periods, it should be remembered that as early as the beginning of the fourteenth century the city of Venice had already acquired many of the characteristics outlined in this chapter. By that time, a range of building types had evolved to suit the particular needs of the city. These were to change only superficially for the rest of the duration of the Venetian Republic, which ended in 1797. Stylistic changes affected little more than the decorative language, both inside and out. The rest of the book will deal chiefly with these transformations, which were guided partly by changes in taste throughout Europe, partly by the personalities of the greatest architects who worked in the city, and partly by internal developments within Venetian society itself.

29 Vittore Carpaccio, 'The Courtesans', *c.*1490, showing noble ladies (probably not courtesans) on a roof top *altana* or balcony. Museo Correr, Venice *(Osvaldo Böhm)*

CHAPTER IV

Gothic

The lifespan of the Gothic style, which dominated Venetian architecture through the fourteenth and fifteenth centuries, coincided with the climax of the political and economic power of the Venetian Republic. This was a period of great expansion in trade, which in turn provided the economic resources needed for territorial enlargement, industrial growth, and population increase. The most rapid rise in prosperity took place in the first half of the fourteenth century. By the onset of the Black Death in 1348 Venice had a larger population than any other Italian city except Naples.[1] As elsewhere in Europe, growth was checked for a time by the effects of the plague and the subsequent economic crisis. This was the first of a series of fluctuations in the fortunes of the Venetian State in the course of these two centuries.

Each phase of increase in trade brought the merchant fleet into competition with its rivals, particularly the Genoese, and fostered the desire for territorial conquest. Throughout the fourteenth century rivalry with Genoa was a major preoccupation, reaching its climax in the Fourth Genoese War of 1378–80. This war, in which the Genoese, with the help of the Paduans, actually captured the lagoon town of Chioggia, brought a very grave threat to the survival of the Venetian Republic. Eventually the Venetians managed to recapture Chioggia, but in the Peace of Turin of 1381 they had to make a number of concessions to the Genoese.

In the long term the War of Chioggia did not prove too damaging, for the period of peace which followed allowed Venice to recover her political and economic stability. By the beginning of the fifteenth century she was again powerful enough to undertake further expansion of her dominion, this time on the Terraferma. Venice was still very much a seafaring nation, with colonies in the Eastern Mediterranean, chiefly in Dalmatia and the Aegean, but very little hinterland on the Italian mainland. Before 1339, when Treviso and Conegliano fell to Venetian rule, she had not even controlled Mestre, the nearest town on the mainland. The main period of Terraferma expansion began with the acquisition of Padua, Vicenza and Verona in 1404–6. Subsequently Venice took over Bergamo and Brescia, but these more distant conquests brought her into conflict with the Milanese. Just as in the fourteenth century, wars with Genoa had repeatedly strained the resources of the Republic, so the defence of the Terraferma made heavy demands on the economy in the fifteenth century. Meanwhile at sea, the struggle against the Ottoman Empire, which had continued on and off since the time of the Crusades, prevented any reduction in the strength of the Venetian navy.

We should not, however, overestimate the strain caused by conflicts between Venice and her rivals. The constant need to finance military and naval efforts was not a remarkable feature of the Venetian Republic at this time. The political map of Italy was continually changing as the fortunes of each state fluctuated, and military expenditure was a normal outlet for a large part of the revenue of every country. Undoubtedly military defeats caused shocks and setbacks, but equally each strategic conquest made trade and shipping more secure, or alternatively increased the self sufficiency of the state by yielding agricultural produce and natural resources.

It is against this background of a progressive rise in prosperity and political security, punctuated, but not halted, by the setbacks of war and plague, that we should view the architecture of the Gothic period in Venice. Most important, there was an enormous boom in the building trade to cope with the rising population. The whole of the central part of the city had been converted from a series of separate island communities into a densely built-up urban area, and land values were rising sharply. Many of the new buildings served relatively mundane purposes as shops and modest dwellings, but the very uneven distribution of wealth among the city's residents meant that a small minority of the population was outstandingly rich and could therefore afford to erect magnificent homes. The tremendous disparity between the richest Venetians and the rest of the inhabitants is revealed by an assessment of property ownership carried out in 1379 during the War of Chioggia, in order to raise forced loans based on individual means. Only about one-eighth of the heads of households were rich enough to qualify for the census, owning property amounting to the value of about 300 ducats or more. This minimum figure was probably equivalent to about three times the annual income of a typical skilled craftsman. Of the 2128 people assessed 1211 were nobles while 917 were not. Even among these families the range of wealth was enormous. Although the balance between nobles and commoners in the survey was fairly even, the financial supremacy of the patrician class is still evident. The fortunes of the richest of them all, Federico Corner, amounted to about 150,000 ducats.[2] In the richest categories twenty-five were nobles while only six were commoners.[3] Virtually every noble family was wealthy enough to qualify for the survey, whereas the great majority of non-nobles were too poor to be assessed. The financial strain caused by the forced loans levied at this time severely reduced the power of the nobility. In consequence, after the War of Chioggia the patrician class, officially sealed off by the closing, or *serrata*, of the Great Council of 1297, was enlarged by the admission of 30 new families to reinforce its political and economic domination. These were the last new families to be admitted to the patriciate before the mid-seventeenth century.

The concentration of wealth and power in the ranks of the nobility throughout the Gothic period is reflected in the nature of the building activity. The Republic itself, governed exclusively by the patrician class, had the resources to carry out the rebuilding of the Doge's Palace, while all the most conspicuous Gothic private palaces were built by members of the nobility. Since virtually every prosperous family wanted the prestige of a fine new home, palace building in this period was carried out on a huge scale, as we can see from the number of Gothic palaces shown in Jacopo de' Barbari's bird's eye view of Venice of 1500. The middle income groups who were rich enough to own land in the city built their own more modest dwellings; and landowners also built artisans' cottages to let to the poorer inhabitants. The wealthier non-nobles, of whom there were a significant number, financed the erection of the city's Scuole or guildhalls. Meanwhile the general overall prosperity of the population, though unevenly distributed, was reflected in the huge scale on which donations were made to the Church, allowing the building of many fine new churches, both monastic and parochial. And, just as their functions and patrons differed so, stylistically, religious and secular Gothic architecture in Venice followed separate paths, leading in a similar direction but rarely converging.

Gothic ecclesiastical architecture: the Mendicant orders

The development of the Gothic style in Venice received a powerful stimulus from mainland Italy as a result of the introduction of the Mendicant orders in the thirteenth century. These new orders broke away from the traditions of older monastic communities such as the Benedictines and the Cistercians, who lived in isolated rural settings supporting themselves by their own agricultural enterprises. (In Venice a Benedictine monastery already existed on the island of San Giorgio Maggiore.) Instead they established themselves in the cities, which were now growing rapidly after the disintegration of the feudal system. As the name 'Mendicant' implies, the orders were financed exclusively by begging; but private donations from rich and poor alike, eager to gain salvation in the after-life through charitable works on earth, swelled their funds and allowed them to erect new churches all over Europe.

The great significance of the Mendicant orders in the architectural history of Venice lies in the fact that, unlike most building patrons, they were not based in the city, but were administered by the superiors of their orders on an international scale. They brought to the city their own traditions of church building, which had already begun to evolve outside the specifically Venetian context, adapted to their particular religious needs. The Mendicant orders aimed, above all, to alleviate the sufferings of the growing masses of the urban poor. The monks dressed simply and lived in austere conditions, so that they could identify as closely as possible with the poverty stricken and the downtrodden. Their days were still punctuated by regular services (which totally dominated life in the more reclusive, older orders), but they had more free time for work outside the cloisters. Thus their churches had to provide not only small secluded chapels for their own private services, but also spacious naves in which to welcome the public into the religious community.

Since the orders were dependent on charity, the Mendicant churches were generally founded on pieces of land donated by private individuals. By the thirteenth century sites were not readily available in town centres, and throughout Europe one finds the new churches scattered around the

30 The Scuola Grande di San Marco, by Pietro Lombardo and Mauro Codussi, begun 1485, and the church of Santi Giovanni e Paolo, begun 1333 (A.F.Kersting)

peripheries of the mediaeval cities, just as railway stations lie on the fringes of nineteenth-century conurbations. This pattern applied in Venice as elsewhere. A map marked with the Mendicant order churches would indicate that not one of them was built in the densely settled Rialto-Merceria-San Marco area. The two most powerful of the new orders were the Franciscans, called the Frati Minori or Lesser Friars, founded in 1210 by Saint Francis of Assisi, and the Dominicans, called the Preacher Friars, founded in 1216. Others included the Augustinians, the Servites and the Carmelites, all of whom established churches in Venice. As we shall see, these churches made a clean break with the local tradition of small, centralized parish churches such as San Giacomo di Rialto.

The most imposing and one of the oldest surviving Mendicant churches in Venice is the huge basilica of Santi Giovanni e Paolo, erected on the northern fringes of the city for the Dominicans or Preacher Friars (Fig. 30). It is said that Saint Dominic himself visited Venice in 1217 and was granted by the Venetian Republic a small oratory, dedicated to San Daniele, which stood on the site of the Cappella del Rosario, adjoining the north transept of the present church. There he founded a small monastic community. However, the order soon outgrew the little oratory, and in 1234 a larger site was donated by Doge Jacopo Tiepolo, supposedly in response to a message in a dream. At this stage the land was still partly inundated, but evidently it was quickly drained, for the new church, dedicated to the Roman martyrs Saints John and Paul, was begun in 1246 and was well advanced by 1258.[4] Nothing is known of the appearance of the original church, for as the needs and resources of the Dominican friars grew, it, too, soon proved inadequate. However, it is

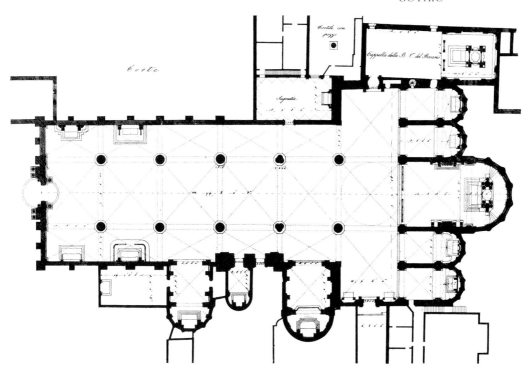

reasonable to postulate that like other Mendicant order churches erected in the Veneto in the mid-thirteenth century, notably San Francesco in Treviso and Santa Corona in Vicenza, it was probably in a simple, early Gothic style.

The present church was begun in 1333; an inscription between the eastern aisle of the nave and the north transept records that this section of the building was completed in 1368. The inscription is decidedly ambiguous, for it may refer to either the east or the west end of the church. Recent close examination of the structure by Herbert Dellwing has suggested that the whole ground plan was probably laid out at one time, but that after the lower portions of the walls had been erected the choir section was then brought to completion first. By the early fifteenth century the whole building was finished, except for interior furnishings such as the monks' choir. The church was finally consecrated in 1430. The dome is unlikely to have formed part of the original scheme, for the crossing piers are too slender and the cupola is not integrated with the rest of the structure. It was presumably added in the fifteenth century to emulate the heightened domes of the Basilica of San Marco. The dome already appears in a print of 1490, as well as in Barbari's map of 1500.[5]

The ground plan (above) reveals a lucid, carefully proportioned design. The nave consists of five square bays, each one the same size as the domed crossing, the two transepts, and the chancel; the side aisles are half as wide as the nave. The chancel has a polygonal apse, echoed on a smaller scale in the two flanking chapels on either side. Although one cannot possibly make claims for the existence of a Dominican master-plan, similarities between the plan of Santi Giovanni e Paolo and that of the sister church in Florence, Santa Maria Novella, founded at about the same date, show that ideas were disseminated rapidly across Italy.[6] In its essential features the Florentine church differs from Santi Giovanni e Paolo only in the two shorter bays which take the place of the fifth square bay of the nave, and in the absence of polygonal apses in the chancel and flanking chapels. The long, spacious nave with side aisles must have impressed the Venetians, for the longitudinally planned basilicas of Torcello and Murano seem to have had no immediate progeny in the city (unless the Cathedral of San Pietro di Castello, which according to Francesco Sansovino was 'in the Greek style',[7] took this form before it was rebuilt in the early seventeenth century).

In cities such as Florence, the Mendicant order churches were founded on the faubourg market places, which formed spacious piazzas to set off the buildings. In Venice there were no such foils for the new churches. At Santi Giovanni e Paolo, founded on an island, the land round about must have been reclaimed little by little. The L-shaped *campo* in front is too small to prevent one from being amazed by the enormous size of the church, which seems quite out of scale with its surroundings. The *campo* was once even smaller, for the present extension along the south side was not opened up until the nineteenth century. Before this time it was blocked off by the Scuola di Sant'Orsola (the original home of Carpaccio's famous cycle of paintings of the 'Life of Saint Ursula' now in the Accademia). But the characteristic Venetian materials – warm red brick and crisp, white Istrian-stone detailing – help the church to blend with its urban context.

The exterior is extremely simple, and clearly reflects the internal configuration (*Fig. 30*). As in other great Gothic churches of the period in Italy, buttressing is provided merely by thickened brick piers placed at regular intervals along the outside walls. There are no flying buttresses to relieve the heavy contours of the solid hulk of masonry. The tall, narrow, two-lancet windows point upward like arrows, enhancing the effect of height yet hardly breaking the continuity of the massive brick walls. The cusped pattern in the brickwork under the cornices is a most effective Italian decorative tradition, perhaps inspired by the defensive machicolations on fortified mediaeval buildings. It seems that the original scheme for the church comprised an articulated façade, but construction never progressed beyond the lowest tier, consisting of a row of blind Gothic arches. The deep recesses of the façade, probably intended for tombs, also form part of the Dominican building tradition. Similar niches are to be found not only on the walls of Santa Maria Novella but also, closer at hand, on the Dominican church of the Eremitani in Padua, as well as in the Franciscan church of San Lorenzo in Vicenza. After a generous bequest in 1458 work on the façade was renewed, but once again the project lapsed not long afterwards. The only outcome was the central portal, with its classical columns supporting a heavy Gothic arch, executed in the studio of Bartolomeo Bon.[8]

When one passes through this grand doorway into the church the effect is magical (*Fig. 31*); but the magic is not the same as the spell cast by the interior of San Marco. This is not an Aladdin's cave full of riches and intricacies. Here there are no flickering mosaics, deep shadows or dancing highlights. The majestic

quality of the vast, silent space lies in its simplicity and stillness. We cannot wonder that the church became the city's principal mausoleum. Its walls are graced with the finest series of tombs to be found in Venice, which in turn add to the dignity of the impression. In general the Mendicant order churches, with their more open sites and greater height, were better lit than the older parish churches, and Santi Giovanni e Paolo is no exception. A serene, even light enters through the clerestory windows and the lancets and roundels of the side aisles. The hefty stone piers which separate the nave from the side aisles are simple cylinders, for the Italian Gothic tradition did not readily assimilate the elaborate clustering effects of Northern Europe. As we have seen, the overall plan, with its cross-vaulted nave and side aisles, adheres closely to the Mendicant order churches elsewhere in Italy. The only obvious concessions to Venetian building traditions are the choice of materials and the provision of extra structural support. Brick and Istrian stone are used alternately for the main roof vaults of the nave, producing a subtle, rhythmic pattern of colour. The ribs of the cross-vaults and the upper pilasters of the nave are in red brick, while the main columns are built up of Istrian-stone blocks. (Single shafts on this scale would have been virtually unobtainable.) The wooden tie beams, which are needed to support the vaults on the unstable Venetian terrain, distinguish the church from its mainland counterparts. Here the cat's cradle effect of the tie beams serves to orchestrate the huge space, but

ABOVE, LEFT
31 Santi Giovanni e Paolo, interior
(A.F.Kersting)

ABOVE
32 Santa Maria Gloriosa dei Frari, begun 1330
(A.F.Kersting)

it also interrupts the soaring height of the nave. Typical of Venetian visual sensibilities is the way in which these strictly functional tie beams are richly decorated as if to justify their existence. The division of the windows of the main eastern apse into two tiers, with a more solid band in the centre, also provides additional horizontal support. The flood of light silhouetting the Gothic traceries of these apse windows gives a dramatic climax to the architecture, and seems to emanate from a divine source. In a setting such as this, the poor and the oppressed, for whose sake the church was ostensibly built, would surely have felt a sense of spiritual repose.

The establishment of the Franciscan order in Venice followed similar lines to the introduction of the Dominicans. The traditional belief that Saint Francis himself visited Venice, and stayed on the island of San Francesco del Deserto, gave an extra stimulus to the movement. After the Saint's death in 1226 his followers set up a community on the little island. Two sites in Venice itself were given to the Frati Minori in the mid-thirteenth century. On one of these plots the friars founded the church of Santa Maria Gloriosa dei Frari, and on the other (a vineyard on the northern outskirts of the city) the church of San Francesco della Vigna. The two original churches must have been very modest, for both were soon replaced by larger structures. In about 1300 an architect called Marino da Pisa began the new church of San Francesco della Vigna. This church is known only from Barbari's view of Venice, for it was again rebuilt by Sansovino in the sixteenth century. Even less is known of the appearance of the first church of the Frari, begun in 1250, although it remained in use until the fifteenth century. It stood in front of the entrance façade of the present church, and was orientated in the opposite direction with its three choir-chapels facing the *rio*. It probably followed in the tradition of smaller, single-naved Mendicant-order churches already founded on the Terraferma, such as the first church of San Nicolo in Treviso. The second, larger church on the site of the Frari was begun in 1330 (*Fig. 32*). As at Santi Giovanni e Paolo, begun just three years later, building proceeded slowly. Here, too, the choir section and transepts were executed first, together with the *campanile*, these parts being effectively completed by 1391. The high altar was finally consecrated in 1469, and the whole church in 1492.[9] As in the case of Santi Giovanni e Paolo we do not know the identity of the architect, though again he was probably one of the monks of the order.

Just as Santi Giovanni e Paolo shows links with the Dominican church in Florence, so the plan of the Frari has affinities with that of its Florentine equivalent, the Franciscan church of Santa Croce.[10] The two plans are broadly similar in layout, both churches having a row of smaller chapels on either side of the chancel. But even more remarkable is the degree to which the Frari resembles its most conspicuous Venetian counterpart, Santi Giovanni e Paolo, as well as Dominican prototypes on the mainland, for ideas spread quickly among the various Mendicant orders. The two exteriors share many components – the plain brick masonry with simple buttressing piers, the two-lancet windows, the dainty Istrian-stone pinnacles crowning the façade, and the cusped decoration under the cornice. The façade of the Frari,

like the nave entirely constructed in the fifteenth century, is at once more complex and more unified than that of Santi Giovanni e Paolo. The swaying curves of the topmost screen walls elaborate the basic scheme, and the fine Gothic doorway harmonizes effortlessly with the whole.

Inside the resemblance between the Frari and Santi Giovanni e Paolo is again evident (*Figs. 33 & 31*). The two choirs with their polygonal apses and splendid two-tier Gothic windows were erected in the same years and are very close in style. The articulation of the nave of the Frari, where again we find hefty stone columns, cross vaults, wooden tie beams and clerestory lighting, is taken directly from the earlier nave of Santi Giovanni e Paolo with only minor variations (although no dome was added to emphasize the crossing). Yet the effect is subtly different, for the Frari seems less solemn and awe inspiring. This is partly due to the survival of the monks' choir in the final bay of the nave, which breaks up the huge space into more intimate compartments. Before the changes associated with the Counter Reformation in the sixteenth century it was normal to find the choir of a monastic church in front of the chancel, but almost all have been removed to less obstructive positions. (That of Santi Giovanni e Paolo was destroyed in 1682.) The warmer character of the interior of the Frari must also be attributed to the effect of Titian's marvellous high altarpiece, the famous 'Assumption of the Virgin' commissioned in 1516. The compelling presence of this pictorial vision, framed by the central arch of

ABOVE, LEFT
33 Santa Maria Gloriosa dei Frari, interior
(*A.F.Kersting*)

ABOVE
34 Santo Stefano, fourteenth to fifteenth centuries; interior
(*A.F.Kersting*)

the choir which concentrates one's attention on the painting and at the same time makes it seem more remote and intangible, draws the eye straight to the focal point of the architecture. Thus discouraged from looking casually around, one is less aware of the daunting scale and spaciousness of the architecture as a whole.

Whereas the Frari and Santi Giovanni e Paolo seem to lack breathing space in their confined surroundings, the Augustinian church of Santo Stefano was endowed with a site on one of the largest *campi* in the city. This church, too, was founded in the thirteenth century, and completely rebuilt in the fourteenth as the needs and resources of the monastery grew. Because of the correct east-west orientation of the building it does not really benefit from its splendid site, for the *campo* offers a view not of the façade but of the south flank. This reveals a characteristically simple brick exterior, with stone used only sparingly. Inside, however, the materials are more lavish (*Fig. 34*). The columns of the nave are not hefty cylinders of Istrian-stone blocks, but slender shafts of red and white marble, the colours arranged in an alternating rhythm. The walls of the nave still preserve their fifteenth-century painted decoration over the arches, in a design of flickering foliage not unlike the crockets on the roofline of San Marco; and the diaper pattern of the brickwork above is reminiscent of the upper walls of the façades of the Palazzo Ducale. But the chief glory of Santo Stefano is the splendid ship's-keel ceiling. Only one other example survives in Venice itself, in the church of San Giacomo all'Orio. (Other examples can be seen on the nearby mainland, for instance in the Basilica of Aquileia and the churches of San Fermo and San Zeno in Verona.) The ceiling construction grandly shows off the shipbuilding expertise of the Venetian people, its woodwork lovingly decorated like the row of tie beams below. The interior has undergone many changes since the original decoration was completed in the fifteenth century. These include the insertion of a clerestory of thermal windows to improve the lighting, similar to those added to the nave of the Frari in the mid-seventeenth century, and the removal of monks' choir from the nave. But the overall effect remains striking. Even after Gothic architecture had passed out of fashion, Santo Stefano was still ranked by Francesco Sansovino among the half dozen finest churches in the city.[11]

Some smaller Gothic churches

By the fourteenth century the Gothic style was used exclusively for all religious architecture, both monastic and parochial. A good example of the way in which the scheme of the great triple-naved monastic church could be adapted to suit the more modest needs of a small parish is the Gothic church of San Giovanni in Bragora, built as late as the 1470s, replacing the earlier church on the site (*Fig. 35*). Here the elements are much reduced in scale, the decoration is simpler, especially on the façade, and a roof of wooden rafters is used instead of a costly vault. The result is a serviceable, less imposing version of the Mendicant order basilicas, a worthy successor to the Veneto-Byzantine centralized parish church.

Monastic churches of the fifteenth century, able to raise funds on a wider scale than the parishes of Venice, enjoyed more generous budgets, allowing them to indulge in the taste for richer decoration which was also prevalent in domestic architecture at the time. This is evident in the case of the lovely church of the Madonna dell'Orto, which belonged to the monastic order known as the Umiliati. The present church was begun in about 1399 (*Fig. 36*). Here the façade incorporates larger window openings with ornate tracery and repeated verticals, while on the roofline statues of the twelve apostles shelter in little Gothic niches. The main portal, commissioned from Bartolomeo Bon in 1460, is crowned by an ogee arch with flame-like relief sculpture, similar to the fifteenth-century decorations on San Marco.[12] The lunette over the door, its semi-circular disc of porphyry ringed with diverging rays like a rising sun, and the columns on high bases on either side, show classical influences already beginning to take root in Venice. This early example is a foretaste of the Renaissance style which was finally to displace Gothic forms in Venetian architecture in the last decades of the fifteenth century.

Gothic secular architecture

As Ruskin himself recognized, the Gothic style introduced into Venice by the Mendicant orders from mainland Italy absorbed little from local Veneto-Byzantine architectural traditions, except for the use of local materials and building techniques.[13] At the same time, just as in civil life Venice was eager to remain aloof from church affairs, so the manner of secular building in the city remained quite distinctive from the ecclesiastical tradition. As we have seen, Venetian parish churches of the fourteenth and fifteenth centuries readily

adopted the essential forms of Gothic monastic buildings, abandoning the Veneto-Byzantine convention of centralized churches. But in civil architecture, when the Gothic style became generally accepted as the normal 'language', it was blended with the legacy of Veneto-Byzantine structural and decorative traditions to form a completely distinctive, secular style. Even the oriental flavour was retained, for the travels of the patrician or merchant class in the Eastern Mediterranean and parts of Asia must have continued to make a deep impression on their artistic sensibilities.

The discrepancy between the architectural language of secular and religious building in the Gothic period shows itself most clearly in the fact that the inflected or ogee arch, which occurs in many different forms in almost every Venetian Gothic palace, and must surely be of Moorish or Eastern inspiration, is relatively uncommon in ecclesiastical buildings. Meanwhile the simple, uninflected Gothic arch, widely used in the churches, generally appears in domestic architecture only in the most solid elements, such as the main portals and the arches supporting external staircases.

Because of local anxieties about the safety of vaulted structures on the unstable Venetian terrain, secular buildings in the city retained their traditional flat wooden-beamed ceilings throughout the Gothic period. Thus the structural *raison d'être* of the Gothic style – to allow the erection of higher and higher vaults, with more flexibility in ground plan – was completely irrelevant in Venice. This must have worried Ruskin, for whom Venetian Gothic was the finest expression of the style, for in his discussion of 'The Nature of Gothic' he affirmed that buildings

> 'are not Gothic unless the pointed arch be the principal form adopted either in the stone vaulting or timbers of the roof proper.'[14]

According to such a definition virtually none of the Gothic palaces of Venice would qualify as 'true Gothic', although Ruskin would never have been so rigid (or so consistent) as to insist on this point. However, we must admit that his elaborate structural justification of the Gothic style has little validity in Venice, where Gothic forms in civil architecture are primarily decorative. The Venetian Gothic surely appealed more to Ruskin's visual and moral sensibilities than to his reason. He loved passionately every delicate stone tracery, every inch of moulding, and every crumbling brick of the Gothic palaces of Venice. And he reinforced this sentiment with a touching faith that the craftsmen had gained as much happiness from creating such artefacts as he did from seeing and drawing them. Uncomprehending of his wife Effie's taste for holding tea parties and dancing with Austrian officers, he spent his days in Venice sketching Gothic capitals for hours on end, reading chronicles of Venetian history, and writing chapters of *The Stones of Venice* in his own inimitable prose.[15] It is to Ruskin's sensitive writings, and his delicate wash drawings skilfully engraved to serve as illustrations, that we owe the nineteenth century 'rediscovery' of Venetian Gothic architecture, undervalued since the onset of the Renaissance.

The Palazzo Ducale

Just as the Basilica of San Marco is the finest manifestation of Byzantine architecture in Venice, so the Palazzo Ducale is the supreme expression of the Gothic style in the city, at least in its external aspect (*Fig. 37*). For Ruskin it was 'the central building of the world', on account of its unique blend of Roman, Lombard and Arab elements.[16] As he recognized, the Palazzo Ducale lies at the focal point where, through centuries of trade, war, crusades, piracy, diplomatic exchanges and voyages of exploration, three of the world's greatest architectural styles – the Classical, the Islamic and the Gothic – met and were combined in a very special way. Most of the classical influences were to be felt at a later period, when the courtyard began to assume its present form in the early Renaissance; but the Gothic exterior, as we shall see, is not simply 'standard' Italian Gothic built of local materials, but is infused with a Moorish predilection for shimmering inlaid surfaces and delicately carved traceries.

Its building history is a long, complicated one, still only partly understood. Since Venice kept her Republican status longer than any other Italian city state, the Palazzo Ducale served the role of ducal residence and political and

37 Palazzo Ducale, Riva façade *c*.1340 onwards, and Piazzetta extension, begun 1424 (*A.F.Kersting*)

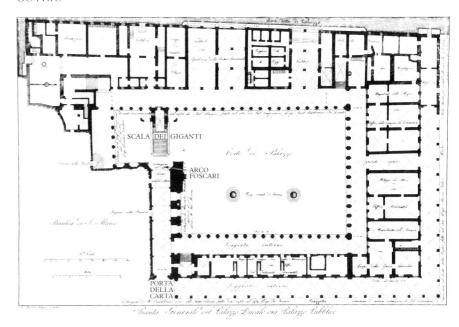

SCALA DEI GIGANTI

Corte cei Palazzo

ARCO
FOSCARI

Loggiato   interno

PORTA
DELLA
CARTA

Loggiato   esterno

Pianta Generale del Palazzo Ducale ora Palazzo Pubblico

Palazzo Ducale, twelfth century onwards, ground plan

legal administrative centre continuously for almost a thousand years. The first palace on the site must have been built when Doge Angelo Partecipazio transferred his headquarters to Rivoalto, as Venice was then known, after his repulse from Malamocco in A.D. 810. From this time until the seventeenth century, extensions and embellishments, successive rebuilding and modernization campaigns, and repairs after fires gradually transformed the original nucleus into the Palazzo Ducale as it stands today.

No visible trace survives of the ninth-century building. Considerable enlargements, including the addition of a Palazzo Comune, were made by the immensely wealthy Doge Sebastiano Ziani (1172–78). Again, we have no visual record of Ziani's palace, but in style it presumably resembled the other buildings erected by the same Doge around the whole of Piazza San Marco, with their two-tier Veneto-Byzantine porticoes, as we see them depicted in Gentile Bellini's 'Corpus Domini Procession' (*Fig. 10*). Probably, like the early Veneto-Byzantine private palaces, the Doge's palace also had corner towers; the so-called Torresella (small tower) now incorporated into the Treasury of San Marco may have been one of these. In this case the towers presumably played a defensive rôle as well as a visual one; one of the corner blocks on the lagoon side is known to have served as an armoury. The palace was built around an internal courtyard, like other communal palaces of the period (*above*). The Palazzo Comune itself occupied the wing along the Molo or waterfront, the Palace of Justice faced the Piazzetta, and the Doge inhabited the portion overlooking the small canal on the opposite side.[17]

The exterior of the Palazzo Ducale owes the essentials of its present appearance to a radical rebuilding programme in the mid-fourteenth century. Despite the famous *serrata* of the Great Council in 1297, when the ranks of the nobility, then comprising about 200 families, were effectively closed to outsiders, the number of male nobles, all of whom were entitled to attend the Great Council, was growing rapidly by natural multiplication. The room provided for their weekly sittings was becoming quite inadequate; and in 1340 it was finally resolved to build a new assembly hall over the office of the Signori di Notte (the night police) on the lagoon side of the palace. Although some older structures were incorporated into the new wing, the renewal of the whole of the Molo façade seems to have been undertaken at this time. The penultimate capital at the Piazzetta end is dated 1344. Building came to a halt after the Black Death in 1348, but a strong sense of Venetian civic pride prompted the rapid resumption of the work. The huge Sala del Maggior Consiglio must have been substantially completed by 1365, when Guariento was commissioned to paint his fresco of the 'Coronation of the Virgin' (destroyed in the fire of 1577).[18]

At this time the Molo elevation continued around the corner along the Piazzetta façade only as far as the seventh great column, marked by the circular relief of 'Justice' on the upper wall. The vast size of the Sala del Maggior Consiglio is evident even from the outside, for it occupies all but two of the large windows which pierce the upper part of the Molo façade. The central balcony on this side, with its fancy Gothic pinnacles and its sculptured figures sheltering in ornate niches, was inserted in 1404 by Pier Paolo dalle Masegne. The continuation along the rest of the Piazzetta façade was not begun until 1424, under Doge Francesco Foscari, when it was finally decided to demolish this section of Ziani's palace; but the new wing copied faithfully the fourteenth-century portions of the façade.

The identity of the architect (or architects) who invented this marvellous elevation still eludes us, although various names appearing in the documents have been put forward. Most critics believe that such a unified and perfectly balanced design must have been the work of a single creative personality – as anonymous as the architects of most of the other Gothic masterpieces of Europe. It is difficult to view such a familiar monument as the Palazzo Ducale objectively, for the eye is adjusted to the proportions as they stand through years of acquaintance. Any change in the appearance would at once look wrong or inharmonious. It is like a great piece of music, every part contributing to the unified whole, in which familiarity can easily hinder understanding. One secret of the success of the design is the way in which the large expanse of solid wall at the top of the building is made to seem light and insubstantial by the shimmering lozenge pattern in the tiles of red and white marble, while the lower arcade, where void in fact predominates over solid, appears robust and strong with its row of stocky columns and plain Gothic arches. There is no sense of top-heaviness, and the balance of light and shade is perfectly controlled.

The origins of this superb composition may be traced back to older structures on the site. Although some of the rooms of Ziani's twelfth-century palace survive in the core of the Molo wing, the double portico which hides them from view was completely remade to support the new Sala. But the rhythm of Ziani's arcades, if we assume them to have resembled those surrounding the Piazza depicted in Gentile Bellini's painting, was not forgotten (*Fig. 10*). The up-dated, Gothic structure preserved the placing of two narrow bays over each of the lower archways. The arrangement violates many of the classical canons which the Renaissance was to reinstate. For example, the stouter columns of the lower portico are shorter than the more slender columns of the *piano-nobile* colonnade. The common mediaeval practice of placing a column over the centre of an arch would also have offended strict Vitruvians, but such slim vertical supports had to be more closely spaced than the fatter columns in order to support the weight of the overlying structure. The lower portico with its stone cross-vaults concentrates the load of the building on the hefty shafts of the great columns, while the light, flat, beamed ceiling of the *piano-nobile* balcony spreads the weight more evenly across the less substantial traceries. Ziani's system was given new life by the flowing lines of the Gothic articulation, with its superbly carved details. On the *piano-nobile* balcony each quatrefoil roundel grows effortlessly from the contours of the ogee arches of the arcade, for the inflected crowns of these

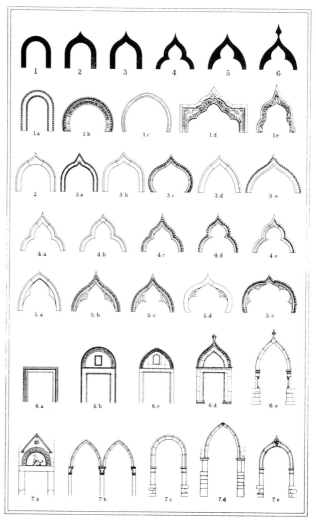

38 Ruskin's 'orders' of Venetian Gothic arches, from *The Stones of Venice*, vol.I, London, 1851 (*University Library, Cambridge*)

arches share the same centres and diameters as the roundels.

The palace exterior also owes much to the layout of the rooms inside. Before the great fire of 1577 the huge Sala del Maggior Consiglio had a ship's-keel ceiling like the churches of Santo Stefano and San Giacomo all'Orio. This type of ceiling was not uncommon in the great civic halls of the Veneto region: other examples can be seen in the Palazzo della Ragione in Padua and in the Basilica in Vicenza. The decision to build the Sala above existing rooms in the Palazzo Ducale was a precondition for the choice of the ship's-keel ceiling, for it would have been inconceivable to build further apartments over a roof of this sort. The fact that the Great Council chamber occupies most of the upper part of the Molo wing had a profound influence on the external appearance, for it implied a huge expanse of wall across the top of the façade. In both Padua and Vicenza the wall mass was hidden behind screening arcades, which provided additional buttressing for the structure, but this severely restricted the amount of light entering the great halls. As Venetians knew well, the largest rooms (like the central *porteghi* of their palaces) needed the best possible illumination. Good natural light was obviously an essential amenity, to reduce the fire-risk resulting from the use of lamps and candles. (Meetings of the Maggior Consiglio were held in daylight – or more exactly, every Sunday afternoon.) The insertion of Masegne's central window in 1404 provided extra lighting inside the Sala del Maggior Consiglio (*Fig. 39*); but its more important function was surely to give a decisive central emphasis to the otherwise uniform rhythm of the Molo façade, and to add a third dimension to the planar wall surface. The two right hand windows are set at a lower level than the others since there are two storeys of smaller rooms in this portion. These are the only windows to have preserved their original Gothic traceries, the rest having been destroyed in the 1577 fire.

The imprint of Islamic culture on the façade of the Palazzo Ducale is unmistakable, though blended with Western Gothic elements (*Fig. 37*). The traceries are as delicately carved as Moorish screen walls, and the whimsical roofline crenellations seem more appropriate to an Egyptian mosque than to an Italian communal palace. The inlaid tiles of the upper wall are reminiscent of the characteristic Persian decorative tradition, brought to Turkey by the Seljuks in the eleventh century and certainly known to Venetians. The key to the magic of the lozenge pattern on the Palazzo Ducale seems to lie in the very centre of each diamond where the regular design is abandoned and the tiles are arranged at random. By this device the apparently regular geometrical pattern is made to vibrate imperceptibly across the vast expanse of wall.

The Palazzo Ducale was built at a time when Republican governments of one kind or another were in power in most of the states of Italy. It was just one of a whole series of civic palaces erected in major cities throughout the Italian peninsula in the thirteenth and fourteenth centuries. Naturally every communal palace reflected local architectural traditions, but the individuality of the Palazzo Ducale is particularly striking. Much of its effect derives from the magnificent site. The view from the lagoon is backed by the great domes of the Basilica which contrast with the simple box-like profile of the palace.

The white Istrian stone and red Verona marble of the waterfront catch the midday sunshine, the light intensified by reflection from the huge expanse of water, so that the arcades seem as dark as night. Not only the materials and the site, but also the articulation of the building betray the Venetian setting. It is almost as if the early type of lagoon house, raised on its wooden stilts, had been petrified like a coral on the sea shore.

The very openness of the structure sets the Palazzo Ducale apart from other Italian communal palaces. There is no suggestion of impregnability in the architecture. The public can wander freely in the lower portico, and even the rooftop crenellations look decorative rather than defensive. The contrast with Tuscan examples, such as the Palazzo Vecchio built between 1299 and 1314 for the Priors of Florence, is particularly revealing. The Florentine palace is effectively a fortress, with its heavy rustication, projecting machicolations and tall lookout tower. Even the Palazzo Pubblico of Siena, finished by about 1344, has a castle-like air, though the stone is smoother and the ground floor windows larger and more accessible.[19] It is hard to imagine that by the fourteenth century the Venetian Palazzo Ducale had need of fortification. Whereas in other Italian cities the Republics were precarious institutions, soon to be replaced by more oligarchic forms of government, in Venice the system was by now so secure that it was to last for a further four centuries. And the Venetian lagoon as a whole was so well protected that invasions from hostile powers were also unlikely. The Palazzo Ducale is a bold symbol of the prodigious rise in prosperity and political power of Venice in the fourteenth and fifteenth centuries.

The interior planning of Venetian Gothic palaces

The characteristic layout of the Venetian palace, developed by the end of the thirteenth century, provided the starting point for Gothic palace design in the city. Most of the changes in domestic architecture during the fourteenth and fifteenth centuries were stylistic and decorative rather than structural, for the arrangement inherited from the early Veneto-Byzantine *casa fondaco* proved so well adapted to the particular social and physical needs of the Venetian patriciate that few modifications were needed. However, as Maretto's detailed studies of palace plans have demonstrated, the very fact that building took place on such a huge scale during this period meant that changes were required to adapt the basic scheme to the denser urban network and to the great variety of shapes, sizes and locations of the new sites.[20]

The chief disadvantage of the block-like plan of the typical *casa fondaco* – such as the Ca' Loredan or the Ca' da Mosto – was that it needed a reasonably open site to admit light to all parts of the building (*p. 41*). More adaptable to continuous urbanization was the L-type plan, with a courtyard at one side of the rear of the palace, which had already begun to appear in some later Byzantine palaces. Quarters where land was scarce and costly could be built up of houses of this type, arranged side by side or back to back, facing in alternate directions. Ideally such developments had a street along one side and

OPPOSITE
39 Palazzo Ducale, Sala del Maggior Consiglio, rebuilt after the fire of 1577 (*A.F.Kersting*)

85

a canal on the other, so that each dwelling could have both land and water entrances. In such a system there was less need for narrow alleys between the houses to admit light and give pedestrian access.

The L-type of plan was well suited to the needs of the smaller palace, where the site was too restricted to allow for complete suites of apartments on either side of a great central hall. A common alternative in the more modest palaces was an asymmetrical interior distribution of rooms, with the great hall stretching back from the façade along one side of the palace, and smaller rooms leading off on the other. Evidence of such asymmetrical planning can be seen in palace façades, where the great window arcades lighting the main *saloni* are placed at one side rather than in the centre, to form a bipartite instead of a tripartite composition. A conspicuous example is the Ca' d'Oro, although as we shall see this palace was in most other respects quite atypical.

Meanwhile the grander palaces still retained the tripartite façade distribution, inherited from the Byzantine era, which reflected the central placing of the great halls and *androne*. By the fifteenth century it became common to insert the courtyard into the centre of one side of the ground plan instead of at the rear of the site. In this way more light could be admitted to the inner parts of the palace, while both land and water façades could be symmetrically arranged. This C-type of plan occurs in Ca' Foscari and the two adjoining Giustiniani palaces, all three of which had large enough sites to allow for additional larger courtyards at the rear (*below*). These three palaces also reveal

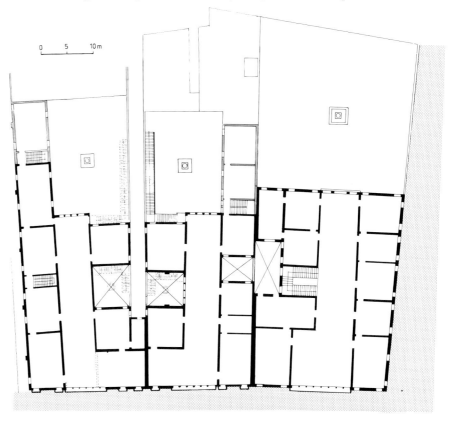

Ca' Foscari (on right) and Palazzi Giustiniani, begun *c.*1450. Second floor *piano nobile* of each. After Maretto

another fifteenth-century tendency, namely the widening of the central hall at one end. This enabled its windows to be placed in the centre of the façade even when the hall itself was not centrally located, and thus allowed a more flexible interior distribution of the rooms.

Naturally, such elaborate plans are not found in more modest, working class housing projects, where the dwellings lacked the space for private courtyards and huge inner halls. In such developments, in the Gothic period as in earlier centuries, houses were arranged either around a communal courtyard containing a well and an external staircase, or along either side of a street. Houses of the latter type, examples of which can be seen for instance in the Calle del Paradiso, had small interior staircases leading to the main living rooms upstairs, above the ground floor workshops and kitchens.[21]

Throughout the Gothic period in Venice external staircases remained a standard feature of every palace of any significance. Conceived originally as a means of saving valuable space inside the buildings, they gradually took on the additional role of decorative show-pieces. The standard means of support for a Gothic external staircase was a series of simple Gothic arches, the lowest placed on or near the ground, the others raised on progressively higher piers. The stone balustrades were formed of slender colonnettes with stone lions' heads or busts placed at intervals along the handrails. One of the most beautiful surviving examples is the staircase in the courtyard of the Palazzo Centani, later the home of the famous eighteenth century Venetian playwright Carlo Goldoni (*Fig. 28*).

Stylistic transformations

The major developments in Venetian domestic architecture in the Gothic period occurred not in the interior planning but in the style and character of the façades, which were the major vehicles for the expression of the wealth, status and taste of their owners. As in the case of the early Veneto-Byzantine *fondaco*-type palaces, our understanding of the evolution of Venetian Gothic secular architecture is very severely limited by the lack of documentation. Not only are we usually ignorant of the identity of the designer – a problem that besets all studies of mediaeval architecture – but rarely, until further researches are carried out, do we have any reliable indication of the dating of the various buildings. For the most part only the later and most prominent palaces can be even tentatively dated from archival evidence, and attempts at dating on a stylistic basis alone are far from reliable.

Ruskin's classification of what he called the 'orders' of Venetian Gothic arches, which attempted to elucidate the transition from the Veneto-Byzantine to the Gothic idiom, also provides us with a scheme for the development of the mature Gothic style (*Fig. 38*). According to the Ruskinian system the first true Gothic arch, inflected on both the extrados and the intrados, forms the third order. (The first and second orders were described in the previous chapter.) The fourth order is a simple, pointed trefoiled arch, while the fifth stage consists of the trefoiled arch contained within the plain pointed arch.

Ruskin added a final sixth order, similar to the fifth but with a decorative finial over the point of the arch. The scheme itself is neat and provides a useful terminology, but as we have seen the actual evolution is not so consistent as the classification would suggest. Ruskin himself admitted that the orders do not follow each other in a clear, systematic sequence, but overlap one another for long periods. The fourth and fifth are the most typical forms of what Ruskin called the mature Venetian Gothic, both lasting from the thirteenth to the fifteenth centuries and often coexisting in the same building.[22]

Despite our ignorance of the chronology and authorship of most Venetian Gothic palaces, some general characteristics and evolutionary patterns can be detected from a study of individual buildings. Of necessity, only a tiny fraction of the thousands of palaces erected in the city during the Gothic period can be discussed here. And it is tempting – even natural – to select the most conspicuous and interesting examples, which are not usually typical of the majority of dwellings erected in the period, although they set the trends followed by other less adventurous builders.

The first Gothic palaces

As we have seen, the first palaces to exhibit true Gothic forms – that is to say arches of Ruskin's third stage pointed in both the extrados and the intrados – are still clearly transitional in style. A typical example is the Palazzo Priuli-Bon at San Stae which retains the solid capitals (here truncated cubes with long corner leaves) and the tall stilted arches of the Veneto-Byzantine period (*Fig. 40*). This palace may date from as early as the mid-thirteenth century, although the divergence in both style and alignment between the water storey and the *piano nobile* suggests two main phases of building at the outset, to say nothing of subsequent alterations. Here, too, as in the Byzantine Palazzo Donà

40 Palazzo Priuli-Bon, San Stae, thirteenth century onwards *(Sarah Quill)*

(*Fig. 16*), we find an early example of the use of a stone or marble framing panel to enclose and identify the main *piano-nobile* window, a convention which was to become one of the most typical and attractive trade marks of Venetian Gothic palaces. Outlined by a dentilled moulding like a serrated postage stamp, the panelled area provides a solid backing from which the windows have been, as it were, cut out, in this case piercing the frame with their tall inflected points.

Gothic palaces in the fourteenth century

Probably by the fourteenth century the heightened, stilted arches had already been largely superseded by a more normal type of Gothic ogee arch, seen, for example, in the façade windows of the Palazzo Zorzi at San Severo, which are lower in profile than those of the Palazzo Priuli-Bon and rest securely within the bounds of their framing panels.

However, all palace building in the fourteenth century was overshadowed by work on the Palazzo Ducale. The huge leap of imagination which the new palace represented brought Gothic secular architecture in Venice to sudden maturity. In theory the two largest of the new Mendicant order churches, the Frari and Santi Giovanni e Paolo, begun only a few years earlier, offered a comparable range of Gothic forms to mid-fourteenth-century builders. These included windows of Ruskin's fifth stage, that is, the trefoil arch within a plain outer arch, and quatrefoil traceries set in roundels or diamonds. But in practice domestic architecture ignored their possibilities. The elongated single or double lancet windows were ill-adapted to the Venetian dwelling house, for they were too tall and narrow to admit enough light, and even their decorative motifs passed unnoticed. Instead it was the flowing rhythmic patterns of the Palazzo Ducale which provided the dominating inspiration, although most builders in the city were slow to grasp the implications of this striking, innovative design. The repeatable bay system, which could be extended to almost any length, made the arcade motif of the Palazzo Ducale a particularly adaptable theme for palace façades, and its impact – at first long delayed – was to last until the Gothic style finally died out at the end of the fifteenth century.

By the end of the fourteenth century Venetian palace building had still absorbed little from the new Palazzo Ducale. A typical example is the Palazzo Priuli at San Severo, near the somewhat older Palazzo Zorzi (*Fig. 41*). This palace reveals a wide range of styles and has obviously been subjected to piecemeal alterations at various times, but the main part of the structure seems to date from the late fourteenth century. This is also implied by the fact that one of the corner windows, clearly later in style than most of the palace, was chosen by Marino Contarini in 1431–34 as the model for three of the windows in the Ca' d'Oro.[23] On the main *rio* façade of the Palazzo Priuli we find windows of Ruskin's third, fourth and fifth stages coexisting, with the third order windows on the second floor *piano nobile*, above those of the fourth and fifth orders on the first floor. Yet, despite a certain lack of order and symmetry, there is no sense of stylistic discordance. The building displays a number of innovations, in

particular the six-light window of the main hall of the *piano nobile* where the two end windows are framed by separate fascias, like the side panels of a triptych, and the daring corner windows which undermine the apparent solidity of the ends of the façade. Only these corner windows, especially the later one over the Rio dell'Osmarin which so much impressed Marino Contarini, show any obvious borrowing from the Palazzo Ducale. Their slim colonnettes carved like twisted cables recall the spirally fluted columns on the corners of the great new palace. In the later window the trefoiled roundels resting between the inflected points of the fifth order arches, and appearing to grow out of them, are derived from the *piano nobile* arcade of the Palazzo Ducale. The pendant arches, however, were a bold new departure. The fact that this palace, now very shabby, was once frescoed by Palma Vecchio, is a poignant reminder of its former prominence.[24]

Fifteenth-century Gothic palaces

Bearing in mind that palaces such as the Palazzo Priuli were considered noteworthy at the beginning of the fifteenth century, we begin to realize how totally remarkable the Ca' d'Oro must have seemed to contemporary Venetians (*Fig. 42*). Indeed, we know from the very full accounts of the building work which have survived for the years 1421–37, that its owner, Marino Contarini, certainly intended his new palace to make the boldest possible impression, despite its modest proportions.[25] This extraordinary palace cannot be seen as typical of Venetian patrician palaces of the period, except in the general disposition of the rooms. But it is important as a pointer of the taste of the

OPPOSITE
41 Palazzo Priuli, San Severo, probably late fourteenth century (*Sarah Quill*)

BELOW
42 Ca' d'Oro, begun 1424 (*A.F.Kersting*)

time, which in Venice was beginning to move towards a more and more decorative, florid Gothic style. The fact that Contarini sought to make an impact by the sheer abundance and lavishness of the decoration, at the expense of harmony between the individual parts, shows that by this time ostentatiousness alone was enough to impress.

Marino Contarini was a member of one of the oldest and most distinguished patrician families in the city. He bought the site of the Ca' d'Oro from the Zeno family in 1412. His first wife, Soramador Zeno, died only five years later, and he probably intended his magnificent new palace, begun in 1424, to serve as a monument to her memory as well as a demonstration of his own wealth and status.[26] This is suggested by the way in which decorative fragments from the Veneto–Byzantine Palazzo Zeno, which was demolished to make way for the new palace, were faithfully preserved and incorporated into the façade of the Ca' d'Oro, in spite of their antiquated style.

The survival of detailed documentation of the construction of the palace gives valuable insight into building procedures at the time, as well as into the particular complexities of the Ca' d'Oro's own history. According to the normal Venetian practice, Contarini himself issued the contracts for individual tasks, and also ordered and supplied most of the materials. As far as one can tell, there was no single unifying design, other than Contarini's own conception of how he wished his magnificent showpiece to turn out. Two main stonemasons' workshops collaborated on the palace, those of the Milanese sculptor Matteo Raverti and the Venetian stonecutter Giovanni Bon. Some parts of the construction were carried out by the two workshops jointly. In other cases, one or other group was responsible for a whole section of the building. The six-light window on the *piano nobile* can for the most part be assigned to Raverti, as well as the external staircase in the courtyard and the portal of the street entrance; both of these were tragically demolished in the mid-nineteenth century, when the palace belonged to the famous ballerina, Mademoiselle Taglioni. Bon's workshop was apparently responsible for the four-light window inside the waterfront portico, the single windows with balconies on the façade, and the cornice and crowning pinnacles.

One of the most remarkable revelations of the documents is the account given of the painted decoration on the façade, entrusted to a French painter called Maistro Zuan di Franza. Here the Venetian taste for polychrome decoration was carried to almost vulgar extremes. The balls of the parapet, the finials of the window traceries, the foliage and lions on the corner capitals, and the mouldings surrounding the circular bosses of coloured marble were all gilded with real gold leaf, while the blue and gold coats of arms on the capitals and the great escutcheon were not only gilded but also painted with two coats of the finest ultramarine. The notion of using such costly materials in the humid, saline atmosphere of Venice was a preposterously extravagant gesture that cannot have failed to make an impact, as long as the decoration survived. The name Ca' d'Oro literally means 'House of Gold'. Meanwhile much of the white Istrian stone was touched up with white lead and oil to give the effect of veined marble, and the red Verona marble was oiled and varnished to bring out the colour.

Ruskin, writing before the discovery of the accounts, was unaware that the palace had once been so richly painted, but he was struck by its magnificence and much distressed by Mademoiselle Taglioni's barbaric alterations:

> 'I saw the beautiful slabs of red marble, which formed the bases of its balconies, and were carved into noble spiral mouldings of strange sections, half a foot deep, dashed to pieces when I was last in Venice. Its glorious interior staircase, by far the most interesting Gothic monument of the kind in Venice, had been carried away, piece by piece, and sold for waste marble, two years before.'[27]

We should be grateful for the attempts of a subsequent owner, Baron Franchetti, at the beginning of this century, to restore the palace to its former condition, building a new external staircase, buying back the well head from the courtyard, sold to a dealer in Paris, and replacing the cusped moulding removed from beneath the cornice. There is, however, no evidence that his other embellishments, such as the polychrome marble wall-facings in the *androne*, replaced earlier decorations of this kind.

Despite the ravages of time the Ca' d'Oro still makes a striking impression, chiefly through the intricacies of its tracings and carvings (*Fig. 42*). Here the full impact of the Palazzo Ducale is at last evident, especially in the six-light window of the *piano nobile*. (We should not forget that the Piazzetta extensions of the Doge's Palace was under construction in the same years.) It is nevertheless possible to detect the foreign hand of Raverti, who brought from Lombardy the tradition of elaborate stonecarving so marked in the great Cathedral of Milan, begun in 1386. There the importation of French and German craftsmen had helped to foster a taste for Northern complexity in the sculptural decoration;[28] and indeed this is reflected by the way in which Raverti's attention to detail conceals the bold, flowing rhythms that are so emphatic in the *piano nobile* arcade of the Palazzo Ducale. The Ca' d'Oro shares with the Doge's Palace the open loggia of the *piano nobile*, not otherwise found in any Venetian palace after the Byzantine period.

What the Ca' d'Oro gained in fine detail it lost through the overall incoherence of the façade. The nineteenth-century scholar, Cicognara, who assumed that the palace was originally intended to be completely symmetrical, with an additional wing on the left to balance the right hand section, ignored the fact that bipartite façades were a common solution in Venice for smaller palaces. Even so, the façade is very loosely organized. The three heightened pinnacles in the middle of the roofline do not coincide with the centre of the façade, marked by the single windows flanking the loggias, nor with the vertical strip of Byzantine carving into which the great coat of arms was inserted, while the dentilled fascias behind the windows are curiously variable in height. Matteo Raverti must have been aware of the search for geometrical harmony which dominated the building of Milan Cathedral, attempting to organize the intricate design into a unified whole; but in the Ca' d'Oro Contarini's concern for elaborate detail obviously precluded such

43 The two Giustiniani palaces and Ca' Foscari, all begun *c.*1450 (*Sarah Quill*)

preoccupations. The magic of the Ca' d'Oro lay instead in the way in which the ever-changing atmosphere of Venice and the dancing reflections from the water played on its highly coloured and richly articulated surface and intensified its deep shadows.

The most conspicuous palace erected in Venice in the middle years of the fifteenth century was the palace of Doge Francesco Foscari, which Ruskin called 'the noblest example in Venice of the fifteenth-century Gothic'[29] (*Fig. 43*). This palace makes its impact in a very different way from the Ca' d'Oro. The property had already had a series of distinguished owners. The previous building on the site was a crenellated Byzantine palace known as the 'House with the two Towers', which was bought by the Republic in 1429 and presented first to the Marquis of Mantua, and then, ten years later, to Count Francesco Sforza. After the latter seized power in Milan in 1450 the State reappropriated the palace and sold it by auction to the Doge of the time, Francesco Foscari.[30] Foscari immediately set about rebuilding the palace in a manner befitting his station. The Venetian diarist Girolamo Priuli reports how the Doge moved the site of the new palace forward on to the bank of the Grand Canal, placing the courtyard where the old one had stood.[31] The huge new palace, which according to Francesco Sansovino contained more rooms than any other in the city, can hardly have been finished when Foscari was disgraced in 1457 and retired to his new home to end his days.[32] He had been Doge for 34 years and had been instrumental in consolidating and extending Venetian domination on the Terraferma. In politics he showed the same bold ambition that he revealed in the building of his palace. However, when Venetian expansion into Lombardy was finally halted by the Milanese, the patriciate began to resent the tax burden imposed by his warfaring policies. The misdemeanours of his son aroused further disapproval, and he was finally voted out by the Senate and deposed.

The two fine palaces of the Giustiniani family, which occupy the adjoining site on the Grand Canal, were rebuilt in the same years, construction work having begun there shortly before 1451[33] (*Fig. 43*). The Giustiniani, too, were among the oldest and most distinguished families of the Venetian patriciate. They had only narrowly avoided extinction during the Crusades, when the Pope gave permission for the one surviving male member, a Benedictine monk, to marry to save his line. Having fathered nine sons and three daughters he then returned to his monastery, while his wife became a nun.[34]

The three palaces, commanding a great sweeping curve in the Grand Canal, form a magnificent ensemble. Foscari's palace dominates the group through its greater height and the prominent display of the Foscari arms over the second floor *piano nobile*, while the two Giustiniani palaces form a unified pair, being arranged symmetrically on either side of their central axis with its huge watergate. The three palaces harmonize with each other through their close stylistic affinity. In all three the *piano nobile* is on the second floor, with the central arcades closely modelled on the façade loggia of the Palazzo Ducale. It is interesting that a whole century had elapsed before really effective use was made of this motif in the design of Venetian patrician palaces. Here, in contrast to the Ca' d'Oro, the bold rhythm of the prototype is not lost through over-articulation. It would, however, be misleading to consider these palaces as small scale imitations of the Palazzo Ducale. All three are firmly rooted in the traditions of Venetian domestic architecture, with their great central window arcades lighting the huge halls behind, flanked by side wings of smaller rooms lit by single windows. The first floor arcades display windows of Ruskin's sixth order, not found before the fifteenth century, with their decorative finials crowning the trefoiled arches within the plain inflected arches. The half quatrefoils, used at the ends of the Palazzo Ducale façades, here exhibit new decorative possibilities in the traceries of the single windows. The Giustiniani palaces take over from the Ca' d'Oro the unusual motif of ornate window traceries with pendant capitals, the only intricate detailing in the whole complex. Unlike the Ca' d'Oro these dignified palaces have well-proportioned, clearly organized façades, unencumbered by rich decoration, and they probably represent the high point in Gothic palace-building in Venice.

By the mid-fifteenth century classical forms were already beginning to infiltrate, albeit very slowly, into Venetian architecture. In the Foscari and Giustiniani palaces this is evident only in the *all'antica* reliefs of putti bearing shields with the Foscari arms, but the process was to accelerate during the second half of the century. As if in resistance to the arrival of the new classical style, a few Gothic buildings of the later fifteenth century were built in an unprecedentedly intricate and florid manner, thus in a sense preparing the way for the death of the style, while others began to exhibit an incongruous blend of classical and Gothic forms. The most extreme example of the elaborate, 'floriated' Gothic style is the little Palazzo Contarini-Fasan, traditionally known as the House of Desdemona (*Fig. 44*). This tiny palace is so small that the miniaturist scale and delicate intricacy of the detail offer no hint of vulgarity. Most effective and most original are the finely carved balustrades with their distinctive wheel motifs. However, further development along these lines would have been inconceivable.

The use of round arches overlapping to produce normal uninflected Gothic arches, which had already appeared in Venice in two much earlier and apparently isolated examples, the south transept of Santi Giovanni e Paolo, and one of the great façade windows of the Palazzo Ducale, finally made its impact on Venetian palace architecture at this time. Possibly the idea was nurtured by the new interest in classical round arches, although the effect is quite unclassical. The use of this arrangement, extended sideways to articulate a whole window arcade, occurs in three splendid mid-or late-fifteenth century palaces, the Palazzo Giovanelli at San Felice, and the Palazzi Cavalli and Pisani-Moretta, both on the Grand Canal. Whereas in the *piano nobile* of the Palazzo Ducale the quatrefoiled roundels are lodged securely between the crowns of the arches, in these three examples they rest on the joints of the arches, as if about to roll across the sweeping curves of the arcade. In the Palazzo Pisani-Moretta the two contrasting systems actually occur together, one above the other (*Fig. 45*). In this palace some explicit references are already made to the classical tradition – for instance, in the pilaster orders which define the ends of the façade, in place of the quoins normally used in Venetian Gothic palaces. Remarkably, the stylistic discordance does not undermine the overall

44 Palazzo Contarini-Fasan, called the House of Desdemona, late fifteenth century (*A.F.Kersting*)

effectiveness of the façade composition, but it does reflect the confusions that tend to accompany a period of transition between one architectural style and another.

The Venetian Scuole

It was in the Gothic period that the Venetian Scuole, or guilds, developed their own particular type of building. The Scuole fell into two main groups. On the one hand there were the so-called Scuole Grandi, the lay confraternities founded as offshoots of the 'flagellant' religious movement of the mid-thirteenth century. The first Scuole Grandi to be established in Venice were the Scuola della Carità, the Scuola di San Marco and the Scuola di San Giovanni Evangelista, all founded in the years 1260–61. The Scuola Grande della Misericordia dates from 1308 and the Scuola di San Rocco from 1478. A sixth, the Scuola di San Teodoro, was raised to the status of Scuola Grande in 1552.[35]

On the other hand there were smaller guilds, known as the Scuole Piccole. These served a variety of different functions. Some were small confraternities with a religious motivation, usually occupying premises attached to a church or convent. Others were centres for colonies of foreign residents in the city, such as the Albanians, the Greeks and the Slavs. The remainder were craftsmen's and traders' guilds. These were broadly similar in function to the guilds or *Arti* found in other parts of Italy, but in contrast to cities such as

45 Palazzo Pisani-Moretta, second half of fifteenth century *(Sarah Quill)*

97

Florence they were not established and dominated by wealthy merchants. Instead they served as instruments for defending the interests of small scale artisans and shopkeepers. In Venice the most powerful merchants had no need of guild representation, for they themselves formed the ruling oligarchy.[36]

The Scuole Grandi had originated as part of the intensely ascetic flagellant movement; but it was not long before the atmosphere of austerity was superseded by a desire for ostentation and display. The essential charitable functions continued, but the Scuole also began to take on a very important political rôle as the organs of self government for the citizen class, who were otherwise excluded from all high government positions except that of Grand Chancellor. In fact the Council of Ten, the smallest, most powerful body in the government, had overall responsibility for the running of the Scuole, but in practice the citizens were allowed at least some degree of control over their own affairs. The nobility, like the clergy, were forbidden to take part in the internal administration of the Scuole, although they could be admitted as members.

The confraternities were financed by donations and subscriptions from their membership. Because of the substantial amount of wealth in the hands of the more prosperous non-nobles, the Scuole Grandi enjoyed generous budgets. The desire for salvation in the after-life prompted many donors to make charitable gifts and bequests, especially at the outset. A further incentive was provided by the sense of competition which grew up between the various Scuole Grandi. This competitiveness was to find its chief expression in the finery of their buildings, works of art, and processional banners.

While the Scuole Grandi promoted the interests of the citizen class, composed mainly of professional people and manufacturers, the Scuole Piccole represented the city's skilled workers, whose incomes were more modest but whose numbers were considerable. Like the Scuole Grandi they took great pride in their buildings and art treasures, and played a prominent part in public processions and pageants. Thus these confraternities – great and small alike endowed with both wealth and a passion for display – came to play a highly important part in the patronage of artists and architects in Venice.

The architectural configuration of all these types of Scuola was similar, for they fulfilled a broadly comparable function as meeting places and as centres for dispensing charity to the more needy of their members. The typical Scuola building took the form of two large halls, one above the other. The upper hall, usually called the *Sala del Capitolo*, was used for important meetings and often contained an altar for services, while the lower hall was used for less solemn, day to day administrative purposes (*Fig. 68*). Because of their more complex function and greater wealth, the premises of the Scuole Grandi were more elaborate than those of the Scuole Piccole. In addition to their two main halls they had a smaller meeting room upstairs called the *albergo*, where the inner committee of 16 members, known as the Banca, dealt with the day to day running of the Scuola (*p. 135*). Those of the Scuole which were endowed with precious relics also needed separate reliquary chapels on the upper floor.

In their early years the Scuole Grandi, like the smaller religious confraternities, were affiliated to churches or abbeys. However, they soon acquired the means to move to separate premises. In the boom years of the early fourteenth century, before the arrival of the Black Death in 1348, the oldest of the Scuole constructed their first independent buildings. (It is notable that this was also the period when work was started on the new Palazzo Ducale and the great new churches of the Frari and Santi Giovanni e Paolo.) For example, in 1343 the Scuola della Carità opened its new headquarters, consisting of two huge rooms, one above the other, on a site adjoining the monastery of the same name (*Fig. 25*). The façade was rebuilt in the eighteenth century, and further alterations were carried out when the Scuola was converted into the home of the Accademia di Belle Arti in 1807. However, the huge *Sala del Capitolo* is still in existence. The Gothic windows have since been replaced by roundheaded ones, but the way in which the ribs of the ceiling coffering are transformed into vaults at the edges of the room, resting on corbels, preserves something of the Gothic character of the room. The ornate gilded wooden ceiling was begun in 1461 and completed in 1484. The eight-winged cherubs which decorate each diamond-shaped panel are thought to symbolize the name of Ulisse Aliotti, who was Guardian Grande, or chief officer of the Scuola, when the ceiling was started.

The *albergo* was added in 1384, and enlarged to its present L-shape in 1442–44. This room, too, still displays its richly carved and painted wooden ceiling, probably dating from the end of the fifteenth century, as well as the wooden benches around the walls. Although it now serves as a passageway for

46   Scuola Vecchia della Misericordia, fourteenth to fifteenth centuries (*Sarah Quill*)

47 Scuola dei Calegheri
doorway dated 1478
(Sarah Quill)

visitors to the gallery, some of whom hardly even pause to notice Titian's great canvas of the 'Presentation of the Virgin', one can still visualize the *albergo* in its original capacity as a small meeting room for members of the Banca of the Scuola.[37]

The most complete surviving example of a Scuola Grande erected in the Gothic period is the Scuola Vecchia della Misericordia, situated on the north-western fringes of the city (*Fig. 46*). The exact date of the foundation of the building is uncertain for it was substantially renovated several times during the fourteenth century. In 1411–12 the members decided to erect a new *albergo*, and the building was further enlarged in the 1430s. In 1441 the Scuola resolved to rebuild the façade. At this time, or possibly earlier, Bartolomeo Bon executed his great relief sculpture of the Madonna della Misericordia, now in the Victoria and Albert Museum, which was placed over the main doorway. The arcade along the waterfront was inserted in the early sixteenth century to provide access to the new almshouses beyond, built in 1504–06.[38]

Some of the masonry of the present structure presumably dates from the fourteenth century, for it was an essential economy measure in Venice to conserve whatever was usable from previous structures. However, the *piano nobile* windows topped by finials and decorated with finely carved traceries are certainly fifteenth century in date. They share with the Ca' d'Oro and the Giustiniani palaces the unusual *motif* of the pendant capital suspended from the centre of the traceries. The alternating cusped and stepped profile of the top of the façade, with its ornate corner pinnacles, is a typical fifteenth-century Venetian Gothic arrangement. However, unlike the window traceries this derives from religious architecture, for the Scuole were in effect the meeting point of secular and religious traditions.

By a stroke of fortune the interior has been little altered since the fifteenth century, because from the sixteenth century onwards the Scuola della Misericordia was preoccupied with the erection of an even more grandiose building nearby to replace it. After the move to the new premises in 1589 the upper room was used by Tintoretto for painting the canvasses for his enormous painting of *Paradiso* for the Palazzo Ducale.[39] That the structure has survived so well is due to a large extent to the thorough and sensitive restoration carried out by the painter and art collector Italico Brass, who acquired the disused Scuola in 1920. The building is now being converted into a state-aided restoration laboratory.

Inside, the small entrance hall containing the simple stone staircase still preserves its pretty coffered ceiling decorated with Scuola emblems. Because of the existence of the cloister of the abbey on one side and the insertion of the early sixteenth century *sotto portego* on the other, the lower hall or *androne* beyond is long, narrow and dark. This makes the effect of the huge, luminous *salone* upstairs all the more striking, its size emphasized by the expanse of glossy *terrazzo* floor and the rhythms of the ceiling beams.

None of the Venetian Scuole Piccole still preserves its Gothic premises intact. The Scuola dei Calegheri at San Tomà, the headquarters of the shoemakers' guild, gives some impression of the Gothic building type, although the structure has since been substantially altered (*Fig. 47*). The central portal, with its slightly inflected arch topped by a finial and its lintel decorated with reliefs of shoes, dates from 1478. The lunette relief, a product of the Lombardi workshop, shows 'Saint Mark healing the cobbler Ananias', a neat combination of State and guild iconography. But in general the competitiveness of the Scuole meant that they were constantly renewing their buildings in emulation of each other. After the Gothic style passed out of fashion all the Scuole with the available funds modernized their premises, leaving only the basic building type as a legacy of their Gothic traditions.

CHAPTER V

Early Renaissance

The Renaissance of the visual arts launched in Florence in the early fifteenth century by Masaccio in painting, Ghiberti and Donatello in sculpture, and Brunelleschi in architecture gradually pervaded the whole of Italy. But its progress was slow. In Venice there was little impetus to supplant local Gothic traditions before about 1460, and even then these died hard. The Venetians had evolved their native Gothic style during the peak of their political and economic power, and had no grounds for considering their own culture deficient or backward. It was natural for Doge Foscari to build his magnificent family palace in the style of the Palazzo Ducale, as if to commemorate his own rise to the highest office in the land, rather than in the style of Brunelleschi, which would have had no such associations for him. As in Milan, where a similar time lag occurred, the Gothic style was so deeply rooted in the city that it continued to flourish and even to develop a new luxuriant growth despite frequent visits by Tuscan artists.

During the first half of the fifteenth century a number of notable sculptors came to Venice from Central Italy. Ghiberti spent a few months in the city in 1424 in flight from the outbreak of plague in Florence, and may have made another short visit in about 1430. Jacopo della Quercia made repeated journeys to Venice to buy materials while he was working on the main portal of San Petronio in Bologna in 1425–27. Neither of these artists was employed in Venice, but a group of minor Florentine sculptors made an important contribution to the decoration of both San Marco and the Palazzo Ducale from about 1415 onwards. They were led by Niccolò di Pietro Lamberti, who had formerly been a master sculptor in Florence Cathedral. With his distinctly Gothic tendencies Niccolò was unable to stand up to the competition of Ghiberti and Donatello in Florence, but his style suited less radical Venetian tastes. He was accompanied by his son Pietro as well as by Giovanni di Martino da Fiesole and a former collaborator of Donatello, Nanni di Bartolo, called 'il Rosso'. Although their sculpture shows many borrowings from Donatello and Ghiberti they lacked a deeper understanding of Renaissance ideas, and as a result their work blended well with that produced in local and Lombard workshops.[1] Even Donatello himself came to Venice in 1453 to make a wooden Saint John the Baptist for the Florentine colony, but this late work is almost Northern in its brutal realism and did little to turn Venetian art towards a more idealized classical approach.

In painting, too, Venice had access to modern Florentine developments through visiting artists. The Venetian love of intricate decoration and flowing

Gothic forms seems to have led to the choice of the great International Gothic painters Gentile da Fabriano and Pisanello to paint frescoes (destroyed in the fire of 1577) for the Sala del Maggior Consiglio in the Palazzo Ducale. More surprisingly, two more severely classical Tuscan painters, Paolo Uccello and Andrea Castagno, were employed in the city. Uccello spent several years designing mosaics for San Marco from about 1425 to 1430; and Castagno came in 1442 to paint a series of monumental frescoed figures in the apse of the old church of San Zaccaria. Shortly after completing his famous treatise on painting, *Della Pittura*, Leon Battista Alberti paid a short visit to Venice in 1437, although this was before the start of his architectural career.

The Florentine artists who visited Venice in the fifteenth century also included the distinguished architect Michelozzo, who accompanied his patron Cosimo de' Medici during his period of exile in the Veneto in 1433–34. Michelozzo himself actually designed a building in the city. This was a library which Cosimo founded at the Benedictine monastery of San Giorgio Maggiore in gratitude for the monks' hospitality. No trace survives of the building, which was damaged by fire and replaced in the seventeenth century by the existing library designed by Longhena. We know little of its appearance. Vasari tells us only that it was 'not only finished with walls, desks, wooden furnishings and other decoration, but also filled with many books'.[2] According to Francesco Sansovino (writing after his father had erected his own splendid Biblioteca Marciana) it was as fine as any other library in the city.[3] Probably the design foreshadowed that of Michelozzo's later library, also founded by Cosimo, in the Monastery of San Marco in Florence, built in 1441–44. At any rate, from our knowledge of Michelozzo's other works it can be assumed that it was a lucid, elegantly proportioned, vaulted hall with classical details and restrained but delicately carved ornament. Yet, as we shall see, local architects showed little interest.

Although, as Fritz Saxl pointed out in two classic lectures in the 1930s, Venetian art does reveal traces of classical erudition from the fourteenth century onwards, her culture tended to resist the importation of Renaissance ideas.[4] Petrarch found an influential contingent in Venice unsympathetic towards his enthusiasm for Latin literature, despite the warm welcome offered by a few enlightened individuals. Unlike Florence, or even the nearby city of Padua, Venice had no strong tradition of humanist studies. The typical education for the young Venetian patrician was a period spent at sea, on merchant galleys or in the navy, rather than a more intellectual training. Some young nobles were taught classical studies by private tutors, but it was not until the middle of the fifteenth century that an official school for the sons of patricians was established, attached to the chancery.[5] By contrast, in Padua, with its ancient university and deep interest in classical studies, artistic patronage had been more enlightened from an early date. Giovanni Pisano worked there in the Scrovegni Chapel at the beginning of the fourteenth century, while in the fifteenth century the presence of Donatello from 1443 to before 1457 and of Filippo Lippi between 1434 and 1437 had a strong impact on local artistic activity.

Possibly we should not think of Venice as conservative in her unreceptive attitude to Early Renaissance culture. The disregard for the achievements of the Florentines was not so much a case of introverted self-absorption or narrow mindedness, as one of rich and varied interests directed elsewhere. As we have already stressed repeatedly, Venetian prosperity depended first and foremost on trade. And this trade was chiefly based on the exchange of merchandise from the Eastern Mediterranean with goods from North of the Alps. Venetian commercial and cultural links were with the Islamic world and Northern Europe, rather than with Florence and the humanist courts of Northern Italy. The oriental influence is reflected in the fact that, whereas there was relatively little interest in Latin studies, the tradition of Greek scholarship was deep-rooted in Venice. Already in the fourteenth century the study of Aristotelian and natural philosophy was well established. In 1468 Cardinal Bessarion of Trebizond left his rich library, including some 500 Greek manuscripts, to the Venetian Republic in recognition of the city's interests. At the end of the fifteenth century, when the Aldine press began to print classical writings in the city, Greek texts were among the most popular titles. Furthermore, Venice was exceptional among major Italian cities in having no Roman infrastructure, although there were conspicuous Roman antiquities on Venetian territory, especially in Verona, Rimini, and the Dalmatian towns of Pola and Spalato. The fact that influential, wealthy Venetians were constantly in contact with two very rich artistic traditions, the Byzantine and the Gothic, probably explains why these two styles had such a profound influence on Venetian art, long excluding what may in retrospect seem more enlightened, namely the culture of the Renaissance.

The beginnings of the Renaissance in Venetian architecture

In Venice, apart from Michelozzo's library which stands on its own, the earliest examples of true Renaissance architecture – in other words, those built in conscious emulation of the style of the buildings of antiquity – date from about 1460. By this time Brunelleschi had been dead for 14 years, and Alberti had already completed the manuscript of his great treatise on architecture *De re aedificatoria*.[6] Renaissance buildings were now rising in many other Italian cities – Rome, Naples, Milan, Rimini, Urbino and Mantua among them – and by the end of the century the Gothic style was to have virtually died out, even in Venice.

One of the very first classical style monuments in the city was the gateway to the Arsenal, erected under Foscari's successor, Doge Pasquale Malipiero, and dated 1460 on the pedestals of the side columns (*Fig. 48*). With its two pairs of free-standing columns flanking a central archway it was surely intended to be recognized as a restatement of the theme of the Roman triumphal arch. Indeed it is modelled on a true antique prototype, the Arco dei Sergi in the Dalmatian town of Pola.[7] This archway, actually a free-standing funerary monument, was certainly well known in Venice, since Pola was then under Venetian rule. In the sixteenth century it was drawn by several architects,

including Fra Giocondo, Falconetto, Serlio and Palladio, although these may not all have visited the monument in person. The way in which the architect of the Arsenal gateway, who was probably Antonio Gambello, transformed the fluted half-columns of the Arco dei Sergi into free-standing smooth columns suggests that he, too, may not have had first hand knowledge of his classical source. The capitals do not conform to an antique type but instead are eleventh-century Veneto-Byzantine capitals taken from an older building. The architect seems to have considered these as part of his classical heritage, just as Tuscan architects of the Early Renaissance turned to their local Romanesque prototypes for inspiration. After the Venetian victory over the Turks at the Battle of Lepanto in 1571 the gateway was turned into a true

TOP
48 Porta dell'Arsenale, attributed to Antonio Gambello, dated 1460 (*A.F.Kersting*)

49 Ca' del Duca, San Samuele, begun by 1460 (*Howard Burns*)

105

triumphal arch by the addition of winged victories and a commemorative inscription. The terrace built in front of the gateway in the late seventeenth century is an unfortunate addition, for it undermines the original function of the monument by obstructing the entrance.

A second extremely innovatory building was begun in Venice at about the same time, although it never progressed very far. This was the Ca'del Duca on the Grand Canal at San Samuele, so called because it was acquired by Francesco Sforza of Milan (*Fig. 49*). The Duke's former palace on the site of Ca'Foscari had been confiscated in 1450 during hostilities between the Milanese and Venetian States, but after the Peace of Lodi he was allowed to take over another Venetian palace, this time one at San Polo which had belonged to the Gattamelata, the famous *condottiere* portrayed in Verrocchio's great equestrian statue at Santi Giovanni e Paolo. In 1458 Sforza sent the best of the architects then under his service in Milan, Antonio Filarete, to make a design for a new house on this site. However, in 1460, acting through his Venetian ambassador Guidobono, Sforza instead arranged to exchange the old house for one on the Grand Canal recently begun by a member of the fabulously wealthy Cornaro family. By this time Filarete was very busy in Milan directing work on his Ospedale Maggiore, so Sforza sent in his place another Florentine architect, Benedetto Ferrini, to prepare a project for the new palace. The foundations laid by the previous owner Andrea Cornaro were not, it seems, ideal, but in 1461 Ferrini began two large-scale models to illustrate his own solution, using the existing structure as the basis for his design.[8]

In the event no more building work was done on the palace after it was acquired by Sforza in 1461, and indeed in 1466 the contract of sale was

50 'House in a Marshy Place', from Filarete's treatise on architecture, Corvinus manuscript, 1484, Biblioteca Marciana, Venice *(Courtauld Institute)*

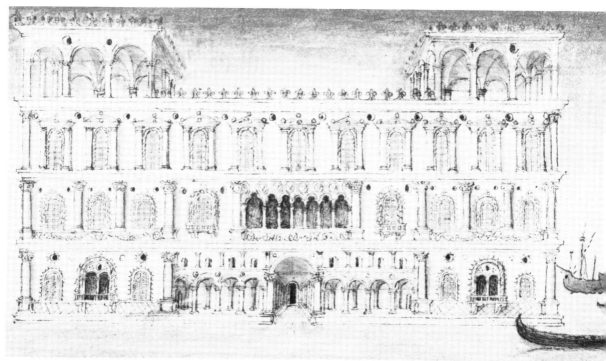

revoked. The letters concerning the sale reveal that the boldly rusticated Istrian-stone basement and the single unfinished corner column, now surmounted by later buildings of no special merit, were the work of none other than the local stonemason Bartolomeo Bon. In no other Venetian building did Bon make so dramatic a leap of imagination. This was the first prominent Venetian building to be faced entirely in Istrian stone.[9] Moreover, the imposing facet-cut masonry *a diamante* would have given the palace an air of impregnability far removed from the characteristic openness of Venetian domestic architecture.

How the palace was to have been completed is uncertain, but there is a strong possibility that the illustration of a 'House in a Marshy Place' in Filarete's treatise may reflect Ferrini's model[10] (*Fig. 50*). This design shares with the executed parts of the building the long frontage on the water's edge, the central water gate, the diamond pattern on the lower walls, and the stocky corner columns. Alternatively it may represent a project for the same site by Filarete himself. The corner towers and waterfront portico are a recollection of the pre-Gothic Veneto-Byzantine tradition, but the forms are those of the Tuscan Renaissance.

How much Venetian architects knew of the scheme is equally uncertain. The manuscript of a Latin translation of Filarete's treatise, made in 1484 for Matthias Corvinus, king of Hungary, was acquired by the library of the monastery of Santi Giovanni e Paolo in 1490;[11] by the sixteenth century it was well known in the city. The craftsmen who made Ferrini's great wooden models in 1461 obviously had precise knowledge of the design, but how influential it proved to be at this early stage is not clear.[12]

51 Palazzo Dario, begun *c.*1487 (*Sarah Quill*)

While some palaces built in the succeeding decades clung to the luxuriant late Venetian Gothic style, others were constructed using purely classical forms. However, their style seems to depend more on direct Lombard influence than on Central Italian ideas brought by Filarete and Ferrini. For example, the delightful Palazzo Dario on the Grand Canal, begun in about 1487 for Giovanni Dario, former Venetian envoy at the Turkish Court, displays neither the classical pediments nor the Tuscan biforate windows of Filarete's 'House in a Marshy Place'. Instead, the windows are simple round-headed openings arranged asymmetrically in the traditional Venetian manner characteristic of smaller-scale palaces (*Fig. 51*). Like the Ca' d'Oro, the Palazzo Dario is jewel-like in its combination of richness and small size. The whole façade is inlaid with fine marbles of various colours, the shimmering, chromatic effect of which must have appealed to the patron with his first-hand knowledge of Islamic decoration. The telephone dial patterns on the flat wall surfaces are a particularly attractive *motif*, borrowed from the designs of Roman floor mosaics, or rather, from their reflections in the pavements of Veneto-Byzantine churches such as San Marco.

Not surprisingly, in the Palazzo Ducale, cradle of Gothic secular architecture in Venice, classical forms were at first used tentatively. Here the Gothic style had recieved what was probably its most extravagant expression in the whole city in the Porta della Carta, the main entrance to the palace, begun by Giovanni and Bartolomeo Bon in 1438 under Doge Francesco Foscari. This gateway, tucked between the south wall of San Marco and the new Piazzetta wing of the Palazzo Ducale, needed an element of flamboyance to draw attention to its important function. But the intricacy of the richly carved pinnacles and crockets also reflects the general move towards a more and more ornate Gothic style in fifteenth-century Venice. Like the Ca' d'Oro, the Porta della Carta was originally richly painted and gilded.

On the courtyard side of the entrance a more sober line was taken in the so-called Arco Foscari, begun under Doge Foscari and continued under Doge Cristoforo Moro (1462–71) probably by Bartolomeo Bon (*Fig. 52*). The central rounded archway, flanked by narrower bays with niches containing statues, is basically classical in style and was surely intended to recall antique triumphal arches. However, in contrast to the Arsenal gateway the inspiration was not a true Roman prototype but instead (far closer at hand) the Basilica of San Marco. It is from the Basilica that the architects borrowed the two superimposed orders with their clusters of columns bordering a great round-arched portal, as well as the continuous balustrade, and the Gothic pinnacles and crowning statues above. The use of this source was not purely a device to harmonize the new archway with its very imposing setting. In Florence, as in other parts of Italy, the first Renaissance architects often turned for specific ideas to the nearest available famous pre-Gothic monument.[13] The underlying intention was certainly to create an *all'antica* style, but by this time even the Romanesque (or in Venice, the Byzantine) heritage had acquired an antique aura and was recognized as a late manifestation of a continuous classical tradition.

ABOVE
52 Palazzo Ducale,
courtyard, showing Arco
Foscari, mid fifteenth
century, and east wing,
1483 onwards
(A.F.Kersting)

LEFT
53 Palazzo Ducale,
Scala dei Giganti, begun
after 1483 *(A.F.Kersting)*

The great fire which damaged the east wing of the Palazzo Ducale in 1483 could have provided the opportunity for a whole-hearted acceptance of Renaissance architectural tenets, but as we shall see, some hesitancy still persisted. After all, the Gothic Palazzo Ducale was a potent symbol of the Venetian Republic at the height of its glory. It is known that the new wing erected after the fire incorporated some of the original structure, but the huge sum of 80,000 ducats spent on the rebuilding suggests that relatively little was preserved. Work was directed by the Veronese stonemason Antonio Rizzo who, improbably, had already received an award for military bravery from the Republic. After he fled to Foligno in 1498 under suspicion of having robbed 12,000 ducats from palace funds, Rizzo's place as *proto* in charge of the building (then at least half-finished) was taken by Pietro Lombardo. The whole wing was finally completed under Antonio Scarpagnino in the mid-sixteenth century.[14]

The high point of Rizzo's contribution was the grand staircase leading from the courtyard to the Doge's apartments on the *piano nobile*, now known as the Scala dei Giganti because of Jacopo Sansovino's two colossal statues placed at the top in 1566[15] (*Fig. 53*). From the beginning the architectural significance of the staircase was recognized. Francesco Sansovino pointed out that not only could the whole flight be seen from the foot of the Campanile through the Porta della Carta, but it was also visible from the Molo entrance of the palace.[16] The staircase was thus the focal point linking these two axes. It also had great ceremonial importance. In 1485 the Maggior Consiglio resolved that the climax of every Ducal coronation, the placing of the *beretta* on the head of the new Doge, should take place at the top of the staircase, after the religious service in San Marco and the grand procession around the Piazza. The same setting was used by the Doge for welcoming ambassadors and important visitors. As a curious extension to the expression of Ducal authority there was a prison cell beneath the staircase.[17]

The form of the grand ceremonial staircase has remarkable precedents among the drawings of Jacopo Bellini, who also bequeathed the same motif to Venetian Renaissance narrative painting. As a painter Jacopo rarely freed himself from the legacy of Gothic and Byzantine traditions, but his drawings show a fine grasp of modern perspective and of classical architectural vocabulary. In his youth he had studied with Gentile da Fabriano, and he may even have visited Florence himself. The triple arch at the top of the staircase, the middle landing, the benches along the sides, the chamber beneath and, above all, the scenic effect of the courtyard setting, are all prefigured in drawings in his British Museum sketchbook. Jacopo died in 1470/71, more than a decade before the Palazzo Ducale staircase was begun, but Rizzo must certainly have known of his ideas.[18]

Like the courtyard façade of the new east wing of the palace, the staircase was the vehicle for a complex iconographical programme glorifying the Republic and the office of Doge. The Barbarigo family arms are also prominently displayed, for much of the sculpture was executed during the reigns of Marco Barbarigo (1485–86) and his brother Agostino (1486–1501).

It seems that the elaborate relief sculpture, which covers the whole wing as well as the sides of the staircase, was intended to be read almost like the illustrations in a book. The romantic humanist novel, Francesco Colonna's *Hypnerotomachia Polifili*, written in Venice in the same years, is perhaps the closest literary parallel.[19] Although we are no longer able to appreciate the full subtlety of the intentionally secretive iconography, we can at least appreciate the high quality of much of the stone carving. Ideas were loosely drawn from a wide range of antique sources, especially from classical gems and sculpture which were already being assembled enthusiastically by collectors in Padua and even in Venice.[20]

The design of the staircase is sufficiently emphatic, coherent, and simple to dominate and contain the elaborate sculptural programme. The same could hardly be said of the rest of the east wing, where the richness of the surface ornament cannot conceal the irregularity and stylistic inconsistency of the whole (*Fig. 52*). The Gothic arches of the *piano nobile* arcade, presumably chosen in deference to the existing Gothic portions of the palace, are inserted between the round arches of the portico below and the classical-style pedimented windows and *all'antica* relief sculpture above. The haphazard arrangement of the windows is governed chiefly by the distribution of rooms in the interior.

Like the edge of a forest the whole composition makes its effect not by bold, regular rhythms, but by the play of light and shade on an intricate and constantly varied frontage. The wing is a graphic illustration of the way in which, in Venice, the North Italian love of rich surface decoration, fostered by Lombard stonemasons working in the city, predominated over the Florentine taste for lucidity and carefully harmonized proportion.

Religious architecture in Early Renaissance Venice

In this period of transition between the Gothic and Renaissance styles in Venice, ecclesiastical architecture once again proved most receptive to ideas from mainland Italy. It was in the church of San Giobbe, rebuilt at the instigation of Doge Malipiero's successor, Doge Cristoforo Moro, that the Tuscan Renaissance first began to make its mark on Venetian architecture. The new church and monastery were founded on the site of a hospital and small oratory dedicated to San Giobbe, to commemorate the visit of San Bernardino of Siena to preach there in 1443. Since 1428 the oratory had been occupied by the Observant branch of the Franciscan order, to which San Bernardino himself belonged. The saint's tremendous popular appeal had brought him a huge audience in Venice. On his visit to the Veneto he had also predicted to Moro that he would one day be Doge. San Bernardino was canonized in 1450, only six years after his death; and in 1470 Moro persuaded the Senate to include him as one of the protectors of the Republic, joining Saints Teodoro and Magno.[21]

The simple aisle-less nave was begun in about 1450 in a late Gothic style, but the choir, where Moro himself was buried, is far more advanced in style (*Fig. 54*). Even at this time the identity of the architect was still considered a relatively unimportant matter, with the result that we do not know who was responsible for the designs. The nave, like the Arsenal gateway, is attributed to the local architect Antonio Gambello. The chancel, choir and chapels were probably finished under the direction of Pietro Solari – known as 'il Lombardo' because he came from Carona in Lombardy – after Moro's death in 1471.[22] The church was consecrated in 1493.

The presbytery of San Giobbe provides the earliest evidence that the achievements of Brunelleschi and Michelozzo were becoming known and understood in Venice. As in the east wing of the Palazzo Ducale the Venetian enjoyment of elaborate surface decoration is still prominent. The piers, capitals and friezes are all skilfully carved with delicate *all'antica* reliefs, probably produced in the Lombardi workshop. But the beauty and richness of the ornament in no way detracts from the clarity and harmony of the whole. The entrance to the chancel forms a great triumphal arch with niches serving as small chapels on either side. The square presbytery is surmounted by a dome hovering just above the crowns of the arches and lit by windows in the drum. The pendentives are decorated with tondo reliefs of the Evangelists attributed to Pietro Lombardo himself.

Of course the domed, centrally-planned space had a long ancestry in

Venice, particularly in funeral chapels and martyria. This form was therefore particularly appropriate for Moro's burial place. Here, however, the elements are not Byzantine but instead derive ultimately from more recent Florentine prototypes such as Brunelleschi's Old Sacristy in San Lorenzo. Evidence of a direct link with Tuscany in the 1470s is provided in one of the side chapels of the nave of San Giobbe, which belonged to a family of silk weavers from Lucca called Martini. The vault of this chapel is decorated with glazed terracotta reliefs from the della Robbia workshop, and the sculpture on the altar is attributed to the school of Antonio Rossellino. This chapel is a miniature, much simplified version of the Cardinal of Portugal's chapel in San Miniato in Florence, decorated by the same artists in the 1460s.[23]

However, the strong Tuscan influence in San Giobbe, so uncharacteristic of Venetian architecture of the period, must also reflect ideas which were widespread among Observant Franciscan communities at the time. The Osservanti were the reformed, more ascetic division of the Franciscan order. San Bernardino himself was a fervent propagator of their ideas and was Vicar General of the branch from 1438 until 1442. In that year the Pope allowed him to resign in order to return to his life as a preacher. His own monastery was the convent of the Osservanza, just outside Siena.[24] In 1423 he had the old church rebuilt, and it was again remodelled at the end of the fifteenth century, probably with instructions from the important Sienese architect Francesco di Giorgio, or his pupil and close friend Giacomo Cozzarelli. In the case of the Osservanza it is difficult to ascertain how much of the design of the present church (restored after severe damage in World War II) dates from before the building of San Giobbe and how much from after. But the similarities between the two churches – the aisle-less nave with side chapels, the domed chancel, and the long retro-choir – are so marked that some link seems inevitable.[25] Probably no previous single-naved churches without side aisles existed in Venice, and even elsewhere in Italy there are few examples before the sixteenth century. As in the case of the first Mendicant-order churches in Venice, it was through the religious orders that new ideas from elsewhere in Italy were most easily imported into the city.

Reminiscences of Tuscan religious architecture are also apparent in Santa Maria dei Miracoli, one of the best-loved churches in Venice, built by Pietro Lombardo between 1481 and 1489[26] (*Fig. 55*). This unusual little church, a simple barrel-vaulted chapel with a raised choir over a crypt at the east end, was built to house a devotional image of the Virgin, which in the year 1480 had supposedly developed miraculous powers. Numerous miracles are recorded, including the removal of all evidence of attack from a woman who had been stabbed and left for dead, and the rescue of a man who had fallen into the Giudecca Canal while washing and remained under water for half an hour. Private donations and votive offerings flowed in, and within six months of the first miracle the foundation stone of the chapel had been laid. The addition of the domed high altar chapel at the east end seems to have been an afterthought. It was begun in 1485 after the decision to build a convent beside the church for nuns from Santa Chiara in Murano.

That the Miracoli was primarily a votive chapel rather than a convent church accounts for some unusual features of the design. The complete marble facing on all four sides helps to draw attention to the church in its cramped urban site, near the wall where the image hung when the miracles began to occur. There are no other examples in Venetian architecture of such a simple barrel-vaulted nave, except in small chapels such as the Mascoli Chapel in San Marco and the Arena Chapel in Padua. The coloured marble decoration of the exterior not only recalls the wealth of precious marbles on the Basilica of San Marco, but also looks to the Tuscan Romanesque tradition. Indeed the arrangement of the two orders of the exterior seems to be borrowed directly from the Baptistery in Florence, popularly believed to be a classical building; and tondo busts like those in the spandrels of the Miracoli also appear on Ghiberti's famous Baptistery doors. As we have seen, the choice of Romanesque models was characteristic of Early-Renaissance architecture in Italy; but the choice in Venice of a Tuscan prototype was still unusual and surprisingly adventurous. Lieberman has recently suggested that Mauro Codussi may have been the designer of the original model and that Pietro Lombardo was merely the executant.[27] There is no direct evidence of Codussi's involvement, and the coloured inlays and elaborate *all'antica* relief sculpture are far more typical of the Lombardo workshop; but on the other hand, Codussi used Tuscan sources more freely than his contemporaries in Venice, as will become clear later in this chapter. Whoever the designer, the Miracoli stands on its own in Venetian architecture of the period – like a richly inlaid jewel box to contain the precious painting.

Mauro Codussi (c. 1440–1504)

One of the most difficult problems in the history of Venetian art is that of disentangling the individual contributions of the various Lombard and Bergamese stonemasons working in fifteenth-century Venice. As a group these mastercraftsmen were responsible for replacing the long established Venetian Gothic style with the new classical forms of the Early Renaissance. For the most part they used *all'antica* elements decoratively and somewhat naively. But among the attractive if provincial buildings which they erected in Venice in the second half of the fifteenth century, a few stand out as indisputable masterpieces.

For 400 years the identity of their architect was lost to posterity. It was not until the end of the nineteenth century that Paoletti, after carefully scrutinizing all the documents which he could trace, finally isolated the name and thus the artistic personality of the most talented of these immigrant stonemasons.[28] He was Mauro Codussi, who was born near Bergamo in about 1440 and died in Venice in 1504. As early as 1581 his genius had already been forgotten: Francesco Sansovino mentions 'Moro Lombardo' only once, as one of two possible architects of the church of San Giovanni Crisostomo.[29] The existence of 'Moro, son of Martino' at the Scuola di San Marco had been known since Temanza's archival researches in the eighteenth century, though

as a mere stonecutter.[30] In contrast to Tuscany, the mediaeval anonymity of artists persisted in Venice right through the fifteenth century, even after the Gothic style had virtually died out in the city.

56 San Michele in Isola, by Mauro Codussi, begun 1469
(A.F.Kersting)

Now that Codussi has been identified with certainty as the architect of such impressive works as the churches of San Michele in Isola and Santa Maria Formosa, the slender white Campanile of San Pietro di Castello, and the masterful double staircases of the Scuole of San Marco and San Giovanni Evangelista, we should ask ourselves what exactly was the nature of his individual contribution to Venetian architecture – so soon forgotten, yet so conspicuous.

Codussi is first recorded in Venice in 1469, the year in which he began the church of San Michele in Isola (*Fig. 56*). This church was erected for a hermitage belonging to the Camaldolese branch of the Benedictine order, situated on the island between Venice and Murano which is now the city's cemetery. We know a good deal about the building history of the church from letters written to the abbot, Pietro Donà, who was repeatedly away in Ravenna, by Pietro Delfino or Dolfin, the monk who took his place during his periods of absence. Delfino's correspondence reveals that Codussi, too, was called to Ravenna by the abbot on several occasions, to work at the Camaldolese abbey at Classe (now destroyed). Despite the day to day practical and financial problems of the building work at San Michele, which Delfino's letters chronicle vividly, the church was inaugurated as soon as 1477. In a letter in that year Delfino described it proudly as second only to the Basilica of San Marco.[31]

It is tantalizing that nothing is known of Codussi's artistic training, nor of how he came to be chosen to design this church. He certainly learned much from his travels. The Byzantine monuments of Ravenna, like the Basilica of San Marco in Venice, must have been viewed by Codussi, as by many of his contemporaries, as an integral part of the classical heritage. Thus the three-aisled nave of San Michele, with its two rows of columns supporting round arches, recalls the much larger Basilica of Sant'Apollinare Nuovo in Ravenna which dates from the early sixth century. On his journey down the Adriatic coast Codussi must also have seen one of the most avant garde Early Renaissance buildings in Italy – Alberti's Tempio Malatestiano at Rimini, begun in about 1450 though never completely finished. The façade of San Michele, with its attic storey crowned by a huge lunette and flanked by convex curves, is strongly reminiscent of the Rimini church, as it appears on Matteo dei Pasti's foundation medal. Huge crowning lunettes were, of course, also a prominent feature of the façade of San Marco. Moreover, some Venetian Gothic church façades had a similar type of lobed profile. However, the fact that the monks themselves seem to have known something of Alberti's theoretical ideas suggests that the resemblance to the Tempio Malatestiano was the result of Codussi's direct knowledge of Alberti's work.[32] Codussi's documented journeys to obtain stone from Istria and Verona must have given himself the opportunity to familiarize himself, too, with real – that is, Roman – antiquity. Although he almost certainly never travelled to Rome, the classical remains of Verona, Pola and Spalato offered a rich supply of all'antica ideas.

In a curious way, tracing the sources of Codussi's style only makes his achievement seem more amazing, for with very limited knowledge of the buildings of antiquity he produced some of the most serene, harmonious, classicizing architecture in the whole of the Italian Renaissance. Already in San Michele he handles classical forms in a most authoritative manner – to organize and explain, rather than to decorate, the structure of the building. Both inside and out, ornament is used with restraint, to highlight the points of emphasis. The individual details are not only beautiful, but are also executed with perfect precision. One has only to look at the exquisite capitals of the nave arcades (each pair different), the shell motifs in the façade, the chain moulding around the large central oculus, and the clean cut rustication which gives texture to the pristine whiteness of the façade. The use of rustication (which normally expressed the defensive character of a building) on the façade of a church was a highly original touch. Codussi obviously knew the rusticated foundations of the Ca' del Duca on the Grand Canal, and must also have heard of rusticated palaces in Florence such as Alberti's Palazzo Rucellai. It is possible that he chose rustication for the façade of San Michele to convey the fact that the island monastery was a hermitage. The extension of the

rustication across the pilaster order was an idea which would rarely be seen in Italy before it became popular with Mannerist architects in the sixteenth century.

It is a commonplace that Venetians enjoyed chromatic richness, in architecture as in painting and mosaics. But Codussi showed that white Istrian stone, without any coloured decoration whatever, could be extraordinarily effective. The church of San Michele, floating like an iceberg in the lagoon, must have inspired Palladio a century later when he designed the façades of San Giorgio Maggiore and the Redentore (*Figs. 87 & 89*). As we have seen, in Venice in the Gothic period churches and palaces alike were usually built of brick, with Istrian stone confined to details such as door and window frames, quoins, cornices and string courses. With the arrival of the Renaissance, architects began to mask brick structures with stone and marble, searching for a more classical effect. (The impressive antique brick constructions in Rome itself were probably little known in Venice at this time.) While his contemporaries, in buildings such as the Palazzo Dario, the Arco Foscari and the church of the Miracoli, were experimenting with coloured marble inlays, Codussi continued to explore the visual and physical qualities of white Istrian stone, which was easy to carve, durable and relatively cheaply imported by sea.

In 1482 he took on the rebuilding of the Campanile of the cathedral of Venice, San Pietro di Castello, situated at the eastern extremity of the city (*Fig. 57*). This commission came from the Patriarch, Maffei Gerardo, a former abbot of the monastery of San Michele in Isola.[33] Because of their long-standing suspicion of ecclesiastical power, Venetians were probably grateful for the remoteness of the site of the cathedral. However, Codussi gave the city a forceful reminder of its presence, in the form of a completely white, lofty bell tower, topped by an elegant octagon. He himself made several journeys to Istria to choose stone from the quarries. Originally the Campanile was roofed by a dome, which unfortunately became unsafe and was replaced by a simple

57 San Pietro di Castello, formerly Cathedral of Venice, rebuilt in the seventeenth century, and Campanile by Mauro Codussi, begun 1482 (*A.F.Kersting*)

pitched roof in the seventeenth century. At this period, all the other bell towers of Venice were built in red brick, so that Codussi's snow white Campanile, sunlit like a beacon against a deep blue sky, would have been all the more striking.

The paired columns and shell niches of the crowning octagon of the tower suggest that Codussi may have had some knowledge – perhaps through drawings or verbal accounts – of the octagonal exedrae which Brunelleschi built around the great dome of Florence Cathedral. As we noted in the case of San Giobbe and the Miracoli, Venice was not quite impervious to Tuscan influence, and ecclesiastical patrons were often those who encouraged the importation of ideas from outside Venice.

While the episcopal seat was answerable to Rome, and monasteries were in regular contact with other members of their orders elsewhere in Italy, the parish churches of Venice were extremely localized in their organisation. It was the parishioners who elected the clergy and financed the erection of new churches. Thus it is not surprising to find that the two parish churches which Codussi built in Venice – Santa Maria Formosa and San Giovanni Crisostomo – were very different in character from his monastic works. Neither contains prominent references to Roman antiquity, or to the work of Brunelleschi or Alberti, but both are rooted in the Byzantine traditions of the Venetian lagoon.

Malipiero's diaries tell us that the foundation stone of the new church of Santa Maria Formosa was laid in 1492, following the design of 'Mauro Bergamasco' (*Fig. 58*). The building was substantially complete by the time of Codussi's death in 1504.[34] This church, which stands on one of the largest and most attractive *campi* of the city, is unusual in that it is almost free standing. Perhaps the challenge of providing a structure which would look effective from all around and which could be entered from three sides encouraged Codussi to experiment with a centralized plan. Barbari's map of 1500 shows that during the Gothic period parish churches, like monastic ones, were normally longitudinal structures, but it also indicates that a number of small Veneto-Byzantine Greek-cross churches, like San Giacomo di Rialto (the only one which exists today), were still standing in the city as a direct source of inspiration.[35] According to Francesco Sansovino's guide of 1581, the previous church of Santa Maria Formosa, built in the eleventh century, was modelled on the central core of San Marco.[36] (Curiously, he makes no mention of the new church.)

Codussi's plan for Santa Maria Formosa shows remarkable dexterity and in-ventiveness (*p. 119*). The Basilica of San Marco, standing as it does only three minutes' walk from Codussi's church, is undoubtedly the chief source of inspiration for the Greek-cross plan, with its three apsed chapels at the east end, its slightly elongated triple nave, and its great central dome over the crossing. The church was badly damaged in World War I, when a bomb destroyed the whole of the roof, and during the repairs the structure was considerably altered. The dome was rebuilt without the high drum which appears in earlier views, and round windows were inserted in the vaults of the nave to replace the windows in the drum. How the building was originally lit

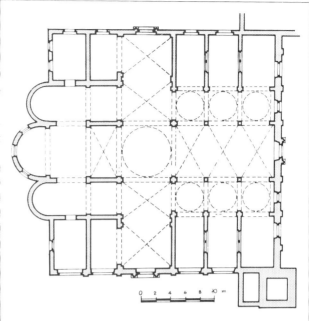

is not clear, for the church had already been reconstructed after an earthquake in 1668.[37] Almost certainly it was fairly sombre, like other pre-Palladian churches in the city, most of which have since been provided with extra windows to improve the illumination.

The ambiguity between the two main axes of the ground plan is consistently exploited inside Santa Maria Formosa, since the worshipper was as likely to enter from the sides as from the east end (*Fig. 59*). The unusually deep side chapels emphasise the cross axis, but this directional force is counteracted by the beautiful device of piercing the walls of these chapels with large biforate openings. To a person moving around the interior these apertures offer a series of constantly changing vistas between the various compartments of the church. Santa Maria Formosa was one of the Venetian churches which was visited annually by the Doge, on the feast of the Purification of the Virgin.[38] In response, Codussi produced a design which was especially effective to the participants of a moving procession.

We know little of Codussi's intentions for the exterior. The façade on the South side dates from the mid-sixteenth century, while the west façade and the Campanile are both seventeenth-century constructions. But Codussi's three swelling apses at the east end, perhaps all the more expressive for their absence of decoration, certainly make a powerful impression on the passer-by moving through the *campo* (*Fig. 58*).

Santa Maria Formosa was a prosperous parish, being among the most desirable addresses in the city. Thus the residents were able to secure a sizeable loan to finance the rebuilding of their church. By contrast the church of San Giovanni Crisostomo, which was rebuilt by Codussi in the same years, had fewer wealthy parishioners and also stood on a very cramped site. It is

ABOVE, LEFT
58 Santa Maria Formosa, by Codussi, begun 1492; view of rear apses *(A.F.Kersting)*

ABOVE
Santa Maria Formosa, by Codussi, plan. After Angelini

ABOVE
59 Santa Maria
Formosa, interior
(A.F.Kersting)

ABOVE, RIGHT
60 San Giovanni
Crisostomo, by Codussi,
begun 1497; interior
(A.F.Kersting)

therefore not surprising that this church was rebuilt on a more modest scale. Funds for the project were raised by ten years of indulgences conceded by Pope Innocent VIII, after the old church had been damaged by fire. The new building was begun in 1497, and was more or less finished at the time of Codussi's death.[39]

Once again Codussi chose a centralized Greek-cross plan, but it was both smaller and simpler than that of Santa Maria Formosa (*Fig. 60*). Inside the church a central dome is supported on free-standing piers, with barrel vaults over each arm of the cross, following the system of San Giacomo di Rialto. Once again, Codussi placed three apsed chapels at the east end, but the central one is flattened because of lack of space. The street façade is a much simplified version of the façade of San Michele in Isola, here built in stuccoed brick defined by elongated Corinthian pilasters. The doorways – executed after Codussi's death but possibly following his designs – are more emphatic in style, framed by fluted half-columns supporting heavy pediments.

At Santa Maria Formosa and San Giovanni Crisostomo Codussi showed how well the ancient Veneto-Byzantine Greek-cross plan suited the needs of parish churches, with their small congregations and intimate services. At Santa Maria Formosa the choice of plan was further justified by a long-established tradition (not universally applied) that Marian churches should be centrally planned, symbolizing the Virgin's womb, as well as her crown in the case of round churches. But apart from these practical and iconographical considerations it is now recognized that the return to the Greek-cross church plan, which Codussi pioneered at the end of the fifteenth century, was part of a much broader Venetian interest in Byzantine culture at this time.[40] In 1468 Cardinal Bessarion of Trebizond had bequeathed to the city his valuable collection of manuscripts, which was particularly rich in Greek codices; and this bequest helped to stimulate a renewed interest in Byzantine studies among the scholars of the city. This is reflected by the large number of Greek texts printed at the famous press established in Venice by Aldo Manuzio in 1494. Painters, too, sought to emulate the art of Byzantium in works such as the Madonnas of Giovanni Bellini, some of which adopt the conventions of icon painting. For the Venetians, with their ancient links with the Eastern Empire, the Byzantine heritage had vivid classical connotations, just as Rome symbolized the world of antiquity elsewhere in Italy. The fact that Alberti's treatise on architecture *De re aedificatoria* recommends the central plan for churches may also have helped to justify the return to Greek-cross plans in Venice.

Codussi's secular work shows the same kind of inventiveness, providing completely fresh solutions to old problems. When the Scuola Grande di San Marco burned down in 1485, a substantial grant towards the cost of rebuilding it was provided by the Senate because of the State's loyalty to Saint Mark. This offered a splendid opportunity for the architects involved. The old foundations were re-used for the sake of economy, so that the main areas for innovation were the façade and the staircase. The first builders appointed were Pietro Lombardo and Giovanni Buora, but after a disagreement with the Scuola officials they were released from their duties. Codussi is first recorded as *proto*, or chief builder, in 1490. By 1495, when his salary was discontinued, the new building must have been largely completed.[41]

The Lombardi-Buora team was certainly responsible for the lower order of the façade with its ornate relief sculpture, intricately carved with flower and foliage patterns, and its coloured marble inlays (*Fig. 30*). The perspective scenes on either side of the two doorways were executed by Pietro's son Tullio. The effect of this charming device is naive rather than impressive, for the illusion only works from a certain viewpoint, whereas the huge *campo* in front of the Scuola allows any number of possible approaches.

It was left to Codussi to give coherence and dignity to the façade, just as he had done at the church of San Zaccaria when he took over the building after the death of Antonio Gambello in 1481. He was probably responsible for the bold triangular and segmental pediments over the *piano nobile* windows of the Scuola. The row of lunettes along the roofline displays one of Codussi's favourite motifs, recalling the great lobes on the façades of San Michele and San Zaccaria. Here the lunettes are multiplied in number as a conscious reference to the profile of the Basilica of San Marco, which shares the same titular saint as the Scuola.

Codussi is usually credited with the invention of the elegant double-branched staircase which led up to the great *salone*. This staircase was destroyed under Austrian rule in 1819, when the Scuola was converted into the civic hospital, but has now been reconstructed on the basis of incomplete evidence of its former appearance. A recent study has shown that the Scuola had planned a double-branched staircase as early as 1486, well before Codussi's involvement.[42] Nearby precedents which could have suggested the idea to the Scuola officials were the exterior double-branched staircases of the Fabbriche Vecchie di Rialto (destroyed by fire in 1514 but visible in Barbari's map of 1500) (*Fig. 66*) and the Palazzo dei Trecento in Treviso.[43] But it was left to Codussi to implement the idea.

As we have seen, at this date all staircases of any importance in Venice were still external structures. The innovation of a covered staircase not only gives better protection from the elements, but also makes the experience of mounting the stairs more dramatic. It ensures that the attention of the person ascending is not allowed to wander, but is focussed on the summit of the staircase. At San Marco the top landing which leads directly into the great upper hall of the Scuola is emphasised by a sail-vaulted dome and by a flood of light from a large biforate window.

In view of the sad destruction of the double staircase at the Scuola di San Marco, we are fortunate that a second example of the same type still survives (*Fig. 61*). In 1498, in the competitive spirit so typical of Scuola patronage, the Scuola Grande di San Giovanni Evangelista employed Codussi to erect a double-branched staircase, similar to that of San Marco, on a newly acquired piece of land alongside their existing building.[44] As at San Marco, the two converging ramps provide access from separate land and water entrances. Codussi ingeniously exploited the oblique angle in the wall of the Scuola di San Giovanni, where the two flights meet, by widening each flight towards the top; but by careful manipulation of the perspective of the cornices and balustrades he concealed this fact. As a result the top landing is more spacious and imposing than that of San Marco. A hemispherical cupola is supported on four broad arches, decorated with classical rosettes and resting on paired, free-standing columns at each corner of the landing. As in the San Marco staircase, a mirror image of the opposite flight is revealed as one climbs the steps, but since the ascent is much less steep the effect is already apparent at the bottom landing.[45]

Just as Codussi added rich new dimensions to Scuola and church architecture in Venice, so, too, he rejuvenated long-established Venetian traditions of palace building. His greatest opportunity in this field was the commission for a new palace for the wealthy patrician Andrea Loredan at San Marcuola, now usually called the Palazzo Vendramin-Calergi (*Fig. 62*). The design is generally attributed to Codussi for stylistic reasons, but the fact that Andrea Loredan was a generous benefactor and protector of the new church of San Michele in Isola makes the authorship of this palace quite convincing. Like Marco Zorzi, who employed Codussi to build his new palace at San Severo, Andrea Loredan was one of a circle of nobles, united by their involvement with the Camaldolese monastery, who adopted Codussi as their favourite architect. Although Andrea began to purchase extra land on the site in 1481 the palace does not appear on Barbari's map of 1500. Building work seems to have begun as late as 1502, and cannot have progressed far before Codussi's death two years later. However, Priuli's diaries in 1509 imply that the building was by then complete, so the patron was probably lucky enough to have finished most of the work by the beginning of the Cambrai Wars. He himself died in battle in 1513.[46]

The palace, now the winter home of the Casinò of Venice, has had a long series of famous owners and an eventful history. In 1581, the year in which Francesco Sansovino described it as one of the four finest palaces in Venice,[47] Andrea's heirs sold it to the Duke of Brunswick. In 1589 it passed to Vettor Calergi, a member of a wealthy family from Crete. In 1658 the Senate decreed that the palace be demolished and its owners banished after three young Calergi brothers had brutally murdered a fellow noble, but the building was reprieved because of its exceptional merit. In 1883 Wagner died there while a guest of the Duke of Chambord who owned the palace at that time.

Francesco Sansovino based his admiration for the Loredan palace on its size and nobility. This was the first Venetian palace façade in which the classical orders expressed the whole structure. The three superimposed Corinthian orders support their entablatures without apparent need of support from the

BELOW, LEFT

61 Scuola Grande di San Giovanni Evangelista, staircase by Codussi, begun 1498 (*A.F.Kersting*)

BELOW

62 Palazzo Vendramin-Calergi, formerly Loredan, by Codussi, begun *c.*1502 (*A.F.Kersting*)

wall surfaces. The choice of pilasters on the water storey, fluted columns on the *piano nobile*, and smooth columns on the second floor, explains the relative importance of each floor, using the most ornate form for the principal storey. The idea of articulating a complete façade with the classical orders derives from Alberti, whose Palazzo Rucellai in Florence has three superimposed pilaster orders. The huge classical cornice, too, was probably inspired by that of the Palazzo Rucellai. The biforate, round-arched windows surmounted by oculi, a favourite motif of Codussi's, must also have been suggested by the windows of Florentine Early Renaissance palaces such as the Palazzo Medici and the Palazzo Rucellai. However, as we have seen, because of the local glass industry and the need to admit light deep into the buildings, windows were by tradition much larger in Venice than in Florence. Enlarging the biforate window-type, Codussi made the form more vigorous and expressive than its Florentine prototype.

With typical ingenuity Codussi applied the lessons of Alberti to the traditional Venetian tripartite palace façade. The three windows in the middle of the two upper storeys light the great central halls or *porteghi*, while the paired columns frame the windows of the smaller rooms on either side. The whole palace is faced in Istrian stone, and although rare oriental coloured marbles and porphyries are used freely to indicate the wealth and prestige of the owner, Codussi characteristically does not allow the coloured decoration to play a dominant rôle and thus to detract from the sober dignity of this astoundingly mature classical façade.

By about 1500 Codussi must have been recognized as the most talented architect in Venice, even outside his inner circle of patrons. For this reason, and on stylistic grounds, he is usually thought to be the author of the Torre

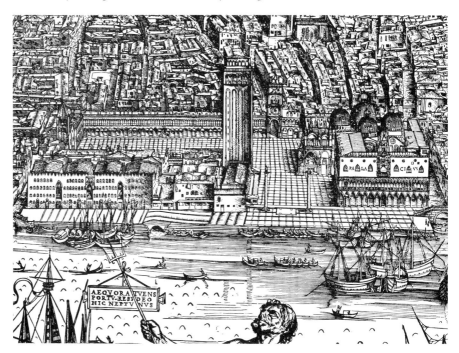

63 Piazza San Marco. Detail from Jacopo de'Barbari's bird's-eye-view map of Venice

dell'Orologio or Clock Tower, which was erected in Piazza San Marco over the entrance to the Merceria (the street leading to the Rialto) between 1496 and 1500 (*Fig. 63*). The side wings, which do not appear on Barbari's map of 1500, were probably added soon afterwards.[48]

This monument plays the important rôle of providing the focal point in the view of the Piazzetta seen from the lagoon. It also indicates which of the numerous arches on the north side of the Piazza leads into the principal street of the city. The theatrical possibilities of arches in public architecture had already been demonstrated in the Porta della Carta and the Arco Foscari of the Palazzo Ducale, which define the main entrance of the palace for processions and other ceremonial purposes. The drawings of Jacopo Bellini and the paintings of Carpaccio, too, show a Venetian awareness of how arches and towers, like stairs, could add to the dramatic qualities of an architectural setting. There was a long-established tradition in Venice of placing arches over the entrances of streets or courtyards, such as that over the *rio* end of the Calle del Paradiso (*Fig. 23*), as a mark of the landlord's ownership. Similarly, Venetians probably interpreted the huge winged lion, guarding the Clock Tower from aloft, as a symbol of the political authority of the Republic.

But the fundamental inspiration behind the conception of the Torre dell'Orologio seems to have been, once again, Alberti. At this time the only towers in Italian cities were *campanili*, defensive towers in fortifications, and the tower homes of feudal lords. Yet in his architectural treatise, *De re aedificatoria*, Alberti describes towers, bearing sundials or wind vanes, as one of the finest attributes of a city. (He was, of course, referring to famous classical prototypes such as Ptolemy's tower on the island of Pharos and the Tower of the Winds in Athens.) Towers, both square and round, Alberti declares, should be built in tiers, each one articulated by the classical orders. Square towers should be six, or in some cases four, times as high as their width.[49] The Torre dell'Orologio, which is exactly four times as high as its width (excluding the side wings), fits Alberti's recommendations so closely that the links can hardly be a coincidence (*Fig. 64*). Even the siting of the tower seems to reveal a conscious attempt to turn Venice into an Albertian ideal city. According to Alberti

> '. . . nothing can be a greater Ornament either to Squares or to the Meeting of several Streets, than Arches at the entrance of the Streets; an Arch being indeed nothing else but a Gate standing continually open. . . . A very proper Situation for an Arch is where a Street joins into a Square, and especially in the Royal Street, by which name I understand the most eminent in the City.'[50]

In other words, the Torre dell'Orologio, 'bearing its sundial decorated with the signs of the zodiac and standing over the entrance to the Merceria, functions both as an Albertian classical tower and as an archway over the entrance to the main street of the city.

As we have seen, Codussi was not the only man who attempted to introduce classical forms into Venetian architecture in the second half of the

fifteenth century. Architects in the city had turned to a wide variety of sources in their search for a new classical idiom. Gambello's Porta dell'Arsenale was an explicit imitation of the Roman arch at Pola. The Byzantine Basilica of San Marco and the Romanesque Baptistery of Florence inspired the Arco Foscari and the church of the Miracoli. The monks of San Giobbe, who had close links with Siena, imported Tuscan ideas in rebuilding their church. Pietro Lombardo's workshop evolved a distinctive classical style, characterized by the profuse application of pretty *all'antica* relief sculpture and by favourite motifs such as free-standing columns on high bases and huge lunettes with tiny scrolls at each corner.

Why, then was Codussi's contribution outstanding? He, too, drew on such classical sources as were available to him, and obviously had some knowledge, whether direct or indirect, of Tuscan Early Renaissance architecture. He also borrowed freely from the Byzantine heritage of Venice and Ravenna. But he used classical forms with a far greater understanding of their underlying logic than any of his contemporaries in Venice. And he showed great ingenuity in applying these classical principles to the established building types, which had evolved to suit the city's physical conditions and the specific needs of Venetian society. There can be no doubt that it was Alberti's treatise which was the fundamental discipline behind Codussi's designs. Whether or not he himself ever consulted a manuscript of the treatise is not known, but as Puppi has shown in his recent monograph, Codussi's circle of patrons, connected by their links with the Camaldolese monastery at San Michele in Isola, shared a keen interest in Alberti's ideas, which they would certainly have passed on to their architect. Codussi was gifted with exceptional artistic imagination and visual sensitivity, but it was through his knowledge of Alberti that he was able to give coherence and dignity to the products of his great natural talent.

Architecture during the Wars of the League of Cambrai

Mauro Codussi died in 1504 leaving behind a series of highly original and beautiful buildings but no name. To a certain extent, the oblivion into which this great architect retreated for almost four centuries is due to the fact that two decades of acute political and financial crisis followed his death. The resulting constraints prevented many of Codussi's ideas from being taken up until after his identity had already been forgotten.

By this time the territorial ambitions of the Venetian Republic had finally exceeded her ability to make conquests and hold the lands she seized. One by one her allies deserted her, and in 1509 they joined forces under Pope Julius II in a pact called the League of Cambrai, to seize Venetian possessions, supposedly in preparation for a great campaign against the Turkish infidel. In the same year the Venetian troops were heavily defeated at the Battle of Agnadello, and even Padua was occupied by Imperial troops. This was the most serious threat to the survival of the Republic until the final collapse in 1797. However, a huge military effort by the Venetians in the wars which followed allowed a partial recovery. In the peace settlement of 1517 Venice

OPPOSITE
64 Torre dell'Orologio, Piazza San Marco, attributed to Codussi, begun *c.*1496, side wings added after 1500 *(A.F.Kersting)*

65 Procuratie Vecchie, Piazza San Marco, by Bartolomeo Bon, begun 1513 *(Deborah Howard)*

regained control of most of her mainland possessions except for the most recent conquests, but the political security of the state was not finally re-established until the Peace of Bologna in 1529.[51]

The vicissitudes of the period are chronicled in vivid detail in Sanudo's famous diaries which he kept continuously from 1496 until 1533, and in the diaries of the banker Girolamo Priuli. Economic hardship was acute. Two of the most important Venetian banks had already failed in 1499 under the strain of military activity on the Terraferma. During the Cambrai Wars the wealthy Venetians had to pay out huge sums in taxes, public loans and voluntary gifts. No interest was paid on existing government bonds, and income from Terraferma property ceased abruptly.

Hardly surprisingly, only the most indispensable or richly endowed building projects were carried out during the period between 1509 and 1529. Architecture was hit harder than painting or sculpture. Not only were the costs much higher, but also, since major buildings took a number of years to complete, an atmosphere of security and public confidence was an essential precondition. Financial pressures alone did not always inhibit the launching of great architectural schemes. In Rome in the same period Pope Julius II began two of the most ambitious projects of all time – Saint Peter's and the Cortile del Belvedere – although the papal budget was severely strained by his warfaring activities. But in Venice, hammered by defeats rather than exalted by victories, there was no scope for such optimism.

The survival of the Republic could only be ensured if public morale were maintained at a high level. Since the buildings of Piazza San Marco and the

Rialto – the political and economic centres of the city – were among the principal expressions of the viability of the state, these had to be kept in good order even during periods of crisis. Thus when, in June 1512, several of the houses on the north side of Piazza San Marco were badly damaged by fire, the Procurators of Saint Mark, who owned the property, made the bold decision to demolish and rebuild the whole north wing

'in order to make it very beautiful for the glory of the land . . . in spite of the war.'[52]

According to Sanudo a model was submitted in 1514 by a Tuscan architect called 'il Celestro'. The building was erected by Guglielmo dei Grigi, a stonemason from near Bergamo (*Fig. 65*). In a contract dated 1517 he was ordered to follow the instructions of his compatriot Bartolomeo Bon, who had been *proto* to the Procurators of Saint Mark since 1505.[53] In his 1581 guidebook to Venice Francesco Sansovino named Bon as the architect of the new wing.[54] However, the *proto* may have followed Celestro's design, at least in part. Bon was a relative of the two older masons Giovanni and Bartolomeo Bon who were widely employed in Venice in the mid-fifteenth century.

The new building was completed by 1526, except for the extra bays on the west side of the Piazza which were added by Jacopo Sansovino in the 1530s (and demolished in the Napoleonic era). It consists of an arcade containing shops, surmounted by two storeys of apartments, all of which were let out to tenants by the Procuracy. According to an inventory compiled in 1569 the apartments were fairly expensive because of the enviable site. The annual rents ranged from 40 to 70 ducats. The shops and mezzanines were much cheaper, costing only 10–20 ducats, and were let to a variety of more modest tenants. Their occupations in 1569 included those of smith, glazier, cobbler, engraver, tailor, spice merchant, painter, cutler and old-clothes seller.[55] A series of 12 small courtyards admitted light into the centres of the houses, while the streets from the north entered the Piazza through three *sottoporteghi*. The building is now known as the Procuratie Vecchie, so called to distinguish it from the Procuratie Nuove, the south wing of the Piazza. This section, where the Procurators themselves lived, was begun by Scamozzi at the end of the sixteenth century, and finished by Longhena in the seventeenth century, following Sansovino's design.

The north wing of the Piazza was the first major public building in Venice to be erected in a purely classical style. Once again a local Veneto-Byzantine model rather than a true monument of antiquity provided the main inspiration. The new wing adhered closely to the form of the previous building on the site, built by Doge Sebastiano Ziani (1172–78), which we know from Gentile Bellini's 'Corpus Domini Procession' and Barbari's engraved view of 1500 (*Figs 10 & 63*). The only important change to the earlier scheme was the addition of an extra storey, in order to increase the rent income of the Procuracy. The design preserves the rhythm of Ziani's building, with two window bays over each archway of the portico; but the architectural language is updated. Here the rooftop crenellations no longer appear defensive, and the tall stilted

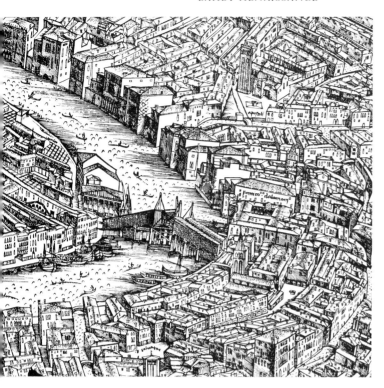

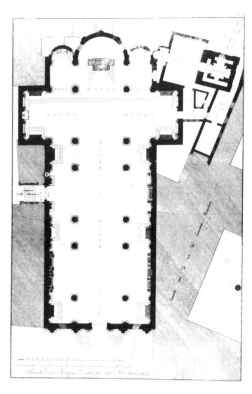

ABOVE
66 Rialto market, before the fire of 1514. Detail from Jacopo de' Barbari's bird's-eye-view map of Venice, 1500

ABOVE, RIGHT
San Salvatore, by Giorgio Spavento, begun 1507, plan

arches of the earlier wing are replaced by more classical semi-circular arches. Simple Doric piers are used to support the ground floor arches, with fluted Corinthian columns on the two upper storeys (*Fig. 118*). The whole composition is restrained and well proportioned, with continuous horizontal string courses to counteract the repeated vertical accents. The intervention of the Tuscan architect Celestro may account for the competent handling of Renaissance forms; but according to the pattern which we see repeated over and over again in the history of Venetian architecture, the overall scheme clings to the local model which had already served the same functions efficiently for more than 300 years.

Less than two years after the fire in Piazza San Marco, the commercial centre of Venice was devastated by a great fire which overran almost the whole of the island of Rialto during a winter's night in 1514 (*Fig. 66*). This fire broke out in bitterly cold weather, with icy winds fanning the flames. Fire fighting was almost impossible because the wells and canals were frozen over, and the blaze burned for 24 hours. The obliteration of the market area in the midst of the wars against the League of Cambrai was so damaging that some people suspected traitors of having started the fire.

The Rialto market had to be rebuilt as quickly as possible, in order not to cut off the city's income from trade. The State fully recognized the need to provide premises for mercantile activity. (Just nine years earlier they had quickly rebuilt the German merchants' centre, the Fondaco dei Tedeschi, when this building, too, was destroyed by fire.) In 1515 four projects for rebuilding the Rialto market were submitted by different architects,

including a highly idealized plan by the humanist architect from Verona, Fra
Giocondo, for a symmetrical rectangular complex surrounded by canals. This
scheme is known from the long description in Vasari's *Lives of the Artists*.
However, the committee of patricians who judged the designs chose the far
more conservative solution by the local architect Antonio Scarpagnino,
which preserved most elements of the previous layout of the market.[56]

The story is remarkably similar to that of the Great Fire of London in 1666.
In each case ambitious replanning schemes were submitted, by Fra Giocondo
in Venice and by Christopher Wren in London; but in each case the legal
problems associated with redesigning the devastated areas proved prohibitive,
for every property owner eagerly reclaimed his own plot of land. Both the
Rialto and the City of London were rebuilt with their former street plans
more or less unchanged, though measures were taken in both cities to make
the buildings less vulnerable to fire.

Scarpagnino's market buildings are strictly functional, with virtually no
ornament apart from continuous horizontal string courses and dentilled
cornices. The arcades, supported on solid piers, were rebuilt with vaults rather
than with wooden beamed ceilings to reduce the risk of fire. As in the case of
the Procuratie Vecchie the need for economy, combined with a certain public
diffidence induced by the Cambrai Wars, led to the choice of a very traditional
model for the new Rialto market.

The religious orders were perhaps less directly affected by the war
emergency than the patrons of public or private buildings. It seems that the
sense of fear which pervaded the everyday world did not prevent the people
of Venice from making charitable donations, hoping to ensure their safety in
the after-life at least. However, even in the monastic institutions, it is certain
that a shortage of funds caused considerable delays in building work. Among
the wealthiest of the Mendicant orders were the Augustinian Regular Canons.
Shortly before the onset of the Cambrai Wars they began to rebuild two of
their Venetian churches, one on the island of Santo Spirito in Isola and one at
the Rialto end of the Merceria. Of the former we know very little. Only two
of its altars were consecrated before the League of Cambrai. The rest of the
church was erected later by Jacopo Sansovino, but was completely obliterated
in the Napoleonic era.[57] The latter was the fine church of San Salvatore,
begun in 1507 by the local architect Giorgio Spavento, and completed in 1534.
After Spavento's death in 1509 the work was supervised first by Tullio
Lombardo and, after 1532 when Tullio himself died, by Sansovino.[58]

San Salvatore is one of the most imaginative and successful designs in the
history of Venetian ecclesiastical architecture (*p. 130*). Spavento took as his starting point the traditional Byzantine centralized plan, with a large central dome
and four smaller domes at each corner. Amid the renewed enthusiasm for Greek
scholarship, this type of plan had been revived in Venice at the end of the
fifteenth century by Codussi and his contemporaries. By joining three of
these domed spaces together, Spavento created the long spacious type of nave
which suited the needs of the religious orders so much better than a small,
centralized structure. In the choice of the three apses at the east end he adhered

to Veneto-Byzantine tradition, yet by lengthening the side arms of the easternmost Greek cross to form transepts, he gave the church a cruciform plan at the same time.

With its succession of three soaring domes, brilliantly lit by lanterns above, and its great piers defined by pilasters on high bases, the interior of the church is grand and imposing, even if some of the details of the articulation have not been clearly organized. Originally the church must have been much darker, for the lanterns in the domes were not added until 1574. In the later sixteenth and early seventeenth centuries, under the influence of the Counter Reformation's desire for greater lucidity in religious buildings, paintings, music and liturgy, additional windows were inserted into many Venetian churches to improve the illumination.[59] However, this fact should not detract from Spavento's own achievement. With its white Istrian-stone detailing and whitewashed walls, the church of San Salvatore was surely never sombre.

The Scuole Grandi, like private individuals, were taxed in wartime. They also had the additional burden of supplying and paying *galleotti* (oarsmen) for naval campaigns.[60] In the Cambrai Wars, which were fought chiefly on land, relatively small sums were levied from the Scuole, but their revenues were hit, too, by the non-payment of interest on government bonds, and by the shortage of ready cash in private hands.

The one Scuola Grande which actually managed to increase its wealth during this period was the recently founded Scuola di San Rocco. After the defeat at Agnadello in 1509 San Rocco was required to pay a levy of only 100 ducats, just half as much as the other Scuole, 'because it is poor'. Yet during the wartime years between 1509 and 1516 as many as 60 new endowment trusts were set up in its favour, including five major bequests.[61]

The Scuola di San Rocco had been instituted in 1478, during an epidemic of plague, under the patronage of the saint who was supposed to give protection from outbreaks of pestilence. In 1485 the saint's body was brought to Venice from Germany, and from this time onwards the cult of San Rocco in Venice grew rapidly. By 1489 the Scuola was large enough to be admitted to the ranks of the Scuole Grandi by the Council of Ten. In the same year a church dedicated to San Rocco was begun on a site leased from the Franciscan friars behind the rear apses of the Frari. The architect of the church, now much altered, was the *proto* to the Procurators of Saint Mark, Bartolomeo Bon.

In 1516 the same architect was appointed *proto* to the Scuola di San Rocco, which had by now raised sufficient funds to begin a grand new building next to the church (*Fig.* 67). The foundation stone had already been laid in the previous year. After a disagreement in 1524 Bon resigned his position, but in 1527 the established local architect, Antonio Scarpagnino, was appointed to replace him.

In 1527 the Scuola di San Rocco was still one of the two poorest of the Scuole Grandi, and regretted having spent so large a proportion of its revenues on building rather than investing for the future. However, this was the year of another severe outbreak of plague. As a result, the number of private donations to the Scuola funds, from people hoping to protect themselves from

the disease, rose to its highest level ever, and gave the impetus to continue the
building.[62] The main structure seems to have been complete by the time of
Scarpagnino's death in 1549. By this time the Scuola had sufficient resources to
employ Tintoretto to paint the remarkable cycle of pictures which decorate the
interior (*Fig. 68*). In his guide of 1581 Francesco Sansovino marvelled at the
wealth of the Scuola di San Rocco, now only a century old yet already the
richest of all the Venetian confraternities.[63]

The Scuola di San Rocco is certainly the most flamboyant building erected
in Venice in the aftermath of the Cambrai Wars. No expense was spared on its
elaborate Istrian-stone façade with its profusion of richly carved detail and its
inlaid panels of precious marble. Nonetheless, the overall design reflects
something of the way in which the inspiration of Venetian architects had been
stifled during the wartime years. For all its complexity the façade has an
undeniably provincial air.

The asymmetrical arrangement reflects the disposition of rooms inside (*p.
135*), with the huge upper and lower halls occupying the three bays on the left

and the smaller *albergo*, or meeting room, the two bays on the right. It is not difficult to distinguish the earlier portions built under Bon's direction from those erected afterwards by Scarpagnino. Bon must have been responsible for the three lower windows which adopt the form introduced to Venice by Codussi. The portal at the right hand end of the façade, crowned by a heavy lunette, is similarly conservative in style – doorways of this type had already been popular in Venice for half a century. Bon must also have been responsible for the layout of the interior with its traditional, colonnaded lower hall.

When he took over in 1527 Scarpagnino tried to bring the façade in line with more modern trends in architecture, but his understanding of classical principles of design was less than his knowledge of individual motifs. The design of the *all'antica* free-standing columns on high bases with their heavy projecting cornices, which define the three bays on the left of the façade, is taken from ancient Roman triumphal arches and gateways. Yet the rings of garlands around the columns serve to undermine, rather than to underline, their rôle as bold framing elements. The use of a single broad pediment to crown each pair of windows on the upper storey also has a respectable antique precedent in Verona. Yet there is little harmony between the upper and lower storeys. Moreover, Scarpagnino failed to disguise effectively the fact that the bay over the great pedimented left hand portal is wider than the other four bays.

One could not deny that with its picturesque detail and high relief the façade is eye-catching and interesting from any approach to the Scuola. However, the presence of an element of fussiness and incoherence, even in a project of such high prestige, shows that Venice was more than ready for the importation of new talent. If the architects of the Scuola di San Rocco showed some knowledge of the antiquities on Venetian territory, they still had only limited understanding of the Renaissance concepts of clarity and harmony.

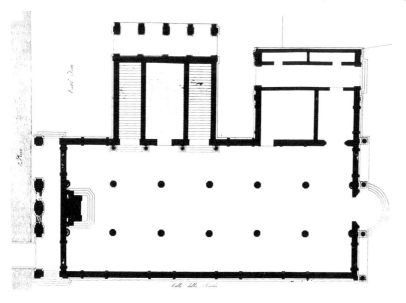

Scuola Grande di San Rocco, by Bartolomeo Bon and Antonio Scarpagnino, begun 1515. Ground floor plan

CHAPTER VI

'Roman' Renaissance

The effect of the Cambrai Wars on Venetian architects of the period was not only to cause lack of employment and financial hardship, but also to stifle artistic imagination. In the state of economic uncertainty which prevailed for almost two decades after the Venetian defeat at Agnadello in 1508, only the most essential schemes could be implemented, using the most conservative models. But less expensive creative outlets could still be found. Some stonemasons and builders survived on repair jobs and smaller scale sculptural commissions (although Scarpagnino, one of the lucky ones, was forced to sell his stonemason's workshop in 1517 because he was so busy with the rebuilding of the Rialto market after the fire).[1] One of the few significant architectural achievements of the war years came not from a stonemason but from a Veronese Dominican friar, Fra Giocondo, whose audacious design for the new Rialto market (mentioned in the previous chapter) was rejected in favour of Scarpagnino's cheaper alternative. Fra Giocondo, a learned humanist, proficient engineer and respected architect, turned his creative impulses to preparing a beautiful illustrated edition of the Latin text of Vitruvius' *De architectura* which was published in Venice in 1511. This was the first printed edition of Vitruvius, which had been known in manuscript since 1415. It preceded Cesariano's Italian translation, published in Como, by a decade. Fra Giocondo was well qualified for the task. He was not only a classical scholar, but had also spent some years studying the antiquities of Rome as a young man. The pre-occupation with the theories of Alberti among Codussi's circle of patrons had prepared the ground for the reception of Vitruvius's ideas in Venice, and Fra Giocondo's edition helped to sustain an interest in architectural theory during the caesura in building activity caused by the Cambrai Wars. More important, it allowed Venetians to give thought to ways of reviving 'authentic' ancient Roman forms of building, as codified by Vitruvius, in their own city.

The Venetian Republic had long aspired to be the true successor to ancient Rome, as David Chambers has shown in a recent lively account.[2] The government, with its constitution moulded on the lines of the Roman Republic, was considered to be a direct continuation of the civilisation of antiquity, since the city had supposedly been founded by refugees at the time of the Barbarian overthrow of the Empire. Moreover, the apostolic Basilica of Saint Mark was thought to be a worthy equivalent to the church of Saint Peter's in Rome. As we have seen, in the later fifteenth century Venice was still turning to Byzantium (which had inherited the role of Imperial capital after the fall of the Roman Empire) for artistic and cultural inspiration. But the search for a visual manifestation of the Serenissima's claim to be the 'New Rome' was to lead eventually to a desire to emulate Rome itself.

The Sack of Rome by Charles V's Imperial troops in 1527 catalyzed this transformation in more ways than one. First, the devastation and political humiliation in Rome itself after 1527 provided a psychological incentive to create a 'New Rome' elsewhere. Second, the fact that the Papal States had long been political rivals of Venice meant that Rome's demise indirectly boosted Venetian self confidence. Third, the Sack coincided with the revival of Venetian fortunes after the Cambrai Wars, to be ratified at the Peace of Bologna in 1529. And finally, the Sack of Rome, scattering the Papal city's artists and architects throughout Italy, brought two important figures to Venice, Sebastiano Serlio and Jacopo Sansovino. Together with Michele Sanmicheli, the Veronese architect who returned to the Veneto from Central Italy at about this time, Serlio and Sansovino were to provide Venice with the new Roman idiom which would symbolize the recovery from the traumatic war years and the epidemics and famines of the late 1520s.

Sebastiano Serlio (1475–1554)

The cheapest, quickest means of communicating knowledge was, of course, printing; and Serlio immediately began to publish engravings of the classical orders, for which he was granted copyright by the Senate in 1528. Meanwhile he started work on his own architectural treatise. By this time Venice not only had a tradition of producing beautifully illustrated printed books, but also boasted an intelligentsia who read architectural treatises avidly. Serlio's first book, Book IV on the orders of architecture, was published in Venice in 1537. The next volume, Book III on the buildings of the ancients, appeared three years later. Serlio then moved to France, where the following volumes of his work were issued, but he had already provided Venice with the essential rudiments of ancient Roman architecture.

Serlio's copiously illustrated treatise offered the city a completely new range of visual ideas as well as his own version of the classical 'grammar' of architecture. In the volume on the orders, in addition to providing details of his recommended proportions for columns, bases, capitals and architraves, he illustrated examples of imaginary doorways, façades, arcades and fireplaces using the various different orders. The book is not, however, a text book in what we now see as classical orthodoxy, for the designs are distinctly Mannerist in style. Bizarre touches such as chimneypieces supported by caryatids with huge clawed feet, boldly rusticated columns, and flaming urns are interspersed with the more conventional classical vocabulary. As he acknowledged in the introduction, Serlio was heavily indebted to the ideas of his master Peruzzi, himself a notable Mannerist architect. Nevertheless, some of the schemes, such as the Venetian palace façades with their tripartite arrangement and flamboyant chimneys, were obviously inspired by Serlio's own personal experiences in the city (*Fig. 69*). These Venetian projects in turn were to be extremely influential in Venice – the 'Serliana' windows lighting the central halls became a favourite motif in sixteenth-century Venetian palace design.

Serlio's volume on the buildings of antiquity gives plans, sections and elevations, as well as architectural details, of the principal monuments of both ancient and modern Rome. The main arches, tombs and temples of antiquity are shown alongside various projects for Saint Peter's, Bramante's Tempietto and Cortile del Belvedere, Raphael's Villa Madama, and Giuliano da Sangallo's palace for the King of Naples. Serlio concludes with an intriguing passage on Egyptian architecture, in which he writes:

> 'In truth the works of the ancient Romans are marvellous to behold; but if we could see those of the Greeks, which have all disappeared by now, though Rome and Venice are richly adorned with their spoils, we should probably consider them superior to the buildings of the Romans.'[3]

Serlio must have gleaned his skimpy knowledge of Egyptian architecture from conversations with Venetian merchants. However, his comment reminds us that despite their trading activities in the Eastern Mediterranean and their deep-rooted respect for Greek culture, Venetians were still totally ignorant of the ruins of ancient Greece.

Sansovino and Sanmicheli

Serlio himself built almost nothing in Venice, but his contemporaries Jacopo Sansovino (1486–1570) and Michele Sanmicheli (c.1484–1559) were both soon so fully employed that they spent the rest of their working lives in the Veneto. Like Serlio, both had studied the antiquities of Rome at first hand and were well acquainted with recent developments in architecture in central Italy. During the first two decades of the sixteenth century the centre of gravity of the artistic life of Italy had shifted from Florence to Rome. The munificent and imaginative patronage of Pope Julius II (1503–13) and Pope Leo X (1513–21) had drawn the most gifted painters, sculptors and architects of Italy to the Papal court. Meanwhile archaeological excavations in the Holy City proceeded apace. In this stimulating atmosphere both Sansovino and Sanmicheli reached their artistic maturity.

Sansovino, whose real name was Jacopo Tatti, was born in Florence. In his youth he was apprenticed to the sculptor Andrea Sansovino and took his name. In about 1506 he went to Rome for the first time and was introduced into Papal circles by his compatriot Giuliano da Sangallo. There he came into contact with such great artists as Bramante, Raphael and Michelangelo. Although he began two churches in Rome and built a palace for the wealthy banker Giovanni Gaddi, he was still primarily a sculptor when he fled to Venice after the Sack in 1527. In that year the painter Lorenzo Lotto described him respectfully in a letter as 'second only to Michelangelo'.[4]

Sanmicheli's artistic origins were rather different. He was born in Verona into a family of professional architects. Both his uncle and his father were architects, and although one of his brothers became a scholar and the other a priest, his cousin Polo and his nephew Giangirolamo also entered the building profession.[5] Like the Sangallo family in Florence, but unlike such great architects as Bramante, Raphael or Michelangelo – or indeed Sansovino – Sanmicheli did not turn to architecture from painting or sculpture, but had a highly professional technical training.

Because their backgrounds were so different, Sansovino and Sanmicheli channelled their energies in different directions in the Veneto. Though they had been subjected to similar artistic influences in central Italy, their approaches to architectural problems remained quite distinct throughout their careers. They certainly knew each other and were to some extent influenced by each other's work. They even shared patrons – for instance, the Venetian patrician Zuanne Dolfin, who was Podestà or chief administrator in Verona in 1532–33, commissioned a new portal for the Palazzo del Podestà from Sanmicheli, and after his return to Venice employed Sansovino to rebuild his family palace.

However, a clear line of demarcation divided their areas of specialization. Following the death of Bartolomeo Bon in 1529, Jacopo Sansovino was employed as *proto*, or chief superintendent of buildings, to the Procuratia de Supra, the body which owned most of Piazza San Marco and was responsible for the upkeep of the Basilica. In the same year Sanmicheli entered the employment of the Venetian Republic to fortify Legnago, the mainland town on the River Adige south-east of Verona. Like his fellow Veronese, Fra Giocondo, who had worked for the Venetian government on the fortification

69 Venetian palace façade, woodcut from Sebastiano Serlio's treatise on architecture, book IV, first published in Venice in 1537

of Treviso and Padua during the Cambrai Wars and on the defence of the lagoon, Sanmicheli had a high reputation as a military architect. He had already been employed by Pope Clement VII on improving the defences of Parma and Piacenza. Vasari recounts that because of his special interest in fortifications, Sanmicheli went to Treviso and then to Padua soon after his return to the Veneto to inspect the new fortresses. But the Republic were suspicious of his behaviour and arrested him. Only when assured of his good faith did they begin to make use of his knowhow themselves. Sansovino, by contrast, seems to have been rarely consulted on military matters. He lacked the technical expertise of Sanmicheli, and tackled engineering problems by a combination of instinct and trial and error. Sometimes he was brilliantly successful, as on his arrival in Venice when he fortified the great domes of the Basilica of San Marco by encircling them with iron rings. On other occasions the results were disastrous. For example, when the first bay of his new Library collapsed in 1545, he was even imprisoned overnight and had to repair the damage at his own expense. Later the church of San Giuliano collapsed while he was having the façade rebuilt.

Sanmicheli was put in charge of the military defences of the whole Venetian Republic in 1535. In this capacity he was employed by the Waterways authority until 1542, when a special magistracy was set up to take charge of the fortifications. The true 'State' architect of Venice was the *proto* to the Salt Office, which financed government building projects, such as the work in the Palazzo Ducale, using revenues from the salt tax. At this time the post was held by the local architect Antonio Scarpagnino, who died in 1549. As we have seen, the State always tended towards conservatism in its patronage. They even turned down Palladio when he applied for the same job in 1554.

As Serlio pointed out in the dedication of Book IV of his treatise, published in 1537, the revival in Venetian architecture during the reign of Doge Andrea Gritti (1523–38) had been carried out chiefly by Sansovino, Sanmicheli and Scarpagnino together. Sansovino and Sanmicheli were not the first architects working in Venice who knew Roman architecture at first hand. Fra Giocondo had studied the antiquities of Rome, and his fellow Veronese, the architect and painter Giovanmaria Falconetto, had made several trips to Rome, as his buildings in Padua show clearly; but the opportunities of both these older architects were badly restricted by the effects of the war years. Doge Gritti's reign provided the perfect atmosphere for architectural innovation. An enthusiastic patron of music and literature as well as the visual arts, Gritti was also a decisive leader who set Venice firmly on the road to recovery. His team of architects, united by a felicitous alliteration as well as by their common aim to restore the grandeur of ancient Rome on Venetian soil, were warmly supported not only by the Doge himself but also by an inner clique of enlightened and influential patricians. In particular, two members of the Procuratia de Supra, Antonio Cappello and Vettor Grimani, could be relied on by both architects to give loyal support.

As military architect to the Venetian Republic, Michele Sanmicheli had many tasks. He was responsible for the defences of the Terraferma, Venetian possessions in the Eastern Mediterranean such as Corfu, Crete and Cyprus, and, of course, the city of Venice itself. He also worked for Duke Francesco Sforza of Milan for some months in 1531, inspecting fortifications in various parts of Lombardy.

This was a period of rapid development in the art of fortification. The typical mediaeval defences – crenellated walls with towers over the gateways – deterred invaders by dropping missiles on them from above. This type of fortification, still visible in Venice in parts of the Arsenal, was made redundant by the introduction of gunpowder artillery, which could attack from much further away. As Vasari points out, Sanmicheli was one of the pioneers in the introduction of the angle bastion, a corner projection from which modern weapons could be used to attack invaders at a considerable distance, while protecting the walls on either side by covering fire.[6]

One of Sanmicheli's most impressive achievements in this field was the construction of a new fortress on the island of Sant' Andrea at the entrance to the Venetian lagoon, opposite the castle of San Nicolò di Lido (*Fig. 70*). This fortress superseded an earlier castle on the site, built in the reign of Doge Michele Steno (1400–13). In 1535 the Council of Ten approved Sanmicheli's recommendation, warmly supported by Antonio Cappello who was Savio alle Acque at this time, to rebuild both castles. Sanmicheli duly provided models for the fortress of Sant'Andrea, but the Council of Ten vacillated, and it was not until 1543 that the go-ahead was finally given. Meanwhile Sanmicheli was dispatched to the Levant to attend to the defences there.

70 Fortezza di Sant'Andrea, by Michele Sanmicheli, begun 1543 (*Sarah Quill*)

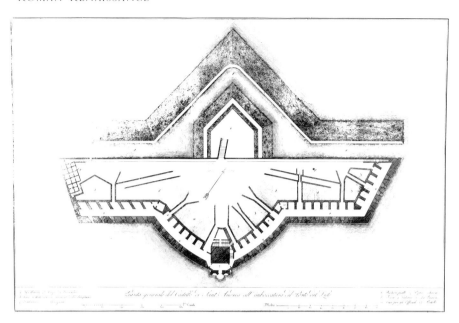

Fortezza di Sant'Andrea, by Sanmicheli, begun 1543, plan

OPPOSITE
71 The Venetian Zecca, or mint, by Jacopo Sansovino, begun 1536 (*A.F.Kersting*)

Although the Council of Ten were characteristically indecisive, the architect received loyal encouragement from the newly instituted magistracy in charge of fortifications, one of the two Provedditori (magistrates) being Vettor Grimani. Considering the scale of the undertaking, the work proceeded with amazing speed. Sanmicheli himself must have visited the site regularly, for in 1545 he was awarded a special allowance to pay for his boat rides. The new Fortezza was largely completed by 1549 when the Council of Ten formally suspended work as an economy measure.[7]

As Vasari explained at length, the technical difficulties were formidable, but Sanmicheli overcame them with dazzling virtuosity. Only in recent decades has constant erosion by the sea begun to cause serious damage to the structure. A typical Vasarian anecdote describes how some critics predicted that the structure would collapse under the weight of its own artillery. To prove its safety a huge quantity of heavy artillery was brought from the Arsenal and fired simultaneously in the fortress.

> 'The building, however, remained firm, establishing the reputation of Michele and confounding the objectors, who had caused such general alarm that pregnant women had left the city.'[8]

The plan of the Fortezza di Sant'Andrea (*above*) shows how carefully the design was controlled by functional considerations. On the seaward side a low wall of rusticated Istrian-stone blocks forms a five-sided projection, the central side curved outwards. Casemates are distributed at intervals around the periphery, like caves at the water's edge, reached by tunnels from the heart of the fortress. Sanmicheli incorporated the old castle into the new fortress to serve as a lookout tower, the rest of the structure being as low as possible to reduce its visibility. An embankment at the back protects the fortress along the edge of a channel used for bringing in supplies and ammunition. At the centre of the

curved projection is a massive rusticated Doric gateway, with imperious keystone heads over each of the three arches, standing guard like the lions' heads over the casemates. The white Istrian-stone blocks are left in their rough hewn state, so that, in Vasari's words, the fortress 'seems cut from a single stone out of the solid rock'.[9] The illusion is highly deceptive, for, of course, the Fortezza was not built on solid rock, but on lagoon sand and mud.

In the Renaissance, military architecture was not purely functional. It was also a vehicle for the imaginative use of conventional classical elements to express the might and status of the territory within. Sanmicheli succeeded in this in the Fortezza di Sant'Andrea, at least for Vasari, who wrote that it 'equals in majesty, the most famous structures of the Romans'.[10] The design of the triple-arched entrance combines the toughness of the Doric order with the roughness of raw stone. The metopes of the Doric frieze contain symbols of Venetian naval superiority, such as galleons, and winged lions. At the corners, hefty square piers reinforce the half columns, protecting the dark, cavernous entrance, lapped by the waves like the haunt of a mythical giant.

Sansovino received his first major commission in Venice for the rebuilding of the Zecca or mint in 1536, the year after Sanmicheli made his designs for the Fortezza di Sant'Andrea (*Fig. 71*). These two buildings were curiously similar in function, and thus brought the styles of the two architects unusually close together. Both buildings had to be secure, fire proof and efficiently organized. Both symbolized aspects of the Venetian recovery – military in the case of the Fortezza, and economic in the case of the Zecca. Both were administered by the State which meant that, although funds were ample, there was an element of instability caused by regular rotations of officers in the magistracies concerned and changing attitudes in the Council of Ten.

The new Venetian Zecca was financed in the most original manner, by the freeing of slaves in Cyprus at 50 ducats a head. The building was begun after the risk of fire and the huge demand for new coins caused by the economic boom made the old mint almost unserviceable. The original design was for a two-storey building, in which gold was to be minted on the *piano nobile* for greater security, and silver on the ground floor. In 1539 an agreement was reached with the Procuratia de Supra, who owned a row of cheese and salami shops on the lagoon side of the mint, to incorporate these shops into the new structure, in order to allow more space for the gold foundries above. A courtyard at the back was surrounded by small workshops for minting, casting dies, and storing coal, while the foundries were located in the front section of the building. A long hall separating these two parts joined the land and water entrances at each side, for the presence of the cheese shops made a front entrance impossible. A third storey was begun in 1558 to provide extra space and to protect the furnaces from the effects of direct sunlight on the roof, which made the heat inside intolerable. The building appears in its original state in two mid-sixteenth century engravings[11] (*Figs 72 & 74*).

It is not clear whether Sansovino was consulted on the design of the weaker third storey, but certainly the two lower storeys form one of the architect's most powerful and confident works. The problem he faced was how to convey

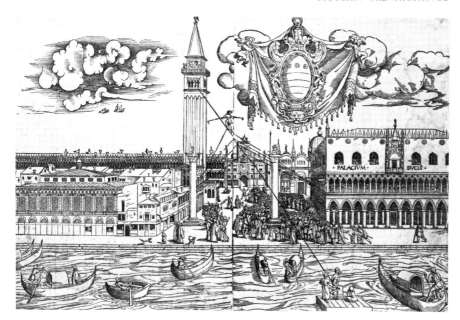

a sense of impregnability while providing large windows on the *piano nobile* to ventilate the furnaces, and a row of open arches on the ground floor to house the Procuracy's cheese shops. He resolved the dilemma by his brilliantly expressive use of rustication. The row of shops is built in the plainest type of rustication, appropriate to the prosaic function. On the *piano nobile* the Doric order, associated with male strength, is boldly rusticated as in the Fortezza di Sant'Andrea, to add an element of robustness. Menacing heavy lintels over the windows are clutched precariously between the ringed half columns.

The rustication of the orders – an intriguing mixture of the sophisticated and the crude, rather like Shakespeare's *Midsummer Night's Dream* – was a favourite Mannerist device. Giulio Romano, in particular, enjoyed using the combination in his buildings in Rome and in Mantua. It also had a respectable classical ancestry in monuments of the Claudian era such as the Porta Maggiore in Rome. Variants of the idea had even appeared long before in Venice, in the Ca' del Duca and Codussi's façade of San Michele in Isola. But for Sansovino, as for Sanmicheli, the rusticated order had a far tougher message to convey. As Serlio wrote in his Book IV, the mixture of rustication and the classical orders

> 'is very pleasing to the eye, and represents great strength. For this reason I consider it more appropriate to a fortress than anything else'.[12]

Contemporary accounts indicate that the Zecca was much admired. Vasari called it the 'finest, richest and strongest of Sansovino's buildings'.[13] But it was also frequently likened to a fortress – for instance, Francesco Sansovino in 1561 called it 'a worthy prison for the precious gold'.[14] Thus it is not surprising to find that Rusconi's design for the city's Prisons, begun in 1566 on the far side of the Palazzo Ducale, was strongly influenced by Sansovino's Mint.

72 'Il Volo del Turco' (a tightrope act which formed part of the Giovedì Grasso festivities), showing the unfinished Library and the two-storey Zecca. Anonymous woodcut, with arms of Doge Francesco Donà (1545–53). *Museo Correr, Venice*

Sansovino's most famous Venetian building was the Library of Saint Mark's. According to Palladio it was 'the richest, most ornate building since Antiquity' which showed the Venetians how to build in the 'beautiful style'.[15] This long structure on the west side of the Piazzetta, facing the Palazzo Ducale, 'collides' with the Zecca on the other side with such apparent rudeness that one cannot help being struck by the difference in style and function between the two buildings[16] (*Fig. 73*). The Library was begun in 1537 to house the famous collection of manuscripts bequeathed to the Venetian Republic by Cardinal Bessarion of Trebizond in 1468.

The Procurators of Saint Mark's, who commissioned the new building,

ABOVE, RIGHT
73 The Zecca and the Library of Saint Mark's, both by Jacopo Sansovino *(Sarah Quill)*

RIGHT
74 Jost Amman: 'The Procession for the Doge's Marriage with the Sea', detail showing the unfinished Library and two storey Zecca. Woodcut, mid-sixteenth century. *Museo Correr, Venice*

146

already owned the existing structures on the site – a row of hostelries and taverns dating from the late twelfth century, with a meat market at the lagoon end and a row of lean-to bakers' stalls in front. These untidy buildings, visible in a late-fifteenth century painting attributed to Lazzaro Bastiani in the Museo Correr in Venice, added nothing to the dignity of the Piazzetta, and in any case were nearing the end of their useful life.

As we learn from Vasari's biography and from contemporary records, the first task which Sansovino tackled when he was appointed *proto* to the Procurators in 1529 was to remove the food stalls and latrines at the feet of the two great columns in the Piazzetta. Thus, from the very beginning, he was dedicated to improving the centre of the city of Venice and removing undignified eyesores. In the event it proved a long and difficult task to find alternative nearby sites for the hostelries, which had to be demolished to make room for the new Library. Because of the delays, only 16 bays were completed before Sansovino's death in 1570. The remainder was completed

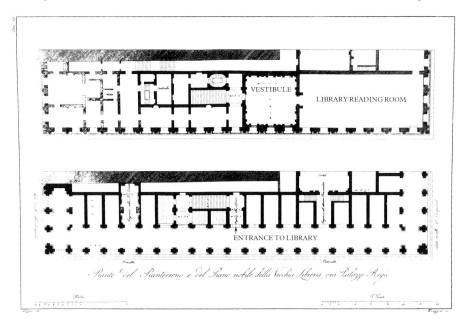

VESTIBULE

LIBRARY READING ROOM

ENTRANCE TO LIBRARY

Piante del Pianterreno e del Piano nobile della Vecchia Libreria, ora Palazzo Regio

afterwards by Vincenzo Scamozzi. The Library appears in its incomplete form in the same two sixteenth century engravings which showed the two storey Mint. That by Jost Amman gives a vivid impression of the sort of use to which the inns were put! (*Fig. 74*)

The Library reading room occupies the seven bays of the *piano nobile* nearest the Campanile, those which were completed first (*above*). The entrance in the central arch of the 21-bay arcade leads by an impressive staircase, its barrel vaulted ceiling richly decorated with guilded stucco and paintings, to a square vestibule which was used as a school for teaching classics to young nobles. The vestibule opens into the magnificent reading-room, brightly lit by the row of large, east-facing windows. It is surely not coincidence that Vitruvius recommends that libraries, like bedrooms, should face the east. The coffered

Library of Saint Mark, by Sansovino, begun 1537. Ground floor and *piano nobile* ceiling contains seven rows of circular paintings by the best artists of the day. The Procurators held a competition to choose the best painting, to be judged by Sansovino's great friend Titian. The prize of a gold chain was awarded to Paulo Veronese for his roundel depicting *Music*. The room originally had rows of reading desks, arranged like church pews on either side of a central aisle, rather like the desks which are still preserved in Michelangelo's Laurentian Library in Florence. The *piano nobile* apartments at the other end of the Library building contained office accommodation for the Procurators. On the ground floor the arcade opened on to a row of shops.

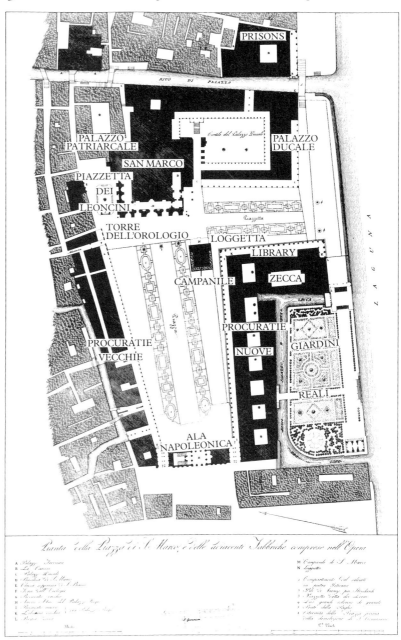

Piazza San Marco in the nineteenth century, plan showing layout after Sansovino's remodelling, sixteenth century

OPPOSITE
75 Piazza San Marco, view towards the Basilica, replanned by Sansovino. (Compare it with the Bellini painting, *Fig. 10*.) (*A.F.Kersting*)

76 Library of Saint Mark's, by Sansovino, begun 1537 (*A.F.Kersting*)

The elevation of the exterior was designed to be continued around the whole of the south side of Piazza San Marco as far as the church of San Geminiano. Thus its design was less strictly related to its function than that of the Zecca, or indeed Sanmicheli's Fortezza. From the outside the spectator is unaware of precisely where in the long façade the library itself is located. The design was conceived as much to mould the open spaces around as to contain the rooms within. Sansovino showed his awareness of the importance of the Piazza and the Piazzetta by the orientation of the new buildings, making the existing Campanile a free-standing monument on the corner between the two adjoining open spaces (*Fig. 75*). As Gentile Bellini's painting of the 'Corpus Domini procession' shows, the Campanile was originally flanked by buildings rather than being free-standing (*Fig. 10*). According to Sansovino's design, the south side of the Piazza was realigned to make the space trapezium shaped. Thus the Basilica became the central feature of the eastern prospect, and the Palazzo Ducale became visible from anywhere in the Piazza (*p. 148*). (Bellini contrived this artificially in his painting by altering the relative positions of the buildings.)

What was it that made the Library façade so famous, both in Venice and elsewhere? (*Fig. 76*) The basic elements of the design – large *piano nobile* windows with balconies over an arcade below – were not revolutionary in Venice. In fact they reproduce the essential features of the previous building on the site. The use of richly carved Istrian stone was not unprecedented in Venice, where there was a tradition of high quality stonecarving. The newly built Scuola Grande di San Rocco, for example, was just as ornate (*Fig. 67*). Moreover, Codussi in Venice and Falconetto in Padua had already shown how to use the classical orders to organize a façade and add an air of classical dignity.

It seems that to Venetians the Library embodied exactly what they were seeking – a transposition of the ancient Roman style of building on to Venetian soil. Classical reminiscences abound – obelisks, keystone heads, spandrel figures, and the rich frieze with *putti* bearing garlands. The correct use of the Doric and Ionic orders with their appropriate friezes, cornices and bases, made the classical allusion yet more convincing to Venetian eyes. The column-arch arrangement derives from well known ancient Roman buildings such as the Colosseum and the Theatre of Marcellus.

In reality, however, Sansovino's Library can hardly be considered 'Roman' in either the Antique or the High Renaissance sense. The contrast with Michelangelo's Capitoline Palaces, designed for the ancient centre of Rome in about 1538, is revealing.[17] Both projects were for two-storey buildings with arcades below and apartments above, crowned by balustrades bearing statues. Both façades were conceived chiefly to articulate and define the open spaces in front. Both designs were conditioned by the Mannerist tendencies of their age, revealed in the window-tabernacles of the Capitoline Palaces and the daring clash with the Zecca at the south end of the Library. Yet the vibrating chiaroscuro of the Library is very different from the hard lines of the yellow travertine palaces on the Capitol. While Sansovino emphasizes the breadth of his façade by means of its two bold entablatures, Michelangelo uses a giant order of pilasters to counteract the width of his elevation. In the Library the half columns are made to appear to support the whole structure, and the wall surface is hardly visible, in contrast to the Capitoline Palaces. Though Michelangelo and Sansovino were both great sculptors, Michelangelo's severe linear design made little use of his sculptural abilities. Sansovino, on the

77 Loggetta at the foot of the Campanile, by Sansovino, begun 1538 (*A.F.Kersting*)

151

other hand, rightly realized that a building richly decorated with *all'antica* sculpture would make a deep impression on the sensibilities of the Venetian nobility, with their long tradition of collecting classical sculpture.

It was his capacity to design buildings in three dimensions which was probably Sansovino's most important contribution to Venetian architecture. The projecting cornices and half columns of the Library give the building a new massiveness and sense of grandeur. The rhythms are slower and more emphatic than, say, those of the Palazzo Ducale opposite. In contrast to the Procuratie Vecchie on the far side of the Piazza the whole façade is not conceived as a wall surface pierced by windows, with the classical orders, as it were, engraved on the plane of the wall. Instead it is a three-dimensional structure, with the deep shadows of the windows and arches enhanced by the play of light on the richly carved white Istrian stone. This sense of volume was not in itself new in Venice – consider, for example, the weighty three-dimensionality of the Basilica of San Marco. But as we have seen, the Basilica was viewed in Venice almost like a work of antiquity; and during the Gothic period the wall surface had re-emerged as an expressive architectural component in its own right.

Sansovino himself designed some buildings of a more sober, two-dimensional character. The Library may be his most famous work, but it is not exactly typical. Indeed, it is difficult to pinpoint Sansovino's contribution to the architecture of Venice, for he was a supremely adaptable architect. Always sensitive to the needs of his patrons, he varied each design according to the specific circumstances of the commission.

Thus, his new Loggetta at the foot of the Campanile was as sculptural and richly coloured as his Fabbriche Nuove, the new Rialto warehouses, were two dimensional and monochromatic. The Loggetta was begun in 1538 for the Procurators of Saint Mark's as a meeting place for nobles (*Fig.* 77), replacing the older loggia which is visible in Bastiani's painting. The Fabbriche Nuove were commissioned by the Council of Ten, and begun in 1554[18] (*Fig.* 78). The Loggetta was expected to provide an eye-catching piece of stage scenery for public processions, like the little coloured marble pavilions in the paintings of Carpaccio. The Fabbriche Nuove, on the other hand, were erected in order to add a more respectable air to an untidy corner of the Rialto market. No expense was spared on the Loggetta, which was built of the richest materials. By contrast, the Council of Ten hoped to recover the cost of the Fabbriche Nuove from the rent of the new shops and store rooms. The Loggetta was the vehicle for an elaborate sculptural programme glorifying the Venetian Republic, while the Fabbriche Nuove have no sculptural decoration whatever. The Loggetta with its red, white and dark green marble and its bronze statues, was perhaps the last important richly coloured exterior in Venice. The Fabbriche Nuove display the Renaissance preference for white Istrian stone, which was to suppress the Venetian love of colour in the city's architecture for at least two centuries. The Loggetta was begun at the end of the reign of Doge Gritti, while Venetian spirits and expectations were still high; but the Fabbriche Nuove were conceived at a time of greater caution

78 Fabbriche Nuove di Rialto, by Sansovino, begun 1554 *(Sarah Quill)*

and realism. Above all, these two schemes were determined by the Renaissance concept of *decorum* – in other words, that the style of a building should be appropriate to its function, just as the behaviour of a person should reflect his position in life. For the Loggetta Sansovino chose the most elaborate of the orders, the Composite, with its columns boldly free-standing, like those of a Roman triumphal arch. But the Fabbriche Nuove revealed their more prosaic function through their simple Doric and Ionic pilaster-orders over a rusticated waterfront arcade.

In addition to their public commissions Sansovino and Sanmicheli also worked for private and ecclesiastical patrons. In this their work was divided geographically. Although Sanmicheli may have designed a palace in Venice for Vettor Grimani as early as 1528, Sansovino held a virtual monopoly of the principal domestic and religious commissions in the city until his position of supremacy was challenged by Palladio in the 1560s.[19] The two fine palaces which Sanmicheli built in Venice were both late works, probably begun only a few years before his death in 1559. Meanwhile Sanmicheli dominated the scene in his home town, Verona, not only as an expert in the art of fortification and designer of imposing city gates, but also as a gifted all round architect. Thus four of the principal towns on Venetian territory received the stamp of a great sixteenth-century architect – Sansovino in Venice, Falconetto in Padua, Sanmicheli in Verona, and later, Palladio in Vicenza. And as we shall see, Palladio was soon to make his mark on Venice itself.

Sansovino's first Venetian family palace was the Palazzo Dolfin, situated on the Grand Canal near the Rialto Bridge (*Fig. 79*, frontispiece). The patrician who commissioned the palace, Zuanne Dolfin, was one of those more fortunate nobles who was still successfully engaged in shipping and commerce. Following the old Venetian practice he combined this with a successful career in public service. He was also lucky in having no brothers with whom to share his father's inheritance. Furthermore, his wife was a member of the wealthy Vendramin family. Thus he had sufficient reserves of capital behind him to trade adventurously and profitably.

His new palace was begun in 1538. As in Sansovino's Zecca, the façade was moved forward to provide more space on the upper floors, in this case incorporating a public street through a *sottoportego* below. The waterfront arcade across the whole façade must have seemed especially appropriate to the mercantile status of the owner, because of its associations with the Veneto-Byzantine *casa fondaco*. The water-entrance was at the side on a narrow *rio*, in order not to obstruct the street, and the land entrance was at the back.[20]

Nothing survives but the façade of this palace, for the rest was rebuilt for the last Doge of Venice, Ludovico Manin, by the Neoclassical architect Giannantonio Selva. The style of the façade must have seemed to Venetians like a demonstration piece in Roman 'correctness' with its Doric, Ionic and Corinthian orders and its row of *all'antica* lions' heads in the uppermost frieze. But the design is also firmly rooted in native conventions of palace building with its tripartite façade and its large windows more closely spaced in the centre. The unclassical use of an even number of bays, with a solid element in the centre (echoing the Gothic Palazzo Bembo next door) affirms the absence of a waterfront entrance.

The position of supremacy which Sansovino rapidly achieved in Venice is clear from the fact that by 1537 he had been asked by the Corner family, the richest in the city and one of the most distinguished, to rebuild their palace on the Grand Canal at San Maurizio, which had been destroyed by fire in 1532[21] (*Fig. 80*). The old Gothic palace on the site had been bought by the Procurator Zorzi Corner, brother of Queen Caterina of Cyprus, before his death in 1527. The Corner family owned vast estates in Cyprus, yielding huge crops of cotton, sugar and wheat. They were one of the so-called *case vecchie*, the original noble families who believed themselves descended from the first refugees from Roman cities on the mainland. Like other *case vecchie*, they maintained close ties with the Papal court, and members of the family held high ecclesiastical office – two of Zorzi's sons and three of his grandsons were Cardinals.

Because of the legal problems involved in dividing Zorzi's huge estate among his four surviving sons, the new palace was not actually begun until about 1545. Having provided Venice with a Roman manifesto in the Palazzo Dolfin, Sansovino was now prepared to treat classical elements more daringly. In particular, the imaginative detailing of the rusticated Doric window-aedicules on the ground floor shows his readiness to create Mannerist effects, as his contemporaries were doing elsewhere in Italy. Sanmicheli in his Palazzo Canossa in Verona had already demonstrated how effectively paired

orders, like those used in Roman High Renaissance palaces such as Bramante's House of Raphael, could be adapted to Venetian palace types. The double order allows more of the wall surface to be concealed, giving greater significance to the columns as structural, rather than decorative elements. As in the Palazzo Dolfin, Sansovino used the tall, round-headed window type which was so popular in Renaissance Venice. However, instead of narrowing the central bays, he made all the bays of uniform width, with the three central windows subtly widened to admit more light to the two long *saloni* or *porteghi* within. This device gives the building a more classical air, while preserving the practical advantages of the local building type.

The ground plan is typically Venetian. A long *androne* in the centre, with store rooms on either side, leads to an inner *cortile*. This courtyard contains the well, but not the main staircase, which is here incorporated into the building where it is better protected from the elements. Before his arrival in Venice, Sansovino had already had the useful experience of designing a palace for a long, narrow, urban site with his only Roman palace, the Palazzo Gaddi.

Sanmicheli's most prominent Venetian palace, designed for the Procurator Gerolamo Grimani shortly before the architect's death in 1559 and built under the supervision of GianGiacomo de' Grigi, was smaller than the Palazzo Corner, yet emphatically grandiose in style[22] (*Fig. 81*). This seems to reflect a certain need for self-assertion on the part of the Grimani family, who did not belong to the *case vecchie*. In fact, they were what one might call (to mix languages) *nouveaux riches*. Antonio Grimani, founder of the family fortune, made his money by cunning commodity-dealing at a time of violently fluctuating

80 Palazzo Corner, San Maurizio, by Sansovino, begun *c.*1545 (*Sarah Quill*)

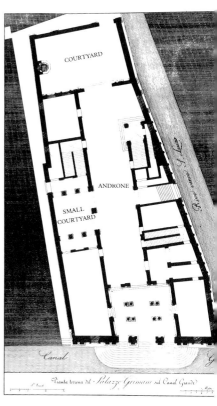

ABOVE
81 Palazzo Grimani,
San Luca, by Sanmicheli,
begun 1559 (*Sarah Quill*)

ABOVE RIGHT
Palazzo Grimani.
Ground plan

prices. He subsequently had a disastrous period as Captain of the Venetian navy, but recovered from his disgrace and was Doge from 1521 to 1523.[23]

Whereas Sansovino took care to make his palace façades seem an integral part of the structure, the façade of Sanmicheli's Palazzo Grimani juts out from the top of the palace, making a bold statement in its own right. The effect of grandeur is heightened by increasing the size of the individual classical elements. By the ingenious use of mezzanines Sanmicheli fitted all the necessary rooms and their windows into three lofty storeys of just five huge bays each. With its three Corinthian orders, paired on each side of the outer bays, the Palazzo Grimani façade looks back to Codussi's Palazzo Loredan (Vendramin-Calergi). However, the triumphal-arch rhythm of the three central bays gives it a distinctly Roman air and adds to the sense of sober dignity. Whereas Sansovino's Palazzo Corner shows a sculptor's enjoyment of varied surface textures, Sanmicheli's is severely architectonic, dominated by its grid of heavy horizontal and vertical components.

Ironically, Sanmicheli's palace is actually far smaller than it appears, for the site becomes rapidly narrower towards the back (*above*). In consequence, the position of the long central *androne* does not correspond with the centre of the façade. As the ground plan shows, its displacement is masked by the colonnaded entrance hall at the water-entrance. Like the Palazzo Corner, the Palazzo Grimani has a grand interior staircase. Because of the narrow site the courtyard is at the very back, for in this case there was less need to admit extra light to the heart of the building by means of an inner court.

In his guide to Venice in 1581, Francesco Sansovino declared that four patrician palaces in the city surpassed all the others in size, grandeur, expense and Vitruvian discipline. These were his father's two palaces for the Dolfin and Corner families, Sanmicheli's Palazzo Grimani, and Codussi's Palazzo Loredan, all of which, he claimed, had cost over 200,000 ducats[24] (*Figs. 62 & 79–81*). Yet we should not forget that the families who commissioned these magnificent buildings represented a tiny minority of the population of the city. The nobility itself were more numerous than at almost any other period, representing about 6% of the total number of inhabitants in the mid-sixteenth century, but already by this stage great wealth was becoming concentrated in the hands of fewer and fewer noble families, while the other patricians were becoming steadily poorer.

Together with the Corner family, the Grimani were perhaps the most active private patrons of art and architecture in sixteenth-century Venice.[25] Both families not only enjoyed great wealth, but also maintained close ties with Rome through their possession of high ecclesiastical offices. Thus both were eager to embrace the new 'Roman' style of Sanmicheli and Sansovino. On the whole the Grimani seem to have been readier to accept radically new artistic developments from Central Italy than the older-established Corner family, who were more deeply rooted in Venetian traditions. But it was Sansovino's design for the Palazzo Corner – so sensitively attuned as it was to Venetian tastes and expectations – which was to prove more influential in Venice in the long run.

Both Sansovino and Sanmicheli are known primarily as secular architects, unlike other great Renaissance masters such as Brunelleschi, Alberti or Bramante. In Venice and the Veneto political and economic power was concentrated as far as possible in secular hands, and the State tried constantly to inhibit the passage of wealth from secular to ecclesiastical ownership. The Doges were not, on the whole, enthusiastic patrons of religious art, except in San Marco, their own private chapel. The Republic tried to keep religious affairs under State control, and had authority over both the nunneries and the parish churches. Only the male religious orders were free from government intervention, and indeed were often the most imaginative patrons of architecture in the city.

Despite the State measures to keep the Church in its place, both Sansovino and Sanmicheli had some interesting religious commissions in the Veneto – Sanmicheli in and around Verona, and Sansovino in Venice. Sansovino's most important religious work – though one of his most undemonstrative designs – was the new church of San Francesco della Vigna, begun for the monks of the Observant Franciscan order in 1534 (*Fig. 82*). The cost of the building was supported by a clique of some of the wealthiest and most influential noble families in the city, who each bought family chapels in the new church. Doge Andrea Gritti himself bought the right to be buried in the chancel.[26]

This was therefore a commission which brought great prestige to the architect. However, as we saw in the case of San Giobbe, rebuilt in the mid-fifteenth century by the same order, the Observant Franciscans exerted strict control over the architecture of their churches. Indeed, Sansovino's design was substantially modified by one of the friars at the Monastery, the humanist scholar Fra Francesco Zorzi. The revisions were made in the light of his views on proportion, acoustics and the need for austerity. Zorzi's ideas on proportion reflected his interest in Neo-Platonic philosophy. For instance, he reduced all the important dimensions to multiples of the number three, which according to Plato was the most perfect number – and also, conveniently, symbolized the Trinity in Christian thought.[27] Like the Camaldolese friars who commissioned San Michele in Isola from Codussi, the monks of San Francesco were eager to embody up to date Renaissance theories in their new church. Though the most influential figures in Venetian monasteries were generally members of prominent noble families, their patronage was at the same time characteristically more enlightened than either the State or individual patricians, who were traditionally conservative in their tastes. Just as San Giobbe had close links with the church of the Osservanza in Siena, so the design of San Francesco della Vigna was modelled on Cronaca's church of San Salvatore al Monte in Florence, begun for the same order at the end of the fifteenth century. Thus Sansovino was strictly constrained, both by Zorzi's intervention and by the need to base his design on this Florentine prototype.

The Observant branch of the order were so called because they attempted to observe the Franciscan ideals of poverty and humility more strictly than the Conventual branch. (In Venice the Conventual friars, or Frati Minori, were based at the church of the Frari.) The search for austerity is obvious in Sansovino's design. Its style is far removed from that of his other buildings of the same period, such as the Library or the Zecca. The flat, whitewashed wall surfaces are adorned only by simple Istrian-stone Doric pilasters, with fluted capitals like those of San Salvatore in Florence. The bright, even lighting, which was unusual in Venetian churches at this time, emphasizes the uniform whiteness of the interior.

The plan (*p. 159*) adheres to the Observant Franciscan convention of a single nave with side chapels, like those of the Osservanza, San Salvatore al Monte, and San Giobbe. As a result, the pulpit and the high altar are clearly visible from anywhere in the nave. The only mysterious element is the long monks' choir, hidden behind the high altar like that of San Giobbe. The large windows on the end wall, which illuminate the choir, actually make it appear dimly lit from other parts of the church because of the *contrejour* effect. This subtle device was taken over by Palladio in his two great Venetian churches, San Giorgio Maggiore and the Redentore. Palladio himself built the façade of the church of San Francesco della Vigna, as we shall see later.

Sansovino's religious commissions were not always so tightly bound to an established tradition. In the case of the church of the Incurabili hospital, begun to his design in 1565, there was no obvious prototype on which to base the project.[28] In the middle of the sixteenth century the four big state-assisted hospitals of the city acquired a very special reputation for their choirs of orphan girls. In Venice a new kind of religious music – the *coro spezzato*, or split choir – was beginning to take over from the mediaeval Gregorian chant,

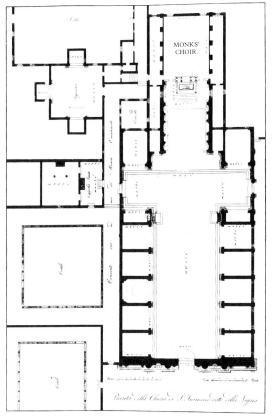

MONKS'
CHOIR

and it soon became fashionable for nobles and foreign visitors to go to one of the four hospitals, or to San Marco, on feast days to hear sung masses performed by such choirs.

The Ospedale degli Incurabili – in fact the syphilis hospital, which had an orphanage attached – was the first to build a new church especially designed for polyphonic choral music. Sansovino chose an oval plan, or rather a rectangle with rounded ends, for which there was no precedent in Venice (*p. 160*). By adopting such a compact form he hoped to avoid confusing echoes, which were such a problem in the cavernous spaces of San Marco. The flat wooden roof was intended to absorb echoes, like the sounding board of a musical instrument, and to project sound back into the church (*Fig. 83*). The choirs sang from three raised galleries, on either side of the nave and over the entrance, hidden from the public gaze by iron grills. The church was built in the courtyard of the hospital, and the little girls reached their places in the church by means of raised passages from their living quarters. The church was built on a very small budget; only 600 ducats was provided by the State and the rest had to be made up from private donations. Unfortunately the church was demolished in 1831, and its contents dispersed, but the hospital still exists on the Zattere, and two of the nave altars are now in the church of San Giovanni di Malta. This efficient and highly original design, one of the elderly Sansovino's last works, became a model from which future orphanage-choir churches in the city would have much to learn.

ABOVE, LEFT
San Francesco della
Vigna, by Sansovino,
begun 1534, plan

ABOVE
82 San Francesco della
Vigna, interior
(*A.F.Kersting*)

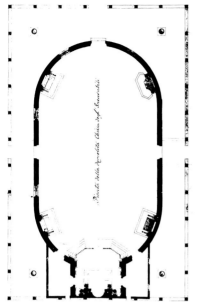

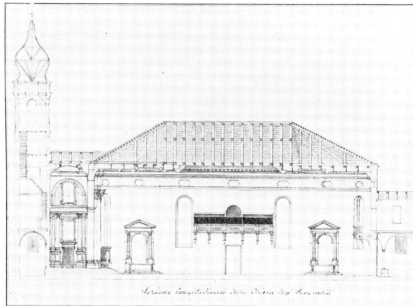

Andrea Palladio

It was not until the last decade of Sansovino's life that Palladio began to receive prominent commissions in Venice. By now the Florentine architect was an old man – he was already 74 in 1560 when Palladio began his first Venetian building, the refectory of the Benedictine monastery on the island of San Giorgio Maggiore.[29] Significantly, in line with the pattern which we find repeated so often in Venetian architectural history, it was the religious institutions rather than the organs of State or the nobility which proved most willing to accept Palladio's bold innovations.

Andrea Palladio (1508–80) was a native of Padua and spent most of his working life in the Veneto. From the 1540s onwards he was erecting magnificent buildings in and around Vicenza. His Vicentine palaces and Veneto villas were greatly admired, but although he had influential Venetian patrons on the Terraferma, the conservative Venetian establishment long resisted the idea of seeing such pioneering architecture in their own city. Jacopo Sansovino had ensured his success in the very special context of Venice by incorporating many aspects of the Venetian architectural tradition into his own style. But Palladio adopted a less compromising approach. In a sense it is more surprising that so small and provincial a town as Vicenza was prepared to accept buildings designed according to such fundamentally new principles, than that the city of Venice viewed Palladio's innovations with suspicion.

After the death of the little known Zuan Antonio Rosso in 1554, Palladio was one of those who applied to succeed him in the position of *proto* to the Salt Office (that is, the architect responsible for the public buildings of the city, especially the Palazzo Ducale). Yet his application was unsuccessful, and instead the insignificant Pietro de' Guberni was appointed to the post. Such was the Venetian attachment to the buildings which symbolized the permanence of the Republic that the predictable skills of a local builder were preferred to the radical ideas of an architect of true genius. Shortly afterwards, Palladio's project for the Scala d'Oro in the Palazzo Ducale, which he submitted in 1555, was turned down in favour of a design by Sansovino; and among the schemes for the new Rialto Bridge produced by various great architects in the same decade, Sansovino's rather than Palladio's seems to have been the one which received most support.[30] (In the event, neither of these schemes was to be the one chosen.)

In the early 1560s Palladio received several important commissions from monastic orders in Venice. Vasari, who visited the city in 1566, was particularly impressed by his project for the Convento della Carità.[31] This new monastery building for the Lateran branch of the Augustinian Regular Canons, begun in 1561, was never completed. It was badly damaged by fire in 1630 and has since been much altered. Moreover, since it has a sober, unremarkable exterior, and the more imposing interior is now little visited, it has been underrated or neglected by many modern writers. The site of the Convento della Carità, much as it must have appeared in Palladio's lifetime, is evocatively recorded in Canaletto's early masterpiece known as 'The Stone-mason's Yard' (*Fig. 25*). In this picture the entrance to the monastery can be seen on the far bank of the Grand Canal between the fine Gothic church of the Carità and the Scuola Grande of the same name. The whole group of buildings is now the seat of the Accademia di Belle Arti.

The elaborate project for the new convent was recorded with evident pride in Palladio's *Quattro libri dell'architettura*, published in Venice in 1570 (*Fig. 84*). As the text explains, the monastery was intended as a re-creation of the houses of the ancients. Palladio's reconstructions of Greek and Roman private houses were already well known in Venice through the illustrations which he provided for Daniele Barbaro's edition of Vitruvius, published there in 1556. Probably the close links which the Lateran Canons maintained with their superiors in Rome led them to accept so strictly classical an idea, and one so apparently alien from mediaeval conventions of monastic building. The account of the project in the *Quattro libri* makes much of the practical advantages, which would also have encouraged the monks to accept the design.

Only the portions on the top right of the published plan were ever built. These consisted of an open colonnaded atrium, the sacristy or *tablinum*, one of the oval staircases, and the east wing of the cloister. The Gothic church, which is not illustrated in the treatise, flanked the right-hand side of the plan. Because of this, the atrium, as depicted in the *Quattro libri*, could only have served as the entrance hall from the church. In reality Palladio would have had to provide an alternative side entrance for direct street access. However, as elsewhere in the treatise, he illustrated an idealized version of his scheme, disregarding the restrictions of the cramped site.

The atrium, with its huge Composite columns, was much admired at the time, but was completely destroyed by fire in 1630. Fortunately the rest of the executed parts of Palladio's project have survived. The east wing of the

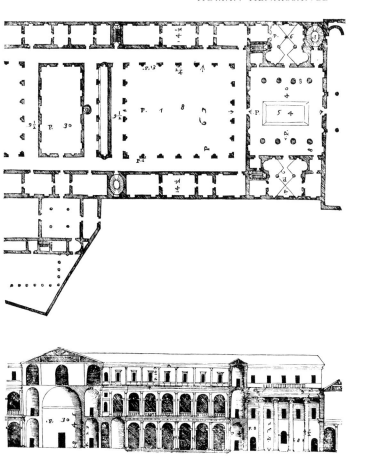

ABOVE
84 Andrea Palladio's project for the Convento della Carità, from his *Quattro libri dell'architettura*, Venice 1570

ABOVE, RIGHT
85 East wing of the cloister of the Convento della Carità, by Palladio, began 1561 (*A.F.Kersting*)

cloister has a two-storey loggia, originally open, with a row of monks' cells above (*Fig. 85*). The Doric, Ionic and Corinthian orders, superimposed one above the other in orthodox succession, are soberly classical in style. However, the use of materials is highly original, with brick used even for the columns and arches. This gives the elevation a characteristically Venetian warm red hue, but at the same time recalls the skilful way in which the ancient Romans used brick in their constructions. The interior parts of the monastery are even more striking. The dramatic oval staircase, with its open well in the centre and its steps cantilevered out from the wall, became justifiably famous, and led to a fine series of imitations both in Venice and in England. The sacristy, called the *tablinum* by Palladio to underline his classicizing intention, has an almost Neoclassical sobriety and purity of form. Great free-standing columns support the heavy vault and help to articulate the otherwise severe interior. The austerity is relieved, too, by the pair of elegant apses, and by the rich Doric entablature – curiously lacking a frieze – which runs around the whole room.

It was surely Palladio's gift for uniting simplicity with grandeur, so evident in the buildings of the Convento della Carità, which gave new life to the architecture of Venice. Sansovino's knowledge of the buildings of Rome had provided the city with a wealth of new motifs as well as a greater understanding of how to handle classical forms coherently and correctly. But the sculptural and chromatic richness of buildings such as the Library and the Loggetta served rather to enliven the surfaces than to emphasize the monumental scale of the structures or the volume of the spaces within. Sansovino's most successful works relied on the dramatic use of surface chiaroscuro for much of their impact. Palladio, on the other hand, could create imposing effects with the sparsest of decoration.

In the same years, Palladio was employed to design the façade of Sansovino's most important Venetian church, San Francesco della Vigna[32] (Fig. 86). The fact that this commission, financed by the Grimani family, was awarded during the lifetime of the older architect, showed convincingly that Palladio's reputation was at last becoming established in Venice. A comparison between Sansovino's design, illustrated on the foundation medals of 1534, and the executed façade, begun in about 1562, reveals how Palladio transformed the basic elements of Sansovino's model into something far more grand and commanding. In Palladio's façade the four half-columns of the main order are elongated into a giant order, which is compressed into the central section as if buttressed by the lower side portions. Both orders are raised on a continuous high plinth, so that the bases of all the columns stand dramatically high above head height.[33] The smaller order indicates the presence of the row of lower side chapels on either side of the nave, although in reality it rises considerably higher than the chapels behind. As the side view shows, Palladio's structure is not coherently integrated with the rest of the church. He was clearly more interested (like his patrons) in creating an imposing monument in its own right, than in compromising his design unduly to fit the existing structure. The unprecedentedly huge scale of the classical forms on the façade of San Francesco della Vigna must have been astonishing in Venice at this time. In the early 1560s there were still hardly any prominent Istrian-stone church façades in the city, with the notable exception of Codussi's San Michele in Isola. Even grand Gothic churches such as the Frari and Santo Stefano were faced relatively simply in brick, while Santi Giovanni e Paolo and San Salvatore still lacked their stone façades. Most parish churches, like their monastic counterparts, had brick exteriors, with Istrian stone confined to the architectural detail. The exteriors of San Marco, and on a smaller scale, the Miracoli derived their effectiveness from the use of rich, colourful materials, rather than from the dignity of their classical elements. Even Sansovino's Istrian-stone façades for the parish churches of San Geminiano and San Giuliano, both begun in the 1550s, were less impressive, for their two-order elevations failed to rival the nobility of Palladio's huge giant order.

That particular quality of Palladio's artistic imagination which allowed him to create majestic effects with such economy of means is vividly illustrated in the new Benedictine church of San Giorgio Maggiore, which he began in 1565[34] (Fig. 87). As early as 1520 the monks had considered rebuilding their old church and monastery. Indeed an anonymous drawing, which seems to be an early project for the same complex of buildings, survives in the Venetian State

ABOVE
86 San Francesco della
Vigna, façade by
Palladio, begun *c*.1562
(*Sarah Quill*)

ABOVE, RIGHT
87 San Giorgio
Maggiore, by Palladio,
begun 1565
(*A.F.Kersting*)

Archives. Francesco Sansovino's guide to Venice, published in 1581, states
that Palladio's design was based on 'a model made some time before'. In other
words, Palladio may even have been instructed to use an earlier project, such
as this one, as his starting point. His wooden model for the church of San
Giorgio was built during the winter of 1565–6. By this time the new refectory
which he had begun for the monastery in 1560 was already finished.
Meanwhile the monks asked permission from the Senate to fell 1,000 oak
trees on their Terraferma property for the new foundations. (Normally the
shipbuilding industry had priority·in the use of the now badly depleted
mainland forests.) The foundation stone of the church was laid in March 1566,
and from then on construction proceeded rapidly. By 1576 the building was
virtually completed, apart from the façade. This was not erected until
1607–11, a quarter of a century after the architect's death, although the
wording of the stonemasons' contract issued in 1607 implies that Palladio's
model was followed strictly.

This was the first complete church which Palladio built, yet it shows a
remarkable sureness of aim. In his treatise he demonstrated his familiarity with

the temples of antiquity, but he was fully aware that these antique models were not entirely suitable for the Christian liturgy. His recommendations on church building distinguish clearly between ideal and reality. 'Since the round (form) . . . is the only one amongst all the figures that is simple, uniform, equal, strong and capacious, let us make our temples round', he writes. But after a long explanation of the advantages of the circular plan he adds: 'Those churches are also very laudable that are made in the form of a cross . . . because . . . they represent to the eyes of the beholders that wood from which depended our Salvation. And of this form I have made the church of San Giorgio Maggiore at Venice.'[35]

Obviously Palladio had thought carefully about more recent traditions of church building as well as about ancient temple architecture. At San Giorgio he had to take special account of Benedictine architectural conventions. In particular he could hardly disregard the huge new church of the most famous Benedictine abbey in the area, Santa Giustina in Padua, which was begun in 1521 and was more or less complete by 1560. This splendid building must at least have inspired the earlier model which Palladio inherited when he took on the commission. From Santa Giustina he borrowed the triple-naved plan with apsed chancel and transepts and great central dome over the crossing (p. 166). What is interesting is the way in which he consistently avoided all those features of Santa Giustina which looked back to San Marco in Venice. For example, he omitted domes from his nave, transepts and chancel. He also replaced the triple apses of the choir and transepts of the Paduan church by single apses. Despite the fact that San Giorgio faced the great Ducal Basilica on the opposite side of the Bacino, he made few concessions to the city's rich Byzantine legacy. We have seen how local architects of the Early Renaissance used Veneto-Byzantine monuments as sources of classical ideas; and even Sansovino did not scorn such precedents. But Palladio's artistic vision was uncompromising.

This is not to say that he was insensitive to the Venetian context and its special qualities and needs. One of the most important lessons which he learned from indigenous Venetian building practices was how to make effective use of white Istrian stone. Codussi's façade of San Michele in Isola, built for another branch of the Benedictine order, must have been the most vivid source of inspiration. In its dazzling whiteness the façade of San Giorgio makes a dramatic impression. Unlike the Scuola di San Rocco or Sansovino's Library, the whiteness is not broken up by arcades acting as wells of deep shadow or by the chiaroscuro of rich sculptural decoration. The situation of the church, as if floating like a ship in a huge expanse of sky and water, emphasizes the frosty whiteness of the façade. In Palladio's lifetime the view of San Giorgio from Piazza San Marco was partly obscured by a row of small houses on the waterfront of the island, which were not removed until after 1609. In that year Doge Leonardo Donà complained that they interfered with his view of the church from the windows of the Palazzo Ducale; but it is not inconceivable that Palladio himself would have wished to have them demolished.

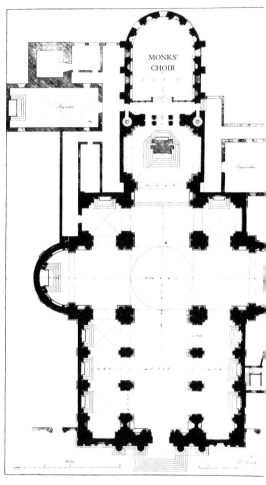

MONKS' CHOIR

ABOVE
ABOVE
88 San Giorgio
Maggiore, interior
(A.F.Kersting)

ABOVE. RIGHT
San Giorgio Maggiore,
plan

A drawing from Palladio's workshop, preserved in the Venetian State Archives, shows a plan of the completed church with a huge free-standing portico in front. In the event this ambitious idea was never taken up. Only in his tiny chapel at Maser, built for the Barbaro family, did Palladio ever build a free-standing temple front on a church. However, the alternative system which he used in his Venetian churches – projecting the elements of the portico on to the plane of the façade wall – was one of his most brilliant inventions. It was probably inspired by his own drawings of classical temples depicted in orthogonal projection, which gave a similar result. The effect was equally impressive, yet the construction was both simpler and cheaper than a true portico. What is more, no wells of shadow could interrupt the gleaming whiteness of the prospect. At San Giorgio, where Palladio designed both the façade and the body of the church, he was able to avoid the stylistic discordance between the exterior and interior which is so marked at San Francesco della Vigna. Here the façade fits more neatly on to the nave, and the large and small orders – the former raised on high bases and the latter resting on the ground – reproduce faithfully the system of the interior.

Inside the church the luminosity is perhaps even more striking than outside

(*Fig. 88*). The combination of white Istrian stone and whitewashed stucco had already been used in the interiors of recent Venetian monastic churches such as San Salvatore and San Francesco della Vigna. What was new in San Giorgio was the use of stronger illumination, perfectly controlled, to stress the almost uniform whiteness, broken only by the subtlest and softest of shadows. Palladio was emphatic about the significance of white in church building:

'Of all the colours, none is more proper for churches than white, since the purity of the colour, as of life itself, is particularly satisfying to God.'[36]

This statement was certainly a justification of his own aesthetic preference, but it also reflects something of the Counter Reformation's desire for greater lucidity in church services, codified in the decrees of the Council of Trent though without specific reference to architecture.

The interior of San Giorgio is so satisfying, so masterful and so original a piece of architecture that it cannot be regarded simply as a manifesto of Counter Reformation ideals. Even in the context of the history of Venetian architecture it seems to stand on its own. Despite his inexperience as a designer of churches there is no awkwardness in the way in which Palladio combined its various components to form a unified whole. In San Giorgio he eliminated the effect of multiplicity resulting from the repetition of apses and domes which characterizes the sister church of Santa Giustina in Padua. From any point in the church one is aware of the presence of the focus of the composition. This is the single great dome over the crossing, placed exactly midway between the entrance and the high altar, and brightly lit by windows in the lantern and drum. The four barrel-vaulted spaces which meet at this point – in the nave, the two transepts and the chancel – are clearly differentiated from the side aisles, which are lower and cross-vaulted, in order to draw attention to the four arms of the cross. In this way Palladio deftly combined his classical preference for centrally planned temples with the Christian ideal of the cruciform plan.

The giant Composite order of half columns and piers and the smaller order of Corinthian pilasters are both carried consistently around the whole church, as well as being echoed on the façade. The smaller order orientates the spectator walking round the church, helping him to relate himself to the huge space. At the same time the giant order, raised on high bases and stressed by a boldly dentilled cornice, serves to articulate more distant vistas.

Great thermal windows admit light to the nave, side aisles and chancel. The thermal window, a lunette divided vertically into three sections, is so-called because of its derivation from Roman baths or *thermae*. The baths were a major source of inspiration for Palladio, not only providing him with individual motifs but also suggesting ways in which spaces of different shapes and sizes could be organized coherently. At this stage the thermal window was still rarely used in Italian architecture, but after Palladio demonstrated its possibilities it became very popular in Venice. From this time on thermal windows became standard features of new churches, and were also inserted into many older ones to improve the lighting.[37]

As in Sansovino's church of San Francesco della Vigna the monks' choir behind the high altar is lit not from above but by windows in the end wall, so that a strong, almost heavenly light seems to spring from this source. In Venice the Observant Franciscan churches of San Giobbe and San Francesco della Vigna had already shown the advantages of the long retro-choir in monastic churches, namely, that this arrangement did not obstruct the view of the high altar from the nave. Palladio, like Sansovino, must also have known Roman precedents such as Bramante's choir in the church of Santa Maria del Popolo. In San Giorgio he adopted the arrangement in spite of the fact that in the new Benedictine church of Santa Giustina the monks' choir was still in front of the high altar. After this time, however, in Venice as elsewhere in Italy, choirs were moved from naves to less obstructive positions – usually to behind the high altar, from where the sacred music could emanate as if from a mysterious, unearthly source.

The monks' choir in San Giorgio was probably a large one (there are 48 choir stalls), and according to Benedictine practice the divine office was sung as many as seven times a day. The importance of their choral music is expressed in the form of the low apsed choir, designed to project sound into the church. It is likely that, on the occasion of the annual visit of the Doge to San Giorgio Maggiore on Saint Stephen's day, the choir of San Marco which accompanied him occupied the two transepts.[38] The church had to provide an effective setting, acoustically speaking, for the *coro spezzato* or divided choir, performing the polyphonic choral music for which San Marco was so famous, as well as for the monks' choir. This must have given Palladio an incentive to refine and simplify the arrangements of the transepts of Santa Giustina, with their multiple apses and domes, as these would have caused confusing echoes. Until this time, flat wooden ceilings, which had the property of absorbing echoes, had been thought to provide the most effective acoustics in church interiors. Sansovino chose ceilings of this type for all his Venetian churches, including that of the Incurabili hospital, begun in the same year as San Giorgio Maggiore and designed with the specific needs of the orphanage choir in mind. However, in Rome in the same years, the idea that a simple barrel vault might project sound more satisfactorily was being tried out in the church of the Gesù, begun in 1568 to Vignola's design; and the notion soon began to take root elsewhere in Italy. In the end it was the low vault rather than the flat wooden ceiling which prevailed in Venice. The later orphanage choir churches of the Mendicanti and the Pietà were constructed with vaulted ceilings rather than flat roofs, and a low vault was constructed in San Francesco della Vigna in 1630, instead of the flat wooden coffered ceiling which had originally been intended.[39]

The second major church which Palladio erected in Venice was that of the Redentore (*Fig. 89*). Like San Giorgio, it can be counted among the architect's greatest masterpieces. Although it has much in common with the earlier church, the very different nature of the commission inspired Palladio to refine and develop his ideas, and to produce a completely fresh design.

The Redentore, dedicated to Christ the Redeemer, was not commissioned

OPPOSITE
89 Church of the Redentore, by Palladio, begun 1577
(*A.F.Kersting*)

by a monastic order, but by the Venetian Senate. It was the outcome of a vow taken before the deliverance of the city from the terrible plague of 1576, in which about 30% of the city's population perished. In 1577 the Senate resolved to spend 10,000 ducats on the construction of a church in honour of the Redeemer. As part of the vow it was also decided that the Doge and the Senate, together with the choir of San Marco, should visit the church every year on the third Sunday in July. Thus the chief function of the church was that of a votive temple, the final destination of the annual procession. Although it was entrusted to the care of a group of Capuchin monks, it was not built specifically to suit their requirements but, rather, to serve as a place of pilgrimage and as a monument to the munificence of the State. Indeed the Capuchin friars, who belonged to a particularly ascetic branch of the Franciscan order, complained bitterly that the church was too lavish.[40]

Because of the commitment of the Senate the church was quickly built. The foundation stone was laid in 1577, and the church was completed within 15 years. The original budget of 10,000 ducats was exceeded by the huge sum of 60,100 ducats, but the advantage of State patronage was that extra expense could usually be met from public funds without long delays for further fund raising.

Like San Giorgio (but unlike San Francesco della Vigna), the Redentore has such a conspicuous position that it has become one of the most famous landmarks of the city. This was not fortuitous. The Senate considered various possible sites before they finally chose the spot on the island of the Giudecca, facing towards the rest of the city. By tradition, in Italy and elsewhere, sanctuaries and votive temples were placed on prominent sites outside city boundaries, for this made processional routes more spectacular. The Venetian sense of spectacle and drama must have guided the Senate in their deliberations. The original route for the Doge's annual visitation passed through a labyrinth of narrow crooked alleys, before emerging on the Zattere (or rafts) on the edge of the Giudecca Canal, facing the new church. This route gave dramatic emphasis to the contrast between the dark, confined passages and the light and space of the Zattere, with the shimmering vision of the brilliant white temple on the far side of the water. A specially erected bridge of boats carried the participants across the Giudecca Canal.[41]

It has recently been perceptively observed by Timofiewitsch that the façade of the church, when seen from afar, almost gives the illusion that a centrally-planned structure lies behind.[42] Outside Venice, sanctuaries and votive temples were often centrally planned. Indeed, the Senate argued intently over the choice between the centralized and longitudinal plan for the new church. In the event a rectangular plan was selected, for it must have seemed most suitable for the final stages of the procession, as well as for the monks' regular services. However, the emphasis which the façade gives to the soaring dome above, with the statue of Christ the Redeemer standing triumphantly on the lantern, preserves something of the character of a more conventional, centralized hilltop sanctuary.

This was the first time that Palladio was able to place a church entrance

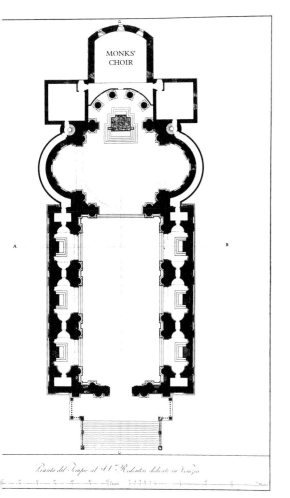

MONKS' CHOIR

Pianta del Tempio al SS. Redentore dedicato in Venezia

above the level of the street in front. Following Vitruvius and Alberti, Palladio himself recommended in the *Quattro Libri* that temples should be raised on steps, but so far he had only achieved this in temple-fronted villas.[43] The flight of steps would have heightened the drama of the final stages of the procession. The façade, executed before that of San Giorgio, but probably designed later, is a yet more elaborate variation on the theme of overlapping temple fronts (*Fig. 90*). The rhythms of the repeated triangular pediments give vigorous visual support to the dome, as well as masking the nave and its hefty buttressing walls. It would need many pages to explore fully the complexities and subtleties of this façade design, with its play of half columns and piers (or pilasters), of triangular and segmental pediments, of plain and dentilled cornices, and large and small orders.

The interior of the church, like that of San Giorgio, is brilliantly lit by huge thermal windows (too often now obscured by heavy red curtains) and by the apertures in the dome (*Fig. 91*). And as in the case of San Giorgio, the interior, like the façade, is entirely of whitewashed stucco and white Istrian stone. Palladio ignored the Venetian love of colour, but in so doing he was able to stress the seriousness and grandeur of the architecture itself. The interior is rich

ABOVE, LEFT
Church of the
Redentore, by Palladio,
begun 1577, plan

ABOVE
90 Redentore, façade
(A.F.Kersting)

in references to the monuments of Rome, both ancient and modern. Over 20 years had elapsed since Palladio's last visit to Rome in 1554, and during this time the city's wealth of artistic ideas had become absorbed into his own personal repertoire of forms. Thus there is nothing derivative about the way in which he turns the system of the drum of Bramante's Tempietto inside out, as it were, for the inside of the great dome over the crossing of the Redentore; or about the way in which the colonnaded apse behind the high altar recalls the wall articulation of the interior of the Pantheon. Once again, as in San Giorgio, the lessons of the Roman baths were fundamental to the design. The way in which the apsed niches emphasize the thickness of the walls, the regular rhythms of the nave elevation, and the linking of varied spatial sequences into a symmetrical, unified coherent whole, are all inspired by Palladio's studies of ancient bath complexes (p. 171). As Ackerman demonstrated, the single-naved church with side chapels was prominent in Counter Reformation church design because of the acoustic and practical advantages of this arrangement for preaching. In this period Vignola's church of the Gesù in Rome and Alessi's San Barnaba in Milan were constructed with similar layouts. However, as we have seen, the type had already been established in Venice, long before the Council of Trent, in the earlier Observant Franciscan churches of San Giobbe and San Francesco della Vigna. However, despite its references to Observant Franciscan traditions, we cannot wonder that the Capuchin monks at the Redentore, with their extreme regard for humility and austerity, were dismayed by the magnificence of Palladio's church. In deference to their feelings, Palladio made their own choir, behind the high altar, as simple as possible. The monks were provided with new monastery buildings at the back of the church; and Palladio therefore ensured that the outside of the main apse of the church, which was visible from the cloisters, was also completely plain. Yet Palladio's own intentions were not irreligious. As he explained in the *Quattro libri*, he believed that temples should be made as fine as one could possibly imagine, in honour of the Almighty, and 'so disposed in every part that those who enter are stunned by their beauty.'[44]

By this time Palladio had acquired respectability in Venice, with the help of influential friends and patrons such as Daniele and Marc'Antonio Barbaro, and was recognized as the city's finest architect. After each of the two great fires in the Palazzo Ducale in 1574 and 1577, he was employed to give technical and artistic advice about the repair of the old palace. Even in this capacity his ideas were as bold as ever. After the more serious fire of 1577 he explained in his report how he believed the Gothic structure of the Palazzo Ducale to be fundamentally unsound – even before the fire damage – since the uppermost walls were twice as thick as the columns which supported them. He therefore submitted an ambitious, radical scheme for the complete rebuilding of the palace in the classical style.[45] His chief supporter was Marc'Antonio Barbaro, who argued Palladio's case in the Senate with great tenacity, but in the end he failed to convince his fellow Senators, just as he had failed to persuade them to choose a centralized plan for the Redentore. It was resolved instead to restore the old structure, which had long represented to

Venetians the ancient traditions and durability of the Republic. This was not the moment to discard such a potent symbol. Public confidence had been badly shaken during the recent, ill-fated war against the Turks in the Eastern Mediterranean, which had led eventually to the loss of Cyprus in 1573, despite the famous Venetian victory at the Battle of Lepanto two years earlier. Once again it was the conservative element in the nobility which dominated.

However, Palladio's artistic legacy in Venice could not be ignored. Within a generation his impressive contribution to the architecture of the city had itself become absorbed into the Venetian heritage. No church builder could in future forget his restrained, yet compelling classical style, or disregard his brilliant solutions to liturgical and practical problems. To the vocabulary and grammar of Roman architecture, already introduced to Venice by Serlio, Sansovino and Sanmicheli, he added a sense of the scale and grandeur of the buildings of the ancients. He showed that majestic effects could be achieved without expensive materials, chromatic richness or elaborate decoration, which would only have obscured the unity and coherence of his masterful conceptions.

91 Redentore, interior
(A.F.Kersting)

173

CHAPTER VII

Baroque

The beginnings of the Venetian Baroque

Sansovino died in 1570, and Palladio a decade later in 1580. Between them, these two architects had provided Venice with a completely new range of visual ideas. While Palladio's activities in Venice had been concentrated in the field of religious architecture, Sansovino had worked mainly for secular patrons. Thus the legacies of the two architects were broadly complementary. The extent and durability of Sansovino's influence was a measure of his special ability to assess the particular tastes and needs of his Venetian patrons. Palladio, on the other hand, was more daring. He inspired Venice, above all, by his capacity to create striking, memorable and satisfying visual effects. Both were sensitive to the theatrical character of the city, integrating their buildings into the urban fabric of Venice like pieces of scenery on a stage. Both based their designs on local building types and used the materials best adapted to the physical setting. Gradually their ideas filtered down through the whole spectrum of the city's architecture, to inspire humbler patrons and lesser builders. Most of their imitators understood little of their precepts of design, but simply applied selected motifs to standard local models. However, the more talented of their successors proved more independent, and began to steer Venetian architecture gently towards the more spacious, rhythmic, flamboyant style known by the convenient, if imprecise, label of Baroque.

Alessandro Vittoria (1524–1608) was Sansovino's most gifted pupil. Best known for his sculpture and stucco decorations, he is usually considered a Mannerist artist because of his liking for bizarre touches such as fireplaces in the form of huge, open mouthed, monstrous faces. But in his Palazzo Balbi on the Grand Canal, built between 1582 and 1590, he moved towards a more relaxed Baroque style, decorating a traditional Venetian tripartite palace façade with exuberant broken pediments and cartouches (*Fig. 98*).

While Vittoria was a former pupil of Sansovino, Vincenzo Scamozzi (1552–1616) was a native of Vicenza and a follower of Palladio. Though his own treatise *L'idea dell'architettura universale*, published in Venice in 1615, makes no mention of Palladio, his work in Venice shows the extent of his master's influence. For example, in the church of San Nicolò da Tolentino, commissioned in 1590 by the recently established Theatine order, Scamozzi based his model on Palladio's own designs for the choir and crossing, adding a nave and side chapels in place of Palladio's portico. (To his great indignation Scamozzi was sacked by the Theatines in 1599 for supposed incompetence.)[1] The ground plan of Scamozzi's hospital of the Mendicanti, begun in 1601, reflects Palladio's interest in symmetrical building complexes (*p. 175*). The

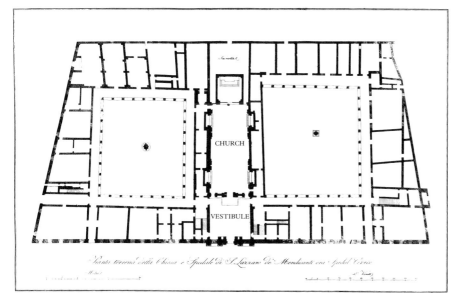

quarters for the inmates – beggars and orphans – are arranged around two cloisters on either side of the central church. The design for the church itself borrows the single nave with four altars and raised singing galleries from Sansovino's church for the Incurabili hospital. But the idea is re-worked on Palladian lines, adding a vaulted ceiling and thermal windows.

Perhaps the most surprising and impressive building of these years was Simon Sorella's new church for the nunnery of San Lorenzo. Light from great thermal windows exposes the bold lines of the spacious, white interior, now disused and stripped of its contents. The unusual breadth of the simple rectangular nave is further emphasized by a triple-arched choir screen, which cuts across the whole church from one side to the other, separating the nuns'

TOP
92 Palazzo Balbi, by Alessandro Vittoria, begun 1582 *(Sarah Quill)*

BELOW
Hospital of the Mendicanti, by Scamozzi, begun 1601

175

choir from the space used by visitors. The side arches of the screen are closed by iron grills, and the central one by the high altar, facing both ways to serve the needs of both the nuns and the public.

The heritage of Palladio and Sansovino, consolidated by such competent followers as Vittoria, Scamozzi and Sorella, provided the artistic background for the city's greatest native architect, Baldassare Longhena. It is a curious irony that Longhena's career coincided with a period in which Venetian painting was heavily dependent on imported talent. The foreign artists who came to Venice in the seventeenth century – such as Bernardo Strozzi from Genoa, the German painters Johann Liss and Johann Carl Loth, and the Neapolitan Luca Giordano – came not so much to learn, as to make their own contributions to the art of the city.[2] Venetian patrons were attracted to their up to date Baroque style, and few local artists were able to compete with these more gifted outsiders. One could protest that the indigenous love of luminosity and a clear bright palette, to which the Venetian eye was attuned by the light and colour of the city itself, made native artists inherently ill-suited to the tenebrism and weight of the Baroque idiom. Yet the fact that Venetian patrons wanted works of this type for their churches and palaces would seem to contradict the idea that there was an innate Venetian antipathy to Baroque chiaroscuro.

The seventeenth century was not a culturally barren era in Venetian history. After all, music, both secular and religious, reached great heights in the hands of such composers as Claudio Monteverdi (1567–1643) and Francesco Cavalli (1602–76), though, admittedly, neither was a native of Venice.[3] Nor was this a period of exceptional political or economic upheavals. During the sixteenth century, in the face of rapidly rising wheat prices and the risky nature of Mediterranean trade, huge amounts of capital had been invested in agriculture in the Veneto, in order to make the Republic more self sufficient in foodstuffs. The Venetian nobility had a long tradition of investing trade surpluses in land on the Terraferma, but in the sixteenth century the productivity of this land was greatly increased by ambitious programmes of land drainage and reclamation. As a result, by the seventeenth century Venice was economically more secure, and far less vulnerable to the effects of war, piracy and storms at sea. Although shipbuilding was hit by the decline in overseas trade and falling supplies of timber, other sectors of manufacturing industry – especially printing and the production of textiles and glass – were expanding. The Republic had recovered from the shock of the loss of Cyprus in 1573 and the terrible plague of 1575–77, and was now beginning to act more confidently on the political front. In 1606 Venice stood out resolutely against the Papal Interdict, which the Pope had hoped would force the Republic to adopt a more subservient attitude towards the Church. At sea, Turkish and Spanish power in the Mediterranean was beginning to wane. Despite the loss of Crete in 1669, Venice generally had the advantage in seventeenth-century naval encounters with the Ottoman Empire, although she had to make concessions to the Papacy in order to gain support in the struggle against the Turks. Venetian survival depended on preserving the

finely balanced political situation in which the Republic found herself, and this fact did not encourage drastic action on the political front. Economically the seventeenth century saw a steady but very gradual overall decline in prosperity, with a few of the richest families still managing to remain extremely wealthy.[4]

The contradictions inherent in the background to Longhena's career serve to remind us that great artists are not simply the products of their environment. Of course, architects in particular are dependent on prosperous, enlightened patrons for their greatest opportunities; but artists need more than patronage and basic competence to produce works of genius. Longhena was an architect gifted with that particular combination of intelligence, ingenuity, technical skill, artistic sensibility and visual imagination, which made his works stand out above those of all his contemporaries in the whole of northern Italy.

Baldassare Longhena (1598–1682)

Longhena was born in Venice, in the parish of San Severo, in 1598, the same year as the birth of Gian Lorenzo Bernini in Naples.[5] His parents came from the Lake of Lugano, the homeland of that other great Baroque architect Francesco Borromini. Longhena's father was a highly respected stonemason, and Baldassare himself studied under Scamozzi. Temanza reports that he was a small man, who always dressed in black and behaved in a dignified manner, and who listened attentively to the opinions of others; but this modest exterior concealed a tenacious and farsighted artistic personality. According to Temanza he was also pleasant and courteous in his relations with others, particularly with his craftsmen.[6]

Longhena's greatest masterpiece was the church of Santa Maria della Salute, which occupied him for most of his long career (*Fig. 93*). In 1630, during the terrible 16-month epidemic of plague in which 46,490 of the city's inhabitants died, the Senate resolved to build a votive temple dedicated to the Virgin, protector of *salute* or health.[7] The city had always been terribly conscious of its vulnerability to epidemics; and this fear manifested itself in the way in which outbursts of plague stimulated some of the city's most extravagant building projects. The building of the church and Scuola of San Rocco, dedicated to the saint who was believed to heal plague victims, had been largely financed through donations from anxious individuals. Huge amounts of public money had been spent on Palladio's church of the Redentore after the great plague of 1575–77. That the church of the Salute was conceived as a seventeenth-century equivalent to the Redentore, is reflected in many aspects of the design, as we shall see.

Of the 11 projects submitted to the Senate, only two were thought worthy of serious consideration. One was a plan for a longitudinal church by Antonio Smeraldi, who was also called 'il Fracao' and whose father Francesco had built the Palladian façade of the cathedral church of San Pietro di Castello. The other was Longhena's centralized scheme, which he himself referred to in an accompanying letter as a 'rotonda machina'. It is significant that the word *macchina*, here meaning a big building, was also used to describe the festive floats used in Venetian regattas. The form of Longhena's model, unprecedented in Venetian ecclesiastical architecture, must have reminded Venetians of these flamboyant, towering, structures, shaped like merry-go-rounds in order to look effective from any viewpoint.[8]

Just as the Senate had argued bitterly over the relative merits of centralized and longitudinal plans in the case of the Redentore, so there was no unanimity over the choice of Longhena's model. This was eventually chosen by 66 votes to 39, to the great indignation of Smeraldi.[9] Longhena was by no means an unknown genius, as posterity would have us believe. Through his father's activities as a stonemason and Scamozzi's teaching, he had already made useful contacts in the city. Indeed he had already been commissioned to rebuild the Cathedral of Chioggia, and was probably responsible for the rebuilding or modernization of four important patrician palaces in Venice at this early stage in his career.[10] Muraro has plausibly suggested that Longhena, who evidently already knew the new Doge Niccolo Contarini on more than professional terms, was supported by the more radical members of the Senate, those who adhered to the policies of Contarini, and the chief advocate of Venetian religious independence, Fra Paolo Sarpi. These were the younger members of the nobility who had backed the Venetian stand against the Papal interdict, and defended her controversial diplomatic, political and commercial links with the Protestant world. Meanwhile Smeraldi's less adventurous model probably appealed to the more conservative element in the Senate.[11]

The important political message which the new church was supposed to convey helped to justify the huge expense. Very quickly, as the church assumed its now indispensable place in the Venetian scene it also became part of the mythology of Venice. A long poem written by a Somascan priest, Lorenzo Longo, and published in 1644, just 13 years after the foundation of the church, related that the Virgin had appeared to the Doge in a vision, bearing a model of the church. The poem also claimed that Longhena, called by Longo 'il nuovo Palladio', was told of the form his design should take in a dream. The miraculous origin is engagingly symbolized by the carved stone cherubs on the waterfront, apparently supporting the platform on which the church stands, as if the church had been carried into place by angels like the legendary transport of the Holy House of Loreto.[12]

The poem's description of the iconography of the church suggests that it was seen as a declaration of Venetian adherence to her own brand of Catholicism, as defended by that persuasive thinker Sarpi. According to the poem, the statue of the Virgin over the entrance was to be flanked by statues of four Venetian saints, Saints Sagredo, Magno, Lorenzo Giustiniani and Gerolamo Emiliani, as if to indicate the self sufficiency of Venetian pastoral life. The church with the statuary described in Longo's poem appears in an engraving by Marco Boschini, published in the same year, 1644.[13] The Republic's stubborn resistance of Papal interference is also reflected in the fact that the church was entrusted to the Padri Somaschi, the only religious order to have been founded in Venice. The Padri Somaschi were responsible for training priests and clerics, and had played a particularly important rôle in the city since the expulsion of the Jesuits after the threat of the Papal interdict in 1606. The Jesuits, who were active in all fields of education, had been seen as unwelcome spreaders of Papal orthodoxy and rigid Counter Reformation ideas.

In the event the Republic was unable to retain this defiant position. Needing the support of the whole Catholic world in her continuing struggle against the Turks, she began to make compromises. The radical element in the Senate began to lose ground against the more conservative members, who traditionally held closer ties with the Papacy, and the Jesuits were finally allowed to return in 1657. The change in government policies is reflected in the way in which the iconography of the Salute was altered to assume a more orthodox Counter Reformation stance. The four Venetian saints were replaced by angels, and on the huge dome a statue of the Virgin with a crown of 12 stars was erected. This figure, standing on a crescent moon, like the vision described in the *Revelation* which was traditionally associated with the Immaculate Virgin, took the place of the Saint Michael which appears in Boschini's engraving. Thus the dominant message of the church became the perfection of the Immaculate Virgin, conceived free of sin, in order to triumph over evil. No longer was this symbol of Counter Reformation ideology rivalled in importance by a patriotic expression of Venice's early-seventeenth-century self assurance.

This highly significant change of emphasis should not allow us to overlook the fact that from the beginning the church of the Salute was dedicated to the Virgin Mary. In his memorandum of 1631 Longhena wrote:

> 'The mystery contained in the dedication of this church to the blessed Virgin made me think, with what little talent God has bestowed on me, of building the church in *forma rotonda*, i.e. in the shape of a crown.'[14]

As we have seen, there was an ancient tradition in Italy for Marian churches to be centrally planned, and Longhena was certainly aware of this. Sanmicheli's circular church of the Madonna di Campagna, outside Verona, was a recent striking example, though Longhena, so to speak, turned the whole model inside out, placing a continuous ambulatory inside the church, rather than a portico around the outside.[15]

Even in the Venetian brand of Catholicism the Virgin Mary was loved and revered. After all, Venetians were not irreligious – their resistance to Papal intervention merely affirmed that they wished to make their own decisions about liturgical and other ecclesiastical matters. According to Venetian mythology the date of the foundation of the city was also the feast of the Annunciation to the Virgin. Her responsibility for the city's foundation as well as Her protection of health is declared in the inscription in the centre of the floor of the nave:

'UNDE ORIGO INDE SALUS'

The Festa della Salute, the date of the Doge's annual processional visit to the new church, was fixed for 21 November, the day of the feast of the Presentation of the Virgin. As Longo's poem makes clear, the flight of 15 steps in front of the Salute was intended as an explicit reference to the Temple of Solomon in Jerusalem, where the Presentation itself was supposed to have taken place. In addition to the complex Marian symbolism, the original function of the church as a means of protection against the plague was not forgotten. In Le Court's group of statues over the high altar, the Virgin is flanked on one side by a personification of Venice, kneeling in adoration, and on the other by a hideous old hag, representing the plague, rushing away to the right.

The notion of the church having been brought by cherubs, and its association with images of regatta floats, are highly deceptive allusions. In reality the huge structure needed the deepest, firmest foundations which could possibly be provided. It is recorded that 1,156,627 piles were sunk to support the new building – 'a veritable buried forest' in Longo's words. By this date the shortage of wood made new foundations almost prohibitively expensive, and most new buildings in the city now re-used existing foundations.

Like the Redentore, the Salute was primarily a votive temple, rather than a monastic church. The processional function is clear from Boschini's engraving, in which crowds of people are seen mounting the steps and converging on the climax of the scene, the high altar, visible through the wide open doorway.[16] Traditionally, as we have seen, sanctuaries and votive temples stood on conspicuous hilltops, such as the basilica on Monte Berico overlooking Vicenza. Like the Salute, this Vicentine votive church was founded during an epidemic of plague and dedicated to the Virgin Mary. The Salute's prominent site, on a narrow finger of land where the Giudecca canal and the Grand Canal join the Bacino di San Marco, was the best equivalent which Venetian topography could offer. The site was symbolic in other ways too. It was already occupied by a church dedicated to the Trinità; and since the Middle Ages the Trinity had been closely associated in Christian imagery with the Immaculate Conception of the Virgin.[17] As Wittkower pointed out, the site also lies at the centre of an imaginary semicircle joining the Basilica of San Marco and the Redentore, the two other great religious monuments erected by the Venetian state. Palladio's church of San Giorgio Maggiore, too, lies on the perimeter of the same circle.[18] Moreover, the new church was situated at the point where the huge triangular complex of the Dogana, the customs' house, joins the rest of the city. This allowed the Salute – a symbol of health and well-being, and of the Virgin's protection of the city – to function visually as an anchor for Venetian trade, at once so risky and so essential to the Republic's survival.

In their final report of June 1631 the committee of five nobles, appointed to advise the Senate on the choice of the model for the new church, summarized the conditions with which the competitors had had to comply. Most of these were predictable requirements – for instance, that the church should make a grand impression, that the interior should be well lit (by this time a general rule in Venetian church-building), and that the cost should not be too exorbitant. The most demanding of the stipulations was more unusual – namely, that while the high altar should be clearly visible from the entrance, the others should come into view as one moved through the church. It was this very awkward pre-condition, designed to make processions more effective, which Longhena's model so brilliantly satisfied, as Wittkower demonstrated in his important analysis of the architecture of the Salute.[19]

In the Redentore Palladio had already showed how effectively the entrance to the chancel could be used to frame the high altar, when seen from the main doorway of the church; participants of moving processions would then gradually see more of the church revealed as they moved down the nave. Longhena took over this dramatic device from Palladio, for like the Redentore the Salute had to serve, above all, as a setting for the annual votive procession. But whereas in the Redentore the spectacle unfolds along a single axis down the nave, Longhena made new vistas open up around the spectator in every direction (p. 183). From the doorway of the Salute none of the six nave altars can be seen, for they are obstructed by the great piers which support the dome. However, from the centre of the nave each one is revealed, dramatically framed by the piers and arches of the ambulatory.

Longhena seems to have derived the idea of using a continuous ambulatory around the nave directly from Early Christian models, such as San Vitale in Ravenna and Santa Costanza in Rome. The only post-Byzantine ambulatory in Venice was the one which runs behind the high altar of San Zaccaria. Longhena probably also knew an attractive variant in a woodcut of the *Temple of Venus* (an appropriate secular parallel) in the famous romantic novel by Francesco Colonna, the *Hypnerotomachia Polifili*, published in Venice by the Aldine Press in 1499.

The Byzantine heritage of Venice provided Longhena with an exciting range of visual ideas. He realized that the sense of mass and the dramatic manipulation of interconnected spaces in Byzantine architecture had a particular affinity with the Baroque approach to design. Furthermore, since the Salute had to serve as the final destination of the important annual procession from the Basilica of San Marco, Longhena sensitively attuned his design to the appearance of the great Ducal church. The soaring central cupola, its outer shell rising high above the inner dome, adopts the system of the double domes of the Basilica; and the elaborate skyline with its profusion of rooftop statuary also links the Salute visually with San Marco.

Palladio, as we have seen, boldly disregarded the example of the Basilica of San Marco in his designs for San Giorgio and the Redentore. To Longhena fell the task of reconciling these two very distinct architectural traditions – the Palladian and the Byzantine – for he recognized the special qualities of each style. Palladio's Venetian churches had become a fundamental source of inspiration, which no religious architect in the city could afford to ignore. Like the Redentore, the rear of the Salute displays a dome framed by two elegant bell towers. Similarly, the side apses of the Salute's presbytery are joined to the dome above in the same way as the rear apse of the Redentore. The side façades of the Salute with their huge thermal windows recall the

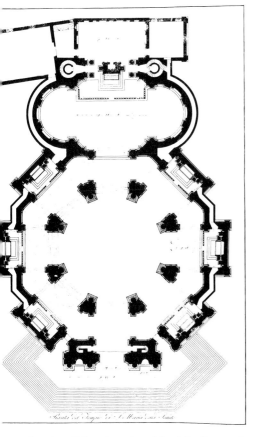

ABOVE, LEFT
Santa Maria della Salute,
by Longhena, begun
1631, plan

ABOVE
94 Santa Maria della
Salute, interior
(A.F.Kersting)

façade of the church of the Zitelle on the Giudecca, also designed by Palladio, though executed after his death. The Salute's central façade, too, with its huge columns on high bases framing niches containing statues, is overtly Palladian in style. In the interior, the Salute has a giant order of Composite half columns on high bases against piers articulated by a smaller order of Corinthian pilasters, all of these elements taken from the interior of Palladio's San Giorgio Maggiore (*Figs. 94 & 88*). And, as Wittkower has shown, the dimensions of the Salute's architecture are linked together in simple mathematical ratios, reflecting Palladio's own interest in harmonized proportions.[20]

Yet the Salute is far more than a catalogue of Palladian and Byzantine prototypes. It is a masterpiece of Baroque architecture in its own right – probably the only Italian seventeenth-century building to rival the creations of Bernini and Borromini in Rome. In some respects Longhena's aims were close to those of his Roman counterparts.[21] Like Borromini he was fascinated by the play of contrasting abstract geometrical shapes. This is clear, for example, from the way in which he effortlessly transformed the nave octagon into a circular dome above by simply continuing the line of the octagon up into the 16 ribs of the dome. Like Bernini in the Piazza di San Pietro in Rome, he evidently enjoyed working on a grand scale, uniting interior and exterior so that the forecourt served as an integral part of the whole dramatic sequence. Like Bernini at Sant'Andrea al Quirinale he turned the hefty buttresses needed to support the dome into visually exciting features in the form of gigantic scrolls, all 12 topped by statues of the Apostles, echoing the 12 stars in the Virgin's crown.[22] Like his Roman contemporaries Longhena was not afraid to break Vitruvian rules for the sake of the overall optical effect. For example, he dared to use Doric pilasters in the dome, *above* the Composite and Corinthian orders in the nave below, and placed two window bays over each of the nave arches. It is as if he wished to state that the dome was a completely separate architectural unit, hovering – almost rotating – over the nave octagon without need of structural support from below. Longhena also showed his awareness of contemporary concepts of urban planning, like those which were developing rapidly in seventeenth-century Rome. The Baroque era brought a growing interest in the possibilities of radiating vistas stretching across whole cities, linked by prominent monuments at the most conspicuous points. With its obvious echoes of features of San Marco and Palladio's churches, the Salute boldly declared its grand visual function as the city's new centre point, drawing the ring of older monuments around itself into a coherent whole.

Despite these affinities with the work of Roman Baroque architects, Longhena's church is unmistakeably Venetian. Like Palladio, and Codussi before him, Longhena took advantage of the special visual qualities of white Istrian stone. Whether sunlit against a deep-blue sky or plunging boldly into storm clouds, the Salute makes an unforgettable impression, casting its huge shadow right across the mouth of the Grand Canal. In the interior, Longhena used white Istrian stone and whitewashed stucco to enhance the bright, even lighting, although now that the stone has somewhat darkened the effect is less marked. It seems that Longhena himself wanted to soften the Palladian severity of the Salute interior, for he intended to have the dome decorated with stucco work and paintings. Ornament of this type would have had greater affinity with Bernini's more figurative decorative schemes in Rome than the dome as it appears today. In the event, this was never carried out, but Longhena's intentions were not so severely abstract and geometrical as some of today's critics like to believe. After all, as we have seen, the iconography of the Salute was as fundamental to its design as that of any of Bernini's Roman churches. With its eight sides facing the eight winds, like the Tower of the Winds in Athens, it served as an inspiration for Venetian seafarers – a powerful symbol of the renewed self confidence and economic strength of the Republic at the time of its conception. If this patriotic message began to weaken later, the Salute remained a gigantic sign of Venetian devotion to the Virgin, and a defiant challenge to future outbreaks of plague.

As the single great Venetian architect of his age, Longhena followed in the footsteps of Sansovino and Palladio simultaneously, for he dominated both secular and religious architecture in the city. In 1640 he was appointed *proto* to the *de Supra* branch of the Procuracy of Saint Mark's, the post held by Sansovino from 1529 until his death in 1570. In this capacity Longhena completed the Procuratie Nuove, the Procurators' houses on the south side of Piazza San Marco. Scamozzi had already begun this continuation of

Sansovino's Library elevation, with the addition of an extra storey to enlarge the Procurators' accommodation. It was left to Longhena to finish this wing, and to build the connecting section joining the Procuratie Nuove with the church of San Geminiano at the far end of the Piazza. This last portion was destroyed when all the buildings on the west side of the Piazza were demolished under Napoleonic rule in 1807 to make way for a grand imperial ballroom (*Fig. 118*).

Meanwhile, Longhena began to work in the Benedictine monastery of San Giorgio Maggiore, for which Palladio had designed the new church, refectory and other buildings. In 1641 the new monastic library was begun, after Michelozzo's famous library had been badly damaged by fire and demolished. Longhena's beautifully proportioned, lofty hall, lit by huge windows opening on to one of the cloisters, retains something of the traditional sobriety of monastic library design, although the heavy, rhythmic forms of the wooden bookcases betray the architect's Baroque leanings.[23]

Two years later, in 1643, Longhena began his grand staircase in the so-called Cloister of the Cypresses at San Giorgio, leading up to the level of the new reading-room (*Fig. 95*). This must surely be one of the most masterful of all his works. The idea of the grand double staircase derives originally from those built by Codussi in the Scuole of San Marco and San Giovanni Evangelista. However, Longhena's is conceived in a totally different spirit. Instead of confining one's attention in narrow, tunnel-like vistas, Longhena opened up

BELOW, LEFT
95 Monastery of San Giorgio Maggiore, staircase by Longhena, begun 1643 (*A.F.Kersting*)

BELOW
96 Palazzo Pesaro, by Longhena, begun 1652 completed by Antonio Gaspari (*A.F.Kersting*)

the whole conception, adding a new spatial dimension. Here the ramps do not converge at the top, but instead part at the bottom and rise on opposite sides of the vaulted staircase hall. Both storeys of Palladio's cloister, brilliantly illuminated by light from the central garden, are revealed through two superimposed arcades. These admit light to the staircase itself, and also provide a luminous goal for those mounting or descending the stairs. The forms of the balusters, like strings of huge onions, give an element of variety to the otherwise restrained style of the architectural detail. Through his brilliant scenographic manipulation of light and shade, space and mass, Longhena gave the San Giorgio staircase that dynamic, dramatic quality which was the great innovation of his age.[24]

Longhena's two greatest opportunities in the field of palace building came so late in his career that neither was completed in his lifetime. The Palazzo Pesaro was begun in about 1652, and finished after his death by an architect of relatively limited ability, Antonio Gaspari[25] (*Fig. 96*). By this stage in Venetian history few noble families had the resources needed for the construction of grand new palaces; and indeed, the Pesaro family's financial ups and downs were to some extent responsible for the long delay in completing the building. The wealthy patrician who commissioned the new palace was Giovanni Pesaro, who obviously intended it to symbolize his family's prominence; he himself was elected Doge in 1658, although he died in the following year. The Pesaro family had long been important patrons of the arts and were still ambitious and adventurous in their patronage.

The planning of the new palace was complicated by the fact that the foundations of three older buildings on the site had to be re-used for the sake of economy. A preparatory drawing by Longhena for the new Palazzo Pesaro is preserved in the Museo Correr in Venice. This shows that the original plan comprised just two storeys, although to give a grander effect, a third storey was implied by a screen wall at the top of the façade, masking the rafters of the roof. The most exciting feature of this early project was the grand central staircase at the end of the *androne*, opening on to the courtyard at the back. In the event, a less conspicuous staircase was incorporated into one of the side wings, for Venetians traditionally showed a great reluctance to waste limited space in their palaces with grandiose staircases. The existing *androne* of the Ca' Pesaro stretches right back to the *cortile*. The final groundplan followed the conventional Venetian arrangement of rooms, which had scarcely changed since the Gothic period, apart from the introduction of the covered staircase in the sixteenth century. As executed the palace was much larger than originally intended. A second living storey was added in the early eighteenth century, and the palace was also extended around the back of the courtyard.

Longhena's façade was more innovatory than the plan, although here, too, he paid tribute to local Venetian prototypes. Sansovino's Palazzo Corner at San Maurizio was the fundamental inspiration (*Fig. 80*). However, Longhena's surface decoration has an even richer texture, with its huge keystone heads, animal masks, and fanciful balustrades. The contrasts of light and shade are intensified by means of free-standing columns on the *piano nobile*, and by the

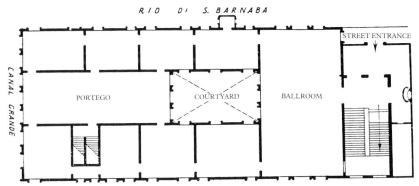

prominent diamond–cut rustication on the water-storey. This feature had not been re-used in Venice since it had been introduced in the Ca' del Duca in the mid-fifteenth century (*Fig. 49*). Longhena's interest in unusual textures extends into the interior. In the *androne* boldly fluted columns and piers are ringed by smooth bands of rustification, reversing the typical play of rough and smooth in sixteenth-century rusticated orders.

The Palazzo Pesaro was Longhena's most idiosyncratic and memorable palace design, and must surely have drawn attention to the eminence of the Pesaro family. Nevertheless, it seems that Longhena felt that this exploitation of dramatic chiaroscuro and new shapes and textures could go no further. His last great palace design, commissioned in 1667 by Filippo Bon, is considerably more controlled, and perhaps in the long term more visually satisfying (*Fig. 97*). This palace, now called Ca' Rezzonico after the family who acquired the palace in 1712, also remained unfinished at Longhena's death in 1682.[26] At that point, only the first *piano nobile* and the side wing along the Rio di San Barnaba

ABOVE
97 Ca' Rezzonico, formerly Bon, by Longhena, begun 1667, completed by Giorgio Massari *(A.F.Kersting)*

BELOW
Ca' Rezzonico, formerly Bon, by Longhena, begun 1667, completed by Massari. *Piano nobile.* After Lorenzetti

187

were usable. The building was completed in the eighteenth century by Giorgio Massari, an architect of far greater ability than Gaspari. Massari's style was lighter and less flamboyant than Longhena's, but in Ca' Rezzonico his work is so perfectly attuned with that of his predecessor that it is difficult to distinguish their individual contributions.

The groundplan of Ca' Rezzonico, like that of Ca' Pesaro, adopts the traditional Venetian arrangement, with its long *androne* flanked by smaller rooms leading to a courtyard at the back (*p. 187*). Its most innovatory features were the contribution of Massari, who added a second *androne*, perpendicular to the first one, at the far end of the courtyard, and a grand ceremonial staircase beyond. Over the rear *androne* Massari built a huge ballroom, decorated with trompe l'oeil frescoes and huge glass chandeliers. As early as the sixteenth century, Venetians had begun to hold great feasts and parties in their ground floor *androni*. This was considered a decadent development by Doge Leonardo Loredan in a speech of 1513, but despite elaborate sumptuary laws the love of such festivities continued to grow.[27] By the eighteenth century, the banquets held by the richest families had become legendary. Those held by the Labia family in their huge new palace designed by Cominelli were perhaps the most famous. As a result, both in Venice and in their country villas, the wealthiest Venetian families began to build sumptuous ballrooms in which to hold their great receptions. The Rezzonico family, who had been admitted to the Venetian nobility as late as 1687, had a meteoric rise in status and power, culminating in the election of Carlo Rezzonico as Pope Clement XIII in 1758.

In the façade of Ca' Rezzonico, Longhena again leaned heavily on the example of Sansovino's Palazzo Corner (*Fig. 80*). Indeed, the style of the later palace has more in common with Sansovino's than that of the more exuberant Ca' Pesaro. The second floor, added by Massari but probably based on Longhena's own design, was completed in 1752. But for Massari's attic, the palace might almost be mistaken for a sixteenth-century building. However, the ringed half-columns on the water storey, which seem to be wrapped in bands of soft fleece, reveal Longhena's interest in varying shapes and textures.

Longhena far outshone other seventeenth-century architects in Venice with his skilful exploitation of dramatic effects of space and light and his fertile visual imagination. But his use of such flamboyant elements was perfectly controlled – it was never merely decorative or pompous. Like other great architects he was most successful in commissions where the circumstantial limitations were strictest – such as the Salute, with its demanding brief from the Senate, or his works at San Giorgio Maggiore, where a certain monastic austerity had to be preserved. Though he worked within the bounds of local architectural traditions and expectations Longhena managed to rise above the provincialism of his contemporaries to assume a distinguished place in the wider context of European Baroque architecture.

Giuseppe Sardi

Only one other architect, Giuseppe Sardi (*c.*1621–99), gained a significant

FACIATA DELLA SCVOLA DI S.TEODORO
Architettura di Giuseppe Sardi
Luca Carlevarys delin et inc.

98   San Salvatore and Scuola Grande di San Teodoro, both façades by Giuseppe Sardi, begun 1649. Engraving by Luca Carlevaris, 1703. *Museo Correr, Venice*

portion of the important commissions awarded during Longhena's lifetime. Sardi was born in Italian Switzerland, a region that had already produced such great architects as Maderno and Borromini. Nothing is known of his training or his artistic background. He emerges from obscurity in Venice in 1649 as the architect of two conspicuous new façades, those of the Scuola Grande di San Teodoro and the adjacent monastery church of San Salvatore, both financed by the bequests of a wealthy Venetian merchant, Jacopo Gallo[28] (*Fig. 98*). The façade of San Teodoro, completed in 1655, is a conservative solution, adhering broadly to the scheme of Sansovino's San Geminiano façade, with its two orders of paired columns. That of San Salvatore, finished somewhat later in 1663, is more inventive, perhaps reflecting the fact that twice as much money (60,000 ducats in all) was provided for this façade. The main order has Palladian reminiscences, with its huge Corinthian columns on high bases and its hanging garlands. The pilasters of the attic storey have masks instead of capitals, while stone figures stand in front of them like detached caryatids, echoing Longhena's use of this arrangement in the dome of the Salute.

After a brief period working on new buildings for the Ospedaletto, only to be superseded by Longhena in 1666, Sardi began the façade of Longhena's church of Santa Maria degli Scalzi in 1672 (*Fig. 99*). The benefactor of this lavish façade, Gerolamo Cavazza, was already a patron of Sardi, which probably explains why Longhena himself was not awarded the commission. Cavazza, who had been only recently admitted to the nobility, contributed the huge sum of 74,000 ducats.[29] Here, too, Sardi leaned on the example of Sansovino, whose vocabulary had now become absorbed into the Venetian tradition. The two orders of paired columns, the statues in niches, and the reclining spandrel figures, are all typical of Sansovino's style. However, the effect is totally

ABOVE
99 Santa Maria degli Scalzi, façade by Sardi, begun 1672
(A.F.Kersting)

ABOVE, RIGHT
100 Santa Maria del Giglio, façade by Sardi, begun 1680
(A.F.Kersting)

different, for the elaborately carved volutes and the huge double pediment with its great central cartouche give the façade a Baroque exuberance.

Sardi was an eclectic and inconsistent architect. It would be difficult to pinpoint his style or define his contribution to the history of Venetian architecture. His last two important commissions, before he died in a state of melancholic insanity in 1699, are so different in character that they could be the work of two different architects. The first, the façade of the hospital church of San Lazzaro dei Mendicanti, begun in 1673 – again with a bequest from Jacopo Gallo – is a simple Palladian design with a giant order of four columns on high bases topped by a single triangular pediment.[30] Only the broken pediment over the door betrays the façade as a seventeenth-century monument. The design seems to have been a deliberate reaction against Longhena's elaborate, three-dimensional façade for the nearby hospital church of the Ospedaletto, begun only three years before.

Sardi's last façade, that of Santa Maria del Giglio, erected in 1680–3, is as ostentatious as the Mendicanti façade is sober (*Fig. 100*). To a great extent its flamboyant character is due to the wishes of the patron, Antonio Barbaro, Proveditore Generale in Dalmatia, who died in 1679 leaving 30,000 ducats for the façade, as a monument to himself and his family. To a certain extent Barbaro felt the need to defend his reputation, as he had been dismissed for incompetence when fighting in the War of Candia.[31] A statue of the donor stands in front of a heavy curtain above the doorway, flanked by statues of Fame, Honour, Virtue and Wisdom; and his four brothers are portrayed by statues in the lower niches. Reliefs of naval battles decorate the bases of the upper columns, while those of the lower order have reliefs of forts and fortified towns then under Venetian rule. The inclusion of Rome in this series seems a splendidly arrogant gesture, but Barbaro had in fact served as ambassador there.

Just as the Mendicanti façade invites comparison with the Ospedaletto, so that of Santa Maria del Giglio seems to have been a critique of the façade of the nearby church of San Moisè, begun in 1668 with a lavish bequest from

101 San Moisè, façade by Andrea Tremignon, begun 1668 *(A.F.Kersting)*

Vincenzo Fini and his brother[32] (*Fig. 101*). The façade of San Moisè, designed by the otherwise little known architect Andrea Tremignon, is a similarly pompous monument glorifying the donor and his family; but here the effect is fussy and the drama confused, while the proportions of the architectural framework are unsatisfactory. Sardi's façade of Santa Maria del Giglio could hardly be described as tasteful, but it has a boldness and coherence lacking in San Moisè. The crowning segmental pediment, breaking through a second one below, and surmounted by a statue of Glory, gives a central emphasis to the design, and the drama is clearly focussed on the person of Barbaro himself, as he would obviously have wished.

In general, the development of the Baroque style is closely associated with expressions of self confidence. The explanation for this is partly economic, for only wealthy patrons could afford to build on such a grand scale, or to employ such flamboyant decoration or rich materials. The financial aspect is particularly evident in seventeenth-century Venice, where all the most conspicuous Baroque monuments were commissioned either by the very richest private individuals or by the State. Other more modest buildings of the period can be distinguished only by the occasional broken pediment or florid balustrade.

However, self confidence of a less material kind was also a prerequisite. The climax of the Baroque style in European architecture was probably reached in mid-seventeenth-century Rome. Here the renewed confidence of the Papacy, which had triumphantly weathered the buffeting of the Reformation and Counter Reformation, was expressed in the magnificent religious architecture of Bernini, Borromini and Cortona. Bernini, in particular, used theatrical devices and Baroque techniques of illusionism to transport the spectator's emotions on to a more spiritual plane, revealing the essential mysteries of the Catholic faith. The success of such effects required a strong commitment on the part of patron, architect and spectator alike. In Venice a certain scepticism had long been present in the religious life of the city because of the city's strong links with the Protestant world. A building like the Salute was certainly a bold expression of self confidence on the part of the Venetian Republic, but Longhena could not expect to play on the emotions of the spectator as Bernini was doing in Rome. Besides, the mystical quality in Bernini's architecture was closely associated with Jesuit thinking – a similar approach is evident in Saint Ignatius's *Spiritual Exercises* – and the Jesuits were banished from Venice for a large part of the seventeenth century. Because of Venetian suspicion of such emotional manipulation, Longhena made no attempt to create such ecstatic, ethereal visions. He simply embraced those characteristics of Baroque architecture – expansive urban vistas, a sense of light and space, and an enjoyment of scenographic effects – which were closest to Venetian sensibilities. To these he added the bold, dynamic forms which best expressed the extrovert self confidence of his patrons. However, in the following century the new intellectual self awareness, with its emphasis on controlled, rational thinking, was to bring this rhetorical, expansive style to an abrupt end.

CHAPTER VIII

Palladianism and Neoclassicism

By the late seventeenth century the traditional balance of Venetian society had begun to change. The fortunes of the patrician class were declining with every generation, as their patrimony was progressively subdivided by inheritance. Forbidden to marry wealthy non-nobles, unwilling to soil their hands with manufacturing industry, distracted by time-consuming diplomatic and government positions, and undermined by the risks of far-flung trading ventures, the old Venetian nobility were no longer the wealthiest sector of the society, even though they still held political power. They were also steadily declining in numbers; by 1797 the patrician class made up only about 3.2% of the city's population, as opposed to about 6.4% in 1520.[1] In consequence, few of the important building patrons were now members of the ancient Venetian aristocracy. Some had been newly admitted to the nobility (which was at last accepting outsiders in return for large payments to government funds heavily depleted by war), others were wealthy members of the citizen class. By this time, as we have seen, the more prominent commissions from laymen were generally not public buildings, nor the palaces of distinguished old noble families, but rather the façades of churches or institutions in conspicuous places, endowed by private individuals eager to leave a lasting imprint on the Venetian scene.

This was also a period in which a number of religious orders in Venice, such as the Dominicans, the Carmelites and the Jesuits, found themselves with the resources for major building projects. The position of the Church in eighteenth-century Venice was somewhat curious, for although the State still maintained its religious independence and vigorously resisted papal intervention in ecclesiastical affairs, the Church in Venice was one of the most fervent defenders of true Catholic orthodoxy.[2] Although clerics were excluded from the government the nobility had considerable control over the religious life of the city, for they monopolized the important religious offices. The Venetian Inquisition, like political censorship, was a powerful instrument for maintaining the traditional values and *status quo* against more radical tendencies. The few remaining wealthy nobles gave strong financial support to the religious orders and even to the parish churches of the city to help finance building projects, partly to glorify their own reputations and partly to consolidate the power of the Church in the city. Furthermore, the suppression of some of the minor orders as a means of raising money for the wars against the Turkish infidel, had led to a kind of 'takeover' situation, allowing certain of the more powerful orders to acquire land, buildings and works of art from the suppressed convents. Thus we find, in the first half of the eighteenth century, a splendid series of new churches, richly decorated with fine paintings and sculpture, rivalling those built in Rome during the Counter Reformation more than a century earlier.

The changing distribution of wealth in Venetian society obviously had its reflections in the architecture of the period. It cannot be denied that buildings such as the façades of Santa Maria del Giglio and San Moisé have a *nouveau riche* quality verging on vulgarity (*Figs 100 & 101*). However, at the beginning of the eighteenth century Venetian architecture began to react sharply against such ostentatious excesses and to follow a course very different from that of architecture elsewhere in Italy – or indeed in Germany, Austria or France. The Rococo style which was establishing itself in various forms in most parts of mainland Europe had a strong impact on Venetian interior decoration, but the actual buildings of the same period show a surprising sobriety and restraint. Whereas the furniture and glassware, the stuccoes and painted decoration, the costumes and the textiles of eighteenth-century Venice display the characteristic Rococo qualities of lightness and elegance, pretty pastel colours and rhythmically curving forms, such features are generally absent in the architecture built to contain them. Nowhere in the fabric of the buildings themselves do we find the virtuoso light effects, illusionistic devices or swaying forms of eighteenth-century architecture elsewhere in Italy, such as the Spanish Steps in Rome, the work of Juvarra in Piedmont, or the villas of Sicily. In Venice the exuberances of the late Baroque were followed not by a lighter, playful, but still decorative idiom, but by a more serious classical style based chiefly on the architecture of Palladio. This Palladian revival, which was to lead directly, almost effortlessly, to Neoclassicism, has its only obvious equivalent in England, though in Venice the movement at first lacked the self conscious intellectual basis of English Palladianism. It is obviously significant that there was a close artistic relationship between England and Venice in the eighteenth century. Not only did English artists visit Venice, but Venetian painters such as Sebastiano and Marco Ricci, Pellegrini and Canaletto visited England and were employed by members of the English nobility.[3]

The growing discrepancy between the styles of the interiors and exteriors of Venetian buildings was a reflection of the fundamental contradiction inherent in the culture of the period. The intellectual and artistic life of the city was evolving in two principal directions. On the one hand there was a yearning for distraction, a need to escape from the realities of a bankrupt treasury exhausted by repeated wars against the Turks, an impoverished nobility, and the rumblings of political discontent. Drama and opera enjoyed huge popularity, and though some *impressarii* were more successful than others, in general the theatres of Venice flourished as never before or since.[4] In the same vein, Venetian painting of the period was theatrical, witty and elegant. On the other hand the spirit of the Enlightenment was alive in Venice, as elsewhere in Europe. There was an intense desire to discuss and to clarify philosophical, scientific and aesthetic questions, and thus, in a sense, to impose order on a seemingly fragile world. Academies were founded to foster the serious study of the arts and sciences. Theoretical treatises were published and read avidly in the search for certainties and absolute values. Despite the attempts of the Government to defend the city against radical thinking, the huge numbers of foreign visitors provided contact with the outside world and its preoccupations.

Rossi and Tirali

The first Venetian architects to react against the extravagant style of the late Baroque were two exact contemporaries, Domenico Rossi and Andrea Tirali (both were born in 1657 and died in 1737). According to their early biographer, the architect Tomaso Temanza, neither of these architects was well-educated or sophisticated – Rossi is described as 'almost illiterate' while Tirali 'could hardly write' – yet both were apparently respected in cultivated Venetian circles.[5]

Rossi was the nephew of Giuseppe Sardi. Like his uncle he was born on Lake Lugano, where his father was a miner. He came to Venice at the age of six or seven, and was trained as a stonemason in the workshops of Tremignon and Longhena. Temanza records that in his youth Rossi was very high-spirited and mischievous (he was also a firework expert), which perhaps accounts for his late emergence as a successful architect. He is first recorded supervising the rebuilding of the church of San Girolamo after a fire in 1705, and working for the powerful Manin family in Udine from 1708 onwards. He achieved his first major success in Venice in 1709, at the age of 51, when he won the competition for the new façade of the parish church of

BELOW, LEFT
102 San Stae, façade project by Giacomo Gaspari, submitted in the competition of 1709. Engraving by Vincenzo Coronelli, *(Museo Correr, Venice)*

BELOW
103 San Stae, façade by Domenico Rossi, begun 1709 *(A.F.Kersting)*

Sant'Eustachio, known in Venetian dialect as San Stae. (This church had been newly rebuilt by an otherwise unknown architect, Giovanni Grassi.) The construction of the façade was to be financed by a bequest from Doge Alvise II Mocenigo. The 12 projects which were submitted to the competition are known from a series of engravings by Vincenzo Coronelli (*Fig. 102*). Evidently the judges were not attracted to the more daring designs, with their swaying curves and showy detail, but preferred Rossi's restrained Neo-Palladian scheme with its four giant columns on high bases supporting a great triangular pediment, reminiscent of his uncle's design for the façade of San Lazzaro dei Mendicanti (*Fig. 103*). The only flamboyant feature is the broken pediment over the door, crowned by animated statues. The rest of the sculpture is neatly contained within niches and relief panels.

Rossi's most important secular work was the reconstruction of the Palazzo Corner della Regina in 1724–27[6] (*Fig. 104*). Once the home of Queen Caterina of Cyprus, this Gothic palace was the oldest of the four huge palaces owned by the wealthy Corner family, one of the few families of the old nobility to have remained prosperous as late as the eighteenth century. Like Longhena in his palaces for the Pesaro and Rezzonico families, Rossi turned to Sansovino's Palazzo Corner at San Maurizio for inspiration for the new palace, but here the effect is cold and inharmonious. The *piano nobile*, lacking a mezzanine level, is uncomfortably low compared with the other two storeys, while the attic windows are inserted awkwardly into the crowning frieze. At first the ever-ambitious Corner family had intended to incorporate the site of the adjacent Palazzetto Grimani into their new palace, filling in the canal separating the two sites in the process, but legal difficulties made this impossible, The eventual plan had to be reduced to fit into the area of the old palace together with some small adjoining houses at the back (*p. 197*). Though the initial scheme was considerably altered, the cramped effect of the final façade still reflects the compression necessitated by the change of plan. The height could not be correspondingly reduced to improve the proportions, for the Corner family had conceived their palace on a scale to rival Longhena's almost-completed Palazzo Pesaro just nearby. The sober classical detail of the façade is indicative of the change under way in Venetian architectural taste, though an element of Baroque extravagance survives in the enormous keystone heads of the *pianterreno*. In the interior Rossi inserted a deliberate Palladian feature into the otherwise traditional Venetian palace plan, placing a colonnaded atrium (probably inspired by the atrium of Palladio's Convento della Carità) in the front portion of the lower *androne*. Temanza's assessment of Rossi as 'highly expert in the technical side of building, but with little or no understanding of artistic good taste' is perhaps a comment on the unevenness which he displayed in his work, but he played an important part in preparing the way for Neoclassicism in Venice.[7]

Rossi's contemporary, Tirali, was born in Venice and trained as a bricklayer and builder. Like Rossi he was renowned for his technical skill, in recognition of which he was appointed in 1688 as *Proto alle Acque*, the engineer in charge of the waterways and sea defences of Venice. In 1721 he became *proto*

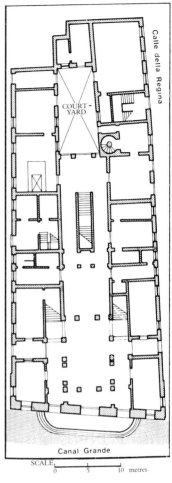

to the Procuratia de Supra, following in the footsteps of such illustrious
architects as Sansovino and Longhena. In this capacity he made some skilful
repairs to the Basilica, and repaved Piazza San Marco, replacing the old
herringbone brickwork with the present squared paving. As an architect
Tirali leant on the example of Palladio even more heavily than Rossi. This is
especially evident in the case of the façade of San Vidal, which is a faithful
restatement of Palladio's San Francesco della Vigna façade. (The building
work is seen in progress in Canaletto's early masterpiece known as 'The
Stonemason's Yard', now in the National Gallery in London, *Fig. 25*.) Tirali's
most inspired work was the façade of the Theatine church of San Nicolò da
Tolentino, which he erected between 1706 and 1714 (*Fig. 105*). This church had
been built by Vincenzo Scamozzi in the last decade of the sixteenth century.
Tirali's solution was to place a classical temple front, raised on a flight of steps, in
front of the huge façade wall. The upper part of the base wall, still visible behind,
should also have been faced and articulated, but the funds, provided by a
bequest from Alvise da Mosto, proved insufficient.[8] Although Palladio had at
one stage considered a portico for the façade of San Giorgio Maggiore, no
projecting temple fronts had yet been built in Venice itself. Tirali's portico,

with its strictly classical fluted Corinthian columns and minimal decoration, is more serious in mood than the only porticoed church façade actually erected by Palladio, that of his Tempietto at Maser, as befits the Venetian headquarters of an important Counter Reformation religious order.

It is important to remember that Palladio's heritage, like that of Sansovino, had become an integral part of Venetian architectural tradition. A Palladian revival in Venice had no need of the backing of learned researches like those carried out by Inigo Jones and Lord Burlington, for the buildings were always at hand as an inspiration for architects. As mentioned, Tirali and Rossi were both almost illiterate, and certainly had no understanding of the theoretical concepts of harmony and proportion contained in Palladio's *Quattro libri*. Their dependence on Palladian prototypes was probably hardly conscious, and certainly did not constitute a deliberate 'revival'. They were simply responding to a growing taste in Venice for a more sober, classical architectural style, and Palladio's buildings were the most obvious, most easily accessible source of ideas in this vein.

Scalfarotto and Massari

As the eighteenth century advanced, architecture began to reflect the growing contradictions inherent in a society on the brink of collapse. It was as if the sober style of the buildings could ill conceal the shallowness and frivolity of the life which they sheltered. The schizophrenic mood of the century is already evident in the parish church of San Simeon Piccolo, rebuilt between 1718 and 1738 (*Fig. 106*). This building is the masterwork of Giovanni Scal-

BELOW
105 San Nicolò da Tolentino, façade by Andrea Tirali, begun 1706 (*A.F.Kersting*)

BELOW, RIGHT
106 San Simeon Piccolo, by Giovanni Scalfarotto, begun 1718 (*A.F.Kersting*)

farotto (c.1670–1764), who was the son in law of Domenico Rossi and uncle of Tomaso Temanza.[9] Inspired by Tirali's newly finished classical portico at the nearby church of San Nicolò, he turned to a true classical prototype, the Pantheon in Rome. There is no evidence that Scalfarotto ever visited Rome himself, and certainly he captured little of the Pantheon's imposing solidity and massiveness. Like Palladio in his Tempietto at Maser, he revived the theme on a diminutive scale, thus disguising the seriousness of his intentions. The proportions, too, are transformed, with the soaring dome more closely related to Longhena's Santa Maria della Salute (*Fig. 93*) at the opposite end of the Grand Canal than to the Pantheon. The brightly lit interior is also a reduced version of the Pantheon, with its pedimented aedicules and its distinctive shallow recesses each containing free-standing columns supporting a straight architrave. However, despite the imposing effect of the huge *all'antica* Corinthian capitals, echoing those of the portico, the mood is light and elegant, and the whole conception is infused with a certain Rococo charm.

By far the most talented Venetian architect of the period was Giorgio Massari, who was born in the parish of San Luca in 1687.[10] He died in Venice in 1766. More than any of his rivals, he succumbed to the influence of Rococo taste, but he absorbed its elements into his architecture with such delicacy and sureness of touch that his style never degenerated into fussy frivolity. Like his great contemporary Giambattista Tiepolo, with whom he collaborated on several occasions, he seems to have accepted the traditional values of Venetian society and culture, ignoring its more degenerate side. In a sense he resolved the contradictions inherent in his background by absorbing both its sober and its lighthearted aspects, without consciously attempting to suppress either tendency.

Massari worked extensively on the Terraferma as well as in Venice. His first Venetian masterpiece was the church of the Gesuati, begun in 1726 and consecrated ten years later (*Fig. 107*). The minor religious order of the Gesuati had been suppressed in 1668, and its buildings taken over by the Dominicans, who decided to rebuild the church and monastery for their own use.

Massari's scheme for the Gesuati was based on the more modest Oratorian church of Santa Maria della Fava, begun by Antonio Gaspari in 1705 and completed by Massari himself. From this church he borrowed the rectangular plan with cut-off corners, and the triumphal-arch rhythm of the nave elevation, its giant order arranged in pairs enclosing niche statues and relief panels, a system deriving originally from Palladio's church of the Redentore on the opposite side of the Giudecca canal (*Figs. 108 & 91*). The single nave, interconnected side chapels, and choir concealed behind the high altar also follow the arrangement of the Redentore. Just as Longhena at the Salute had risen to the challenge of siting his church with Palladio's two masterpieces, San Giorgio and the Redentore, in full view, so Massari had to respect these Palladian precedents in his design for the Gesuati. Like Longhena he borrowed from the Redentore the motif of the domed chancel flanked by twin bell towers, but the more pointed dome and the onion-shaped *cupole* of the little turrets betray the eighteenth-century context. The façade, too, is a tribute to

ABOVE
107 Santa Maria del Rosario, called the Gesuati, by Giorgio Massari, begun 1726 *(A.F.Kersting)*

ABOVE, RIGHT
108 Gesuati, interior *(A.F.Kersting)*

Palladio, with its four giant Corinthian half columns supporting a great triangular pediment, but unlike Sardi's San Lazzaro and Rossi's San Stae, which adopted the same simplified Palladian scheme, there are no Baroque legacies – no broken pediments, no crowning statues. Here, instead, the characteristic sobriety of eighteenth-century Venetian exteriors prevails.

The interior of the Gesuati is a fine blend of classical and Rococo elements (*Fig. 108*). The giant Corinthian half columns, echoing those of the façade, replace the flat pilasters of the interior of Gaspari's Santa Maria della Fava, to give a greater monumentality. But in the ceiling, where delicate, curving Rococo frames, designed by Massari himself, surround Tiepolo's fresco decorations, the solidity evaporates into a still lucid daintiness. It is significant that the paintings in no sense conflict with the architecture nor undermine the essential architectonic structure by means of the illusionistic devices which Tiepolo so often enjoyed. The slender ribs of the ceiling vault continue the verticals of the wall elevation; and the bright, even lighting, once again recalling Palladio's Venetian churches, enhances the clarity of the design.

The stylistic unity of the Gesuati, where the architecture, sculpture and painted decoration were all completed within a few decades, also characterizes the church which Massari erected for the foundling hospital of Venice, the Ospedale della Pietà. Established in 1346, this was the oldest of the four big State hospitals, and by the eighteenth century its ancient buildings were in a shameful state of repair. Like the other three hospitals the Pietà was famous for its choir of orphan girls, who also had a high reputation for instrumental playing. Many of Vivaldi's finest *concerti* and choral works were written for the Pietà. But the hospital was becoming conscious of the deficiencies of the shabby setting in which the musicians had to perform, especially since its rivals, the Incurabili, the Mendicanti and Ospedaletto, all had the advantage of newer churches erected by celebrated architects.

In 1736 Massari won a competition for the design of the new church and orphanage of the Pietà, the two other entrants in the competition being the aged Tirali and an amateur architect and geometry teacher called Padre Pietro Foresti. Massari's design survives in a drawing in the Museo Correr (*Fig. 109*). In the event the hospital buildings were never erected, despite the fact that part of the old orphanage had been demolished to make way for the new church and its inmates lodged with Venetian families. The church itself was begun in 1745 and completed in 1760, although the façade was not built until the early twentieth century.

Defending himself against his most fervent rationalist critic, the Franciscan friar, Carlo Lodoli, Massari admitted that he had tried to base his design on established Venetian traditions, because he believed this would be more acceptable to the public than a totally revolutionary conception. The rectangular plan with rounded corners, the four nave altars, and the separate raised chancel, are derived from Sansovino's Incurabili church, though Massari chose a low vault in place of Sansovino's flat wooden ceiling (*pages 160 & 202*). Like Scamozzi at the Mendicanti he added an entrance vestibule, similar in shape to the choir of the Gesuati, to prevent street noise from disturbing the concerts (*p. 175*). As in the Gesuati, Massari used a paired order to articulate the nave, but in this case the huge half columns are replaced by a small pilaster order, to emphasize the simplicity of the oval space (*Fig. 110*). Once again, Massari himself designed all the details of the interior decoration, including the pretty Rococo pulpit and confession boxes and the wrought iron screens of the raised choir galleries. But here, too, the integrity of the architecture is strictly

109 Massari's design for the new church and hospital of the Pietà, 1736. *Museo Correr, Venice*

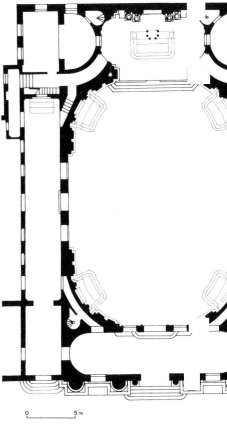

ABOVE
110 Santa Maria della Pietà, by Massari, begun 1745; interior (*A.F.Kersting*)

ABOVE, RIGHT
Santa Maria della Pietà, plan. After A.Massari

preserved. The ceiling frescoes, again executed by Giambattista Tiepolo, are contained in simple compartments, the great central oval reflecting the groundplan of the nave.

That the style of the interior of the Pietà is more restrained than that of the Gesuati in part arises from the more modest circumstances, for the State hospitals could not expect the wealth enjoyed by the Dominican order. However, there is no doubt that the desire to impress was one of the principal aims of the Pietà in rebuilding their church. The contemporary records speak of the church as if it were a concert hall, while its religious function fades into the background. A huge sum of money was spent on widening the Riva in front of the hospital to create a grander prospect, yet the more urgent project, the new orphanage, was put aside for lack of funds. The sobriety of the Pietà interior therefore suggests that, despite his overt dependance on older traditions and his enjoyment of fine decorative detail, Massari himself was responding to the ever-increasing desire for a more severe style of architecture in mid-eighteenth century Venice.

Massari's most important secular work was the huge palace which he built for the Grassi family on the Grand Canal at San Samuele[11] (*Fig. 111*). Such commissions were by this time extremely rare, for few Venetian families now had the resources with which to build fine palaces. The Grassi, originating from Chioggia, were very recent members of the Venetian patriciate – they had

been admitted to the nobility as late as 1718. In this palace, begun in 1748, Massari again showed his respect for older traditions. Like Rossi in the Palazzo Corner della Regina, he based the façade on Sansovino's Palazzo Corner at San Maurizio, reducing the scheme to its simplest elements. However, with a broader site at his disposal Massari was able to avoid the cramped proportions of the façade of the Palazzo Corner della Regina. Like Rossi, too, Massari felt himself challenged by the example of Longhena, whose Ca' Rezzonico stood on the opposite bank of the Grand Canal. In the interior he borrowed Rossi's idea of the colonnaded atrium, while the imposing double staircase must be inspired by Longhena's monumental staircase in the monastery of San Giorgio Maggiore. The plan is not typical of Venetian palaces, but is more characteristic of Terraferma architecture with its courtyard in the centre of the block, the position favoured by Sansovino but otherwise rarely found in the city. The court is completely surrounded by a portico of severe Doric columns supporting a straight architrave, its frieze decorated only by trighyphs and panels of coloured marble (*Fig. 112*). The austerity contrasts sharply with the pretty Rococo decorations of the interior of the palace. Intended to imitate the private houses of Antiquity, the courtyard is the most classical feature which Massari ever introduced in his work, and indicates that although committed Neoclassicists disapproved of his Rococo leanings, he went far towards satisfying their demands at the end of his life.

111 Palazzo Grassi, by Massari, begun 1748 (*A.F.Kersting*)

Visentini and Temanza

In comparison with Massari, the architectural output of Antonio Visentini (1688–1782) was fairly insignificant, although he had great influence.[12] He was trained as a painter in the studio of Pellegrini and was also a proficient engraver. Nowadays he is chiefly remembered for his engravings after Canaletto's views of the Grand Canal and his book of illustrations of the islands of the Venetian lagoon, the *Isolario Veneto*. His only important building was the small palace on the Grand Canal which he designed for the English connoisseur and collector, Consul Joseph Smith, the famous patron of Canaletto (*Fig. 113*). The façade of Smith's palace, which was completed in 1751, was greatly admired at the time, but it is not a memorable composition. Its sober classical elements are combined in a somewhat awkward manner, giving a crowded effect in the elevation of the *piano nobile*. (The top floor was added later by Visentini's most successful pupil, Giannantonio Selva.)

The chief contribution of Visentini to Venetian architecture was a didactic one. He was a founder member of the Accademia di Belle Arti, where he taught 'architettura prospettica' from 1761 to 1778. He was the author of numerous theoretical works on architecture, most of which exist only in manuscript, but which give some account of the ideas which he propagated. His approach was dogmatic, pedantic and strictly classical. His criticisms were

OPPOSITE

112 Palazzo Grassi, courtyard *(A.F.Kersting)*

113 Palazzo Civran, built for Consul Joseph Smith by Antonio Visentini, completed 1751 *(Sarah Quill)*

vehement – he disapproved of Piranesi for his *capriccio* element, of Massari for his Rococo tendencies, of Rusconi for his misinterpretations of Vitruvius, and of Andrea Pozzo for corrupting the taste of young architects. His admiration was chiefly reserved for Palladio and the ruins of Antiquity, including the works of the Ancient Greeks which were finally becoming known in Venice through the publications of the English authors, Stuart and Revett and Robert Wood. Ironically, despite his rigid views, Visentini himself never succeeded in discarding a fanciful, decorative element (inherited from Pellegrini) in the frames and frontispieces of his engravings, though unlike Massari he would not have admitted the fact. Once again we are reminded of the contradictory forces at work in Venetian culture of the time.

Tomaso Temanza (1705–89) is a significant figure in the history of Venetian architecture, though like Visentini his importance lies more in his writings and teachings than in his work as a practising architect. His scholarly, authoritative book, the *Vite dei più celebri architetti e scultori veneziani*, published in 1778, is probably his greatest personal achievement. This work, modelled on Vasari's *Lives of the Artists*, is an indispensable source for students of Venetian architecture or sculpture. Like Visentini he was also a stimulating teacher of architectural students at the Accademia, taking a special interest in his most talented pupil Giannantonio Selva.

Temanza began his architectural career in the studio of his uncle Giovanni Scalfarotto, and like many other native Venetian architects before him he spent most of his life in Venice itself. His technical knowledge appears to have been sound; he was, for example, the architect consulted over the restoration of Sansovino's Fabbriche Nuove di Rialto.[13] The only two buildings worthy of note which he himself erected in the city are the church of the Maddalena, much loved by Venetians especially as a setting for weddings, and a gardener's house behind the Palazzo Zenobio at the Carmini.

The Maddalena is a small, circular, domed church situated on one of the prettiest *campi* in the city (*Fig. 114*). Like his uncle's design for San Simeon Piccolo this church is evidently inspired by the Pantheon, which Temanza himself never saw in person. Here the restricted site did not allow space for a free-standing portico, and instead the pediment over the entrance is supported by four Ionic half columns. The Ionic order, with its feminine connotations, was obviously suitable for a church dedicated to Mary Magdalene, but Temanza chose the plainest possible architectural elements. The effect of austerity contrasts sharply with the richness of the Corinthian porticoes of San Simeon Piccolo and San Nicolò da Tolentino (*Figs. 105 & 106*). The interior is boldly articulated by pairs of three-quarter columns enclosing niches. Like San Simeon Piccolo, the Maddalena has a domed chancel with apsed ends. The four nave altars are set in deep rectangular niches, as if to emphasize the thickness of the walls.

The same paring down of architectural detail, which was to be one of the principal qualities of full-blown Neoclassicism, is also apparent in the little gardener's house (*Fig. 115*). This was not as modest a commission as one might imagine, for the Zenobio family, nobles since the mid-seventeenth century,

were said to be the richest in the city. They were enlightened and enthusiastic patrons, and their palace was decorated by the finest painters of the day. Nevertheless, Temanza's garden pavilion is visually far less satisfying than the Maddalena. The large blank expanse of wall of the upper storey, articulated only by slim Corinthian pilasters, rises unhappily above the projecting loggia below. With its four Ionic columns and unusually designed balustrade, the loggia is more elegant, but the overall composition remains somewhat awkward. The large piers on either side of the loggia have no order whatever, showing that Temanza was responding to the new interest in functional rather than decorative architecture.

Giannantonio Selva

The introspective, almost inbred character of Venetian architectural activity in the seventeenth and eighteenth centuries seems curious when one considers that Venice was one of the great tourist centres of Europe, a city where encounters with foreigners must have been a daily occurrence. While painters and musicians travelled widely, architects showed little inclination to expand their horizons beyond Venice and the Veneto. A rare exception was Piranesi, who was trained as an architect in Venice and who travelled to Rome in 1744, but once there he soon gave up architecture to become an engraver.

The first Venetian architect proper since the time of Palladio to study intensively outside the Veneto was Giannantonio Selva (1751–1819), who brought Neoclassical architecture in the city to fruition at the end of the eighteenth century.[14] His father, the State optician of Venice and a well known maker of optical instruments, enthusiastically supported his son's career as an architect and financed his travels abroad, being content to place his two other sons in the family business. At first Giannantonio studied architecture at the Venetian Academy where his teachers included Visentini and Temanza. In 1778 he set off for Rome where he studied for three years. Throughout this time Temanza kept up an affectionate correspondence with his pupil, but undoubtedly the greatest influence on the young architect came from the group of artists of various nationalities then working or studying in Rome. He formed a close friendship with his compatriot Canova and also became a friend of Quarenghi, the architect who later made his career in Russia. After his stay in Rome, Selva travelled widely around Europe, visiting France, England, Holland and Vienna before he finally returned to settle once more in Venice.

This was the period in which the great *risorgimento* of the arts, which we now call the Neoclassical movement (the name applied to it in the mid-nineteenth century) united artists throughout Europe in a joint quest for a new, rational, austere style purged of Rococo frivolity and prettiness.[15] Although artistic ideas were diffused rapidly across state boundaries over much of Western Europe, the Venetian Republic held out as long as possible against the influx of new, enlightened ideas, which it resisted by means of censorship and the State Inquisition. Despite the city's insularity, one of Europe's most radical thinkers on architecture in the first half of the eighteenth century had been a Venetian, the Franciscan monk Padre Carlo Lodoli.[16] As a young man Lodoli travelled to Rome and other parts of Italy, before returning to Venice in 1720 to open a private school. There he taught the most modern scientific and philosophical ideas and influenced a whole generation of young Venetian patricians. The Republic was somewhat suspicious of his activities, although he was later accepted and even appointed chief Censor. He was a regular visitor at the house of Visentini's patron, the English Consul Joseph Smith, which was one of the few places in Venice where new and unorthodox ideas were freely discussed. As far as we can judge from contemporary accounts of his ideas, Lodoli's views on architecture were radical in the extreme. He rejected any kind of decoration that was not strictly functional, even daring to criticize such venerated models as the architecture of antiquity and that of Palladio. At a time when a sober neo-Palladian style was becoming established in Venice his ideas were too extreme to gain wide acceptance, but as the century advanced it became more and more difficult for Venice to insulate herself against radical currents from outside. By 1787, when Lodoli's former pupil, the Venetian noble Andrea Memmo, published his *Elementi dell'architettura lodoliana*, at last presenting the public with a reasonably accurate version of his master's views, the Venetian intelligentsia was ready to understand and even to accept some of these innovatory doctrines. It was in this more open-minded climate of ideas that Selva began his architectural career. The international *risorgimento* of the arts was at last beginning to penetrate the conservative Venetian mentality.

In the atmosphere of political ferment which pervaded Europe in the late eighteenth century this artistic quest gathered momentum rapidly, although its precise links with ideas in the political spectrum are extremely hard to define. The huge scale on which many Neoclassical architects conceived their grandiose ideas meant that they depended on the wealthiest, most powerful patrons to implement their designs, and thus could not ally themselves easily with the cause of popular, or even bourgeois, revolution. Selva's first important work, the new Fenice Theatre in Venice, provides a fascinating illustration of the complexity of the relationship between art and politics at the end of the century.[17] In retrospect this would appear to have been a highly unpropitious time for the founding of a great new theatre, but in the event all the obstacles facing this ambitious project were overcome with astonishing ease and rapidity.

According to the city's sumptuary laws, the Republic had restricted the number of theatres in Venice to seven. One of these was the theatre of San Benedetto which was leased by a group of wealthy nobles and citizens known as the Nobile Società. In 1787, finding themselves obliged to give up possession of the San Benedetto theatre, the Società resolved to found a new one to rival the greatest opera houses of Europe. It is an indication of their power and influence in the city that within only a few months the Senate had granted permission for the erection of an eighth theatre 'to add to the beauty and dignity of the Dominion.' A sizeable if irregular site in the centre of the city, near the church of San Fantin, was purchased, and in 1789, at the very climax of the French Revolution, the Società invited architects to submit designs for the new theatre, clearly oblivious of the far-reaching implications of the political upheavals in France.

Four projects were short listed, two by Venetian architects and two by outsiders. Eventually the design of Giannantonio Selva was selected, to the intense annoyance of his Venetian rival, Pietro Bianchi, who vigorously contested the decision, claiming that only his own design satisfied all the requirements set out in the original brief. After months of wrangling a compromise was reached by which Bianchi was awarded the prize of 300 sequins, while Selva's design was the one actually adopted. Despite its élitist patronage the new theatre aroused great popular interest, evidently fired by this colourful dispute. Bianchi, son of a gondolier poet, certainly did not lack popular support, although in the end Selva's theatre itself became a focus of civic pride for the Venetian people.

The scheme was, of necessity, an elaborate one, involving the demolition of existing buildings on the site, the excavation of a canal to provide access for theatregoers arriving by boat, and the laying of foundations capable of supporting the huge structure. Yet the whole project, including the decoration of the interior, was completed within a mere twenty-seven months. The theatre opened on 16 May 1792 with an opera by the Neapolitan composer, Paisiello, only five years before the Fall of the Venetian Republic. The cost, which amounted to over 400,000 ducats, was met by the members of the Nobile Società, each one making a contribution proportional to the value of his own box in the new theatre. Although the financial state of the Republic was by this time extremely precarious, and numerous noble families

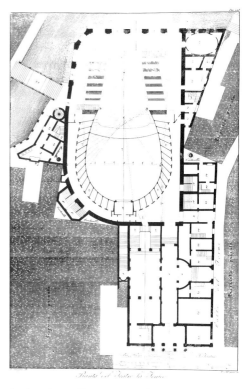

ABOVE
116 Teatro la Fenice, by
Giannantonio Selva,
begun 1790, façade
(A.F.Kersting)

ABOVE, RIGHT
Teatro la Fenice, plan

were impoverished, a select few obviously still commanded considerable wealth. It is typical of the eighteenth-century Venetian order of priorities that they should have chosen to devote such a large sum to the building of an opera house, as if refusing to recognize the insecurity of their position.

Selva's original design was substantially altered during the nineteenth-century modifications to the interior, but the two principal façades, one facing Campo San Fantin, the other overlooking the new canal at the back, are virtually unchanged. It is indicative of the changing artistic climate of the city that even the Nobile Società, which was effectively an organ of the Establishment, preferred Selva's innovative project to Bianchi's more conservative design, which was a variation on the theme of Palladio's Basilica in Vicenza. Selva's writings stress his admiration for the architects of sixteenth-century Venice – Sansovino, Sanmicheli, Palladio and Scamozzi – but in his own work he drew on a far wider range of ideas. Like other more avant-garde Venetians of this time he felt a particularly strong sympathy with English culture; he owned a volume of drawings by Inigo Jones and was enthusiastic about the work of Robert Adam. Neoclassical architects of his generation in Rome were learning to select only the most sober and dignified ideas from the works of the ancients, and evidently Selva, too, carried out his studies of Roman antiquities with discrimination. In common with many of his contemporaries elsewhere in Europe he was also a great admirer of ancient Greek architecture which, in spite of centuries of trade with the Byzantine Empire and Venetian colonization in the Eastern Mediterranean, had never before had a direct influence on the architecture of the city.

210

In the exterior of the Fenice we see evidence of his search for a new, severe idiom suited to the seriousness and moral conviction which projected the Neoclassical movement (*Fig. 116*). As we have seen, the reaction against the Baroque had begun long before in Venice, but it was Selva who finally cast off the superficial trimmings of the Rococo and freed himself from Palladio's powerful example. The façade on Campo San Fantin, which leads into the main foyer and ante rooms of the theatre, has the restraint and stately bearing which characterize the best of Neoclassical architecture. Here, more than at any stage in Venetian architecture since the Gothic period, the flat wall surface plays an expressive part in the design. No attempt is made to mask the weight-bearing walls behind a veneer of classical columns or pilasters and sculptural decoration. The decorative elements are confined to the central section. In the upper part statues of Music and Dance are surmounted by masks representing Tragedy and Comedy, the main divisions of the antique theatre. A relief of a phoenix, the emblem of the new theatre, fills the lunette over the central window, while the panel above states simply SOCIETAS MDCCXCII, commemorating the Nobile Società and the date of completion of the theatre. The projecting Corinthian portico below adds grandeur to the main entrance, raised on a flight of steps, and gives an emphatic third dimension to the façade at its climax. Elsewhere decoration is reduced to a bare minimum, the pilasters at either end having neither bases nor capitals. Selva's teacher, Temanza, had already used this simplified pilaster order in his Loggia Zenobio, which also prefigured the central projecting portico and flat upper wall surface; but the effectiveness of the earlier design was reduced by its distracting details and awkward balance of forms. At the rear of the Fenice a simple rusticated waterfront arcade, surmounted by a plain upper wall articulated only by a

117　Teatro la Fenice, auditorium, by Selva, rebuilt with modifications after the fire of 1836 (*A.F.Kersting*)

rudimentary Doric frieze and pierced by three plain pedimented windows, encloses the great stage of the theatre. Distinguished visitors arriving by boat were deposited at a side entrance beside the slender staircase turret. The bareness of the Fenice exteriors would certainly have made a deep impression on Venetian artistic sensibilities, long attuned to theatrical, heavily encrusted Istrian-stone façades. Some conservative critics objected to Selva's unconventional use of classical language, but in general Venetian taste was now ready for innovation and change.

In the interior, the horseshoe-shaped auditorium was widely appreciated, for it not only created a grand, imposing space but also allowed most of the spectators to see and hear easily (*p. 210*). Selva claimed to have borrowed this form from the Teatro Argentina in Rome, although much closer at hand Maccaruzzi's Teatro Balbi in Mestre, built some ten years before, had a similar plan. The original appearance of the auditorium is now known only from Selva's groundplan and from written accounts. However, we can assume that with its elaborate painted decoration it did not echo the austerity of the façades, repeating yet again the contrast between exterior and interior that had characterized so many eighteenth-century Venetian buildings.

The first really successful production to be staged at the new theatre was Cimarosa's opera *Gli Orazi e i Curiazi* early in 1797, on the eve of the Fall of the Republic. The collapse of the Venetian *ancien régime*, which was to lead to far-reaching changes in the appearance of the whole city, actually disrupted the activities of the Fenice remarkably little. The Nobile Società survived the upheavals, though threatened by serious economic difficulties; and when Napoleon visited the city in 1807 Selva himself was employed to convert six of the central boxes into a single, grand Imperial Box. Operas by such composers as Rossini, Bellini, and Donizetti assured the theatre of survival, until in 1836 a disastrous fire destroyed a large section of the building. The theatre lived up to its emblem, the Phoenix, and was completely restored in the following year. Selva's interior was changed in a number of respects and the whole theatre was redecorated in a florid, late Empire style (*Fig. 117*). The chief alteration to the fabric was the diversion to the centre of the auditorium of the main entrance from the ante rooms, which Selva had placed at one side because of the peculiar shape of the theatre's site. Further modernizations followed in 1854 and 1878, while a succession of operas by Verdi and later Wagner and Puccini (to name only a few) sustained the artistic life of the opera house. The masterpieces actually commissioned by the Fenice included Verdi's *Rigoletto*, *La Traviata* and *Simon Boccanegra* – as well as *Attila*, of course! (Paradoxically *I Due Foscari*, which is so quintessentially Venetian, was first performed in Rome.)

Like the fortunes of his theatre, Selva's own career as an architect was little disrupted by the Fall of the Republic; but since, like all Neoclassical architects, he depended chiefly on public patronage to implement his monumental ideas, the rest of his activity is best considered in the context of the very different political situation of the early nineteenth century.

CHAPTER IX

Venice since the Fall of the Republic

The end of the Venetian Republic in 1797 was not a glorious event. Only a few gestures of opposition hindered the Napoleonic troops as they overran the Veneto. In Verona the people staged a brave resistance, which became known as the *Pasque Veronesi* because it took place at Easter. Later, at the entrance to the Venetian lagoon, an invading French schooner, the 'Libérateur', was bombarded and captured by a Venetian ship. But by 30 April French guns on the mainland were audible in the Palazzo Ducale as the last Duke of Venice, Ludovico Manin, conferred with his advisors. On the following day, 1100 years after the appointment of the first Doge, the Republic simply voted itself out of existence, when the Maggior Consiglio agreed to Napoleon's request for a change in the constitution by the overwhelming majority of 598 votes to 74.

Napoleon had shrewdly taken advantage of the nascent spirit of revolution in Italy, and this made the Venetian nobility all the more aware that their élitist government had no future. The aristocracy were declining in wealth and numbers. They had managed to remain in office so long, thanks only to a policy of strict political censorship, aided by the innate conservatism of the Venetian people. Realizing that the charade had to end, they merely wished the termination to be as painless as possible. Ironically, it was the ordinary people of Venice who protested against this submission, but their cries of *Viva San Marco!* were ineffectual.

In the event, the new municipal democracy instituted by the French troops was short-lived. At the Treaty of Campoformio in October 1797 most of the Veneto was handed over to Austria. This first phase of Austrian domination lasted until 1805. In that year Napoleon, spurred on by his brilliant victories at Vienna and Austerlitz, took over the Veneto as part of his new Kingdom of Italy. By this time he had abandoned any pretence of democratic government. In the previous year he had declared himself Emperor of France, and his new administration in Italy was unashamedly regal. In 1807 he made a triumphal entry into the city of Venice to pay a ten day visit.

The Napoleonic Kingdom (1805–14)

The period of Napoleonic rule was one of great political, social and economic upheaval in Venice. Despite the poverty of some members of the nobility, the Venetian economy as a whole had not declined too seriously during the eighteenth century. Manufacturing industry, shipping and overseas trade were all still profitable, and the long period of peace from 1718 to 1797 did not necessitate huge outlays on warfaring.[1] But after the Fall of the Republic the economy collapsed. Major commercial ventures were unthinkable in the atmosphere of uncertainty and political turmoil. More than 100 merchant ships were broken up, and many prosperous Venetian families were ruined. Trade slumped as the domination of Adriatic shipping passed to Trieste. The monetary system was put in chaos and the land market crashed, allowing numerous Venetian palaces to fall into foreign hands. The social order of the city was turned upside down, leading to a dramatic fall in population. Parish boundaries were altered, with flagrant disregard for their great antiquity. Smaller parishes were amalgamated, and some of the more prominent monastic churches, such as the Frari and San Francesco della Vigna, were converted into parish churches. The religious orders and *scuole* were ruthlessly suppressed, and their property seized and redistributed. Many of their finest works of art were sold or removed to France, while monastic churches were demolished or put to use as warehouses, mills, or ammunition dumps.[2]

These iconoclastic aspects of the Napoleonic administration in Venice are well known. It is perhaps less often realized that they went hand in hand with policies of a more constructive and enlightened kind, intended to improve the urban environment of the city, though these, too, were implemented with little sensitivity. By its very nature Venice was ill-adapted to the ideals of Neoclassical city planning fostered in Napoleon's dominions. There was far too little space on the archipelago for broad, straight avenues and imposing public monuments. By no stretch of the imagination could Venice be made to resemble Paris or Milan. Of course, these ideals were not all ill-conceived. Badly needed improvements to street lighting and fire fighting equipment, repairs to streets, bridges and *fondamenta* (waterfronts), and the dredging of canals were all given high priority. It was also resolved to spend at least 100,000 *lire* annually on modernizing the port facilities.

The plans for improving the appearance of Venice were formulated by a body called the Commissione all'Ornato. It was the Venetian architect Giannantonio Selva who emerged as the moving spirit behind these ambitious policies.[3] At last he had the opportunity to realize some of his more grandiose Neoclassical ideas. His overall plan for Venice is lost, but his design for the new gardens at Castello gives some sense of his bold, uncompromising approach. A broad, straight, new highway, the Via Eugenia, called after the Viceroy (now renamed the Via Garibaldi), was made by covering over the Rio di Sant'Anna, in order to create a grander approach to San Pietro di Castello. Selva's elaborate formal gardens, which led off the new street, occupied the site of several convents and monasteries, which were obliterated. Although Selva himself was dismayed by Napoleonic demolitions of Renaissance monuments in the city, he offered no protest at the destruction of the mediaeval heritage, for the Byzantine and Gothic styles were so alien to his Neoclassical taste. The Giardini at Castello, now the home of the Venetian Biennale exhibitions, have been much altered since Selva's time. However, their original appearance is known from nineteenth-century maps, which

show a complex arrangement of long, stately avenues and more intimate *ronds points*.

It is hardly surprising that so vigorous and uncompromising a new régime should have wished to make its imprint on Piazza San Marco. The whole Piazza was a symbol of the power of the Serenissima. Its traditions and its ideology were documented, directly or indirectly, in every building, every stone carving and every mosaic. But the Doge of Venice had never been a monarch; and no Doge – or indeed any other Venetian – had ever been commemorated on a public monument in the Piazza. Naturally, the Napoleonic government felt the need to give a more regal air to the city centre; and this was done with a predictable sureness of aim and characteristic disregard for the artistic heritage of the Venetian Republic.[4]

The Procuratie Nuove on the south side of the Piazza were speedily converted into the new royal palace. As well as the rearrangement and redecoration of the rooms, this conversion also led to the destruction in 1807 of the historic granaries on the south side, on the quayside site known as the Terra Nova. This huge crenellated brick building was demolished because it obstructed the view of the lagoon from the royal apartments. Its massive form had for centuries been an imposing landmark in the view of Venice from the Bacino, and the pretty walled garden which replaced it did little to fill the gaping void on the waterfront, nor to improve the amenities of the city, for it was reserved for residents of the palace (*p. 148*).

The chief deficiency of the new royal palace was considered to be the absence of a grand ballroom for imperial receptions. Eventually it was decided to locate the ballroom in a new wing to be built on the west side of Piazza San Marco, facing the Basilica. This involved what was perhaps the most notorious of all Napoleonic demolitions in Venice; despite strong local opposition the existing buildings on the site – the church of San Geminiano, together with the adjoining sections of the Procuratie Nuove on one side and

118   Ala Napoleonica, Piazza San Marco, by Giovanni Maria Soli, begun 1808, and Procuratie Vecchie, by Bartolomeo Bon, begun 1513 *(Sarah Quill)*

the Procuratie Vecchie on the other – were razed in 1807. The façade of San Geminiano was Jacopo Sansovino's most conspicuous church façade, and Venetians still felt a sense of loyalty to the great sixteenth-century architect who had made so deep an imprint on the configuration of their city. Fortunately, when the church was demolished, the abbot Moschini managed to rescue the architect's remains and take them to the safety of the Somascan monastery at the Salute.[5]

Work on the new west wing of the Piazza started in 1808. This range of buildings, called the Ala Napoleonica, was designed by an architect from Modena, Giuseppe Maria Soli, who took over the project in 1810 (*Fig. 118*). It was largely completed by 1814, when a huge bronze 'N' was erected in the centre of the attic. The ballroom itself, reached by Soli's grand ceremonial staircase in the centre, was completed by the Sienese architect Lorenzo Santi after the return of the Austrians.

The Piazza elevation of the Ala Napoleonica was in some respects not insensitive. The two main storeys reproduced the forms of the repeatable bay system of Sansovino's Library, in order to harmonize the new wing with the rest of the buildings in the Piazza. The design was brought up to date by the addition of a high attic, needed to conceal the lofty vault of the ballroom. This was overtly Neoclassical in style, with its statues of Roman emperors and *all'antica* reliefs. What Santi failed to provide was a visual replacement for San Geminiano, that is to say, a strong central emphasis to serve as a foil for the great Basilica at the opposite end of the Piazza. The bronze 'N' obviously had to be hastily removed in 1815 – together with a colossal statue of Napoleon which had been erected in front of the Palazzo Ducale in 1813 – and without the Emperor's initial the western side of the Piazza was left without a focus.

The rebuilding of the nearby parish church of San Maurizio, modelling its interior on that of the demolished church of San Geminiano, did little to reconcile the city's inhabitants to their loss. San Maurizio, begun in 1806, was the work of Giannantonio Selva and the secretary of the Venetian Accademia, Antonio Diedo (*Fig. 119*). The façade of the new church makes no reference to that of San Geminiano, but is a sober Neoclassical demonstration piece. Its plain, rectangular wall surface, defined by a rudimentary serliana, is decorated only by two inset panels with relief carvings and by a simple pedimented door and window frames. The crowning pediment encloses a relief depicting the deaths of Saint Maurice and the soldiers of his Roman legion in Gaul, after refusing to take part in heathen sacrifices, a subject which was perfectly suited to the Neoclassical liking for stoical stories in antique settings.

Selva left few other traces of his creative activity in Venice. His dignified design for the new cemetery on the island of San Michele – the outcome of the new régime's desire to end the unhygienic practice of burial in the city itself – suffered from a pompous remodelling in the 1870s. And his scheme for a huge studio on the Zattere for his friend, the sculptor Antonio Canova, was never executed. A number of his drawings preserved in the Museo Correr record other bold and imaginative schemes which he produced in these years. But in general his conceptions were too ambitious to come to fruition during such a

short-lived reign. The eminence which he reached in Napoleon's eyes is clear from the fact that he was commissioned in 1813 to design an enormous monument to the Emperor to be built on Mont Cenis in France. This, too, came to nothing because of Napoleon's fall.[6]

The motive for erecting the colossal statue of Napoleon in the Piazza was ostensibly to commemorate the establishment of a free port on the island of San Giorgio, where goods could be traded without the burden of customs duties. The prosperity of Trieste, which had been a free port since the eighteenth century, was evidence of the advantages of tariff-free trading at this time. Although the statue of Napoleon was soon removed from Piazza San Marco, a more permanent mark was left on the island of San Giorgio itself. Improved harbour facilities and quayside buildings were provided, and the new status of the island was symbolized by two Istrian-stone lighthouse towers designed in 1813 by Selva's pupil Giuseppe Mezzani, himself a professor of architecture at the Venetian Accademia[7] (*Fig. 120*). These are perhaps the most attractive legacy of the Napoleonic period in Venice. Standing guard beside Palladio's church of San Giorgio Maggiore, the towers pay tribute to the earlier master, with their windows set into rusticated walls like those of Palladio's Villa Malcontenta. Even at the height of the Neoclassical period, Palladian ideas still played an important part in the teachings of the Venetian Accademia. However, the elegant simplicity of the open lanterns which surmount the two lighthouses bear the stamp of Neoclassicism.

ABOVE, LEFT
119 San Maurizio, by Selva and Antonio Diedo, begun 1806 (*A.F.Kersting*)

ABOVE
120 Lighthouse tower at San Giorgio Maggiore, by Giuseppe Mezzani, designed 1813 (*A.F.Kersting*)

ABOVE, LEFT
121 Caffè Florian, Piazza San Marco, décor by Ludovico Cadorin, 1858 *(Sarah Quill)*

ABOVE, RIGHT
122 Corpo di Guardia, Arsenal, by Giovanni Casoni, designed 1829 *(Sarah Quill)*

Although Napoleon's Kingdom of Italy was short-lived, it established certain attitudes towards the architectural heritage of the city which were to survive through much of the nineteenth century. The most significant of these were a continuing readiness to demolish historic buildings and a bold policy of modernization. The Neoclassical movement, which had formulated an idiom so well-suited to Napoleonic ideals, had provided the style adopted by the Establishment. As the chief propagator of Neoclassicism, the Venetian Accademia di Belle Arti was given full recognition, and in 1807 Giannantonio Selva was given the task of converting the former Scuola and monastery of the Carità into their new premises. Meanwhile, a new organizational framework for local government in the city was founded to replace the Republic's numerous magistracies. Thus the Kingdom of Italy not only bequeathed its policies, but also the administrative machinery with which to implement them.

The second and third periods of Austrian rule (1814–48 and 1849–66)

With the return of the Austrians a period of recession and economic hardship set in. A trade blockade in 1813–14 had only aggravated the already precarious financial situation. The cumbersome bureaucracy established during the Napoleonic period proved incapable of tackling the huge social problems caused by the economic decline – poverty, infant mortality and unemployment. The changing social conditions in the city are reflected in the fact that the number of people in domestic service fell by as much as 90% in the early nineteenth century. Heavy taxation penalized property owners so severely that many palaces and houses were demolished, simply because their owners could not afford to maintain them. The Commissione all'Ornato lamented the decay in the fabric of the city, but had few powers to remedy the situation.[8]

Eventually, however, trade began to make a partial recovery. In 1830 the whole city was granted the status of a free port, and a new class of rich Venetians began to grow up, consisting of the more enterprising members of the *borghesia*. Nevertheless, for the Austrians Trieste remained the principal Adriatic seaport. Venice was valued more for her strategic and military importance than as a major commercial outlet for the huge Hapsburg Empire. To strengthen the city's defences, the lagoon fortifications were modernized and extended. The Arsenal, no longer important for the construction of merchant ships and galleons, became the chief headquarters of the Austrian armed forces. The severe Neoclassical portico of the Corpo di Guardia, designed in 1829 by the engineer Giovanni Casoni, is a potent visual reminder of the Austrian presence in the Arsenal[9] (*Fig. 122*). The baseless Doric order, drawing its inspiration from Greece rather than Rome, reflects the archaeological interests of the scholarly Casoni. The Greek Doric order, one of the favourite themes of Neoclassical architects throughout Europe, is here reduced to its most basic geometric shapes. Such severity – appropriate to the original function of the building (but perhaps less so now that the building has been converted into a cinema!) – was not to be seen again in Venetian architecture until the Age of Fascism.

As part of the Austrian Empire Venice was effectively under occupation. Even the office of Patriarch became a Hapsburg appointment. Although Austrian influence can still be detected in the city today, particularly in the wares of the *pasticcerie*, the Venetian people maintained a separate identity throughout the period of Hapsburg domination. While Austrian officers frequented the Caffè Quadri on the north side of the Piazza San Marco, Venetians remained loyal to the rival Caffè Florian on the opposite side. Florian's provided an *ambiente* which felt intimate, old fashioned, and above all, utterly Venetian (*Fig. 121*). This atmosphere was reinforced by the present décor, the work of the architect Lodovico Cadorin, which dates from 1858.[10] The style is ostentatiously eighteenth-century, though with richer, more sombre colours. It was at Florian's that Daniele Manin's revolutionary government was formed during the night following the dramatic overthrow of the Austrians on 22 March 1848. This new democratic Venetian Republic lasted until August 1849. The Venetians defended their liberty to the bitter end with extraordinary tenacity and courage, but they did not have the military strength to resist indefinitely.[11]

Unlike her rival, Trieste, Venice did not acquire a 'Viennese' style of architecture during the years of Austrian occupation. State patronage was mainly confined to the building of bridges and streets, and private building was characterized by a stylistic reticence and artistic uncertainty. In this period of political and intellectual oppression there was little scope for creativity. The death of Selva in 1819 left an artistic vacuum which was hard to fill. The few imaginative buildings of the period, such as Lorenzo Santi's Patriarchal Palace

ABOVE
123 Coffee house in the
Giardini Reali, by
Lorenzo Santi, *c.*1838
(A.F.Kersting)

ABOVE, RIGHT
124 Rio Terà di
Sant'Agnese, canal filled
in in 1863 *(Sarah Quill)*

on the Piazzetta dei Leoncini to the north of the Basilica of San Marco, were isolated phenomena. The ability of Santi, Sienese by birth but trained in Rome, can also be seen in his delightful little white Istrian-stone coffee house on the corner of the new Giardini Reali [12] (*Fig. 123*). The idea of building a coffee house on this spot dates from the Napoleonic period, but the rhythmic lightness of the decoration of the executed building suggests a certain concession to Austrian sensibilities. This elegant garden pavilion is well-attuned to its recreational purpose. It has a festive character more reminiscent of a regatta flat than of, say, the earnest Neoclassicism of Casoni's Corpo di Guardia.

Despite the relatively subordinate position of Venice in Austrian eyes, the wheels of progress turned inexorably. The Napoleonic policies for improving the city's network of streets and canals were continued almost without interruption. [13] Streets were widened, bridges restored or rebuilt, and canals dredged. By 1843 gas street-lighting was in operation. A new development was the selling off of little-used public streets and courtyards to private buyers. Little by little, the ancient configuration of the city was being transformed. The simplest, cheapest method of creating new streets was the filling in of canals, and it was under Austrian rule that most of the city's *rii terà* were created. These 'land canals' are among the most attractive of the streets of Venice, being unusually wide, yet preserving ancient waterfront façades alongside. For example, the Rio Terà di Sant' Agnese, filled in in 1863, forms a broad thoroughfare between the Grand Canal and the Zattere, passing alongside the former Convento della Carità (*Fig. 124*). Gradually the Austrians were beginning to realize the need for a more constructive approach to local government in Venice, if the city which they had coveted for so long was not to become a picturesque ruin. Their new attitude manifested itself, for example, in the reopening of some de-consecrated churches and the restoration of others, and the building of a major new slaughterhouse at San Giobbe.[14]

In 1846 the city effectively lost its insular status, when the first railway bridge across the lagoon was opened, providing a direct rail link with Milan. Gustav Aschenbach in Thomas Mann's *Death in Venice* mused that 'to come to Venice by the station is like entering a palace by the back door.'[15] But every Venetian palace had to have both land and water entrances. Similarly, in the city as a whole, the advantages of direct land access were quickly realized. The commercial possibilities were enormous, and tourism, now one of the city's most profitable industries, was given a great boost. In 1860 a stretch of historic buildings on the Grand Canal, including the church of Santa Lucia from which the station derives its name, were ruthlessly demolished to make way for new terminal buildings.[16]

Perhaps the most striking visual legacy of the Austrian period is the magnificent series of iron bridges which they built in Venice. No less than 17 were erected between 1850 and 1870, most of these replacing existing wood or stone structures.[17] The two most impressive examples were the two new bridges across the Grand Canal, the Ponte dell'Accademia, built in 1854, and the Ponte degli Scalzi erected four years later. The Ponte dell'Accademia, designed by a gifted English bridge builder called Alfred Neville, was a brilliant feat of engineering, for the wide expanse of the Grand Canal was spanned by straight iron girders without vertical supports below or suspension from chains above. The Ponte degli Scalzi, near the new railway terminal, was modelled on Neville's bridge. The two iron bridges no longer exist, for both were rebuilt in 1933–34 by the Comune's civil engineer Eugenio Miozzi. The Ponte degli Scalzi was replaced by a stone bridge, and that of the Accademia by a temporary wooden structure which also still survives today. It is important to remember that before 1854 the Rialto was the only pedestrian crossing point on the whole length of the Grand Canal. Despite the loss of the two longest iron bridges, other smaller examples can be seen all over the city. For example, the Ponte di Ghetto Nuovo, one of the last iron bridges erected by the Austrians, shows the splendid wrought-iron-work railings which were such an attractive contribution to the Venetian urban scene (*Fig. 125*).

By the time that Venice was liberated from Austrian domination in 1866, the face of the city had changed considerably. The period is often remembered for the tragic demolitions of notable historic buildings, but as we have seen there were also many constructive changes.[18] After all, Venice could not have preserved her mediaeval way of life unchanged in the context of modern Europe. Techniques of building and modes of transport, which had been little altered for a millennium or more, had to be modernized if the city were to survive at all. The new industrial age, manifested in Venice in the arrival of the railway and the erection of iron bridges, had to be adapted to the special circumstances of the Venetian lagoon, rather than warded off indefinitely.

125 Ponte di Ghetto Nuovo, 1865–66 *(Sarah Quill)*

Venice as part of Italy: 1866 – World War I

In 1866, after the Austrian defeat in the Austro-Prussian War, the Veneto was finally freed from Austrian rule and handed over to Victor Emmanuel II of Italy, who had formed an alliance with Prussia. In a referendum held in that year the people of the Veneto voted by the overwhelming majority of 674,426 votes to 69 to join the newly-formed Italian nation. This did not immediately bring the utopian democracy which the electorate had hoped for, and at the outset there was much confusion and uncertainty. However, the policies for modernizing the city, initiated by Napoleon and kept in motion by the Austrians, were given new life by the greater commitment of the new Italian administration. High priority was given to the creation of new streets. In 1867 a decree of Victor Emmanuel II provided a special fund for steeet widening in Venice. A new commission was set up to study means of improving the street and canal network, and numerous projects were assembled and considered.[19]

The first new highway to be forged through the dense urban network of Venice was that linking the Rialto with the new railway terminal. This new street, the Via Vittorio Emmanuele II, was solemnly opened in 1871. Not surprisingly, the ponderous title was soon forgotten, and the street has always been known since that time simply as the Strada Nova. Two sections of the new route had already been created under Austrian rule by the filling in of canals; but the new project was more radical, more decisive and more ambitious. Two straight stretches of roadway, each a full ten metres wide, meeting each other at an angle at the church of San Felice, were cut through the city by demolishing all the existing buildings on the route.[20] Similarly, between 1870 and 1875 the Via 22 Marzo, named after the date of the 1848 revolution, was constructed on the path of an existing narrow *calle* between San Moisè and Santa Maria del Giglio (*Fig. 126*).[21] These new thoroughfares were different in character from the *rii terà* created by the French and the

Austrians, for they were flanked not by ancient waterfront façades, but by generally unremarkable nineteenth-century buildings in a variety of styles, with shops along both sides.

A much-needed outcome of the newly imposed Italian rule was the impetus given to the development of Venetian industry. This was provided both by the general sense of liberation and, more constructively, by the greater involvement of the new administration. The Austrians had already considered the need for a railway terminal with port facilities for handling goods traffic. The final decision to construct a Stazione Marittima in the south-west corner of Venice was taken in 1868. Work began a year later, and the new facilities were opened in 1880, providing rail access, quays, warehouses, offices and a customs house.[22] This development finally confirmed the end of the Rialto market as a major centre of international trade. The rôle of the Grand Canal as the main route of entry for seafaring ships was taken over by the much wider Giudecca Canal. While the scope of the Rialto had been reduced to that of a local food market and emporium for the sale of lace, glass and leather for tourists, the Stazione Marittima became the focus of new industrial development and led to a dramatic revival in overseas trade.

In the last two decades of the nineteenth century the population grew from about 130,000 to 150,000 (compared with the all-time low of less than 100,000 in 1821). Although the former importance of Venice as a shipbuilding centre was never recovered, the ancient glass industry boomed, becoming the means of livelihood of about 10% of the people of Venice and Murano at the end of the century. Other traditional craft industries – leather-working, wood-carving, and specialized textiles (lace, ropes and linen) – prospered, and the more recently introduced manufacture of matches and tobacco flourished. The most dramatic new industrial ventures were the huge cotton factory at Santa Marta, near the Stazione Marittima, and the Mulino Stucky, the great

126 Via 22 Marzo, 1870–75 *(Sarah Quill)*

127 Mulino Stucky, additions by Ernst Wullekopf, begun 1895 (*Sarah Quill*)

flour-milling complex, on the opposite bank of the Giudecca Canal.[23]

With its prominent site and imposing architecture the Mulino Stucky has made the more conspicuous contribution to the urban scene of Venice (*Fig. 127*). The factory was established by Giovanni Stucky, son of a Venetian mother and a Swiss father who owned a water mill near Treviso. The young Giovanni had travelled widely in Central and Northern Europe studying the most modern milling techniques. Steam-powered flour mills already existed in Venice – for instance, the Austrians had converted the de-consecrated church of San Girolamo for this purpose, using the former *campanile* as the factory chimney![24] But Stucky's mill had two great advantages. It had the most up to date equipment possible; and above all, it could be reached by large cargo boats importing grain in large quantities. Stucky's enterprise was an immediate success, and the original factory soon became impossibly cramped. In 1895 Stucky applied for planning permission for a major programme of enlargement and modernization. This project was not only commercially bold; it was also more artistically ambitious. The original solid brick building, with its plain Istrian-stone window frames, was to be completely masked by the immense Neo-Gothic brick 'castle', topped by turrets and crenellations, which still exists today, now abandoned and desolate. This new addition was designed by an architect from Hanover in North Germany, Ernst Wullekopf, apparently chosen because of Stucky's admiration for German expertise in flour milling. Not surprisingly, there was considerable local opposition to the scheme, especially in the Commissione all'Ornato, which felt that it was out of character with the rest of the city. However, Stucky was by now sufficiently powerful to get his own way. In 1908 he established his status in the city when he bought Massari's Palazzo Grassi, one of the largest and most magnificent palaces in the city (*Fig. 111*). Only two years later, to the great shock and sadness of the people of Venice, he was assassinated by one of his workers in the forecourt of the railway station.[25]

Stucky left the city with a noble piece of nineteenth-century industrial architecture, created at the period when industrialists throughout Europe

were becoming aware of the exciting visual possibilities of factory buildings. Despite local chauvinistic reservations, Wullekopf's Neo-Gothic brick construction, with its expansive waterfront façade and repeated vertical accents, was not entirely alien to Venetian architectural tradition. It even recalled aspects of the mediaeval granaries of Terra Nova, destroyed under Napoleonic rule, though its style had a distinctively north European streak of fantasy. Stucky would be dismayed to know that he bequeathed to the city what is now one of its most romantic ruins. After World War I capital investment was diverted to the new industrial zone of Porto Marghera on the nearby mainland. Like the cotton factory at Santa Marta the Mulino Stucky became an imposing symbol of the last short-lived but brave attempt to revive industry within the confines of the city of Venice.

128 Albergo Excelsior, Lido, by Giovanni Sardi, begun 1898 (Sarah Quill)

Throughout Europe industrialization was giving new prominence to the middle classes. So, too, in Venice, where the more enterprising members of the *borghesia* – industrialists and tradesmen – were forming a new collective identity as the most prosperous social group. The aristocracy were still respected, but on the whole no longer powerful, inhibited by a deep-rooted prejudice against becoming involved in manufacturing or shopkeeping. Meanwhile many members of the working classes were suffering terrible poverty and living in slum conditions.

The most significant architectural manifestation of the rise of the *borghesia* was the development of the Venetian Lido, both as a middle-class suburb of Venice and as one of Europe's most fashionable resorts. When Goethe had visited the Lido in 1786 the long sandy island had been inhabited only by a few fishermen and the Benedictine monks of San Nicolò di Lido. Shifting sand dunes were threatening to bury the Hebrew and Protestant cemeteries, placed there because they were not allowed on consecrated ground. On the lonely windswept beach the fine, pale yellow sand was strewn with shells and exotic seaweeds.[26]

The first bathing establishment on the Lido was opened in 1857, a whole century after sea bathing had first become popular in the colder, rougher waters of Southern England. In the comprehensive plan of 1886–91 for the revival and preservation of Venice, a substantial sum of money was set aside for the building of streets on the Lido.[27] By the time that Thomas Mann published his story *Death in Venice* in 1912, the Lido had become one of the bourgeois playgrounds of Europe. Aschenbach's impressions of the shore were very different from those of Goethe a century earlier:

> 'He delighted, as always, in the scene on the beach, the sight of sophisticated society giving itself over to a simple life at the edge of the elements. The shallow grey sea was already gay with children wading, with swimmers, with figures in bright colours lying on the sand-banks with arms behind their heads. Some were rowing in little keelless boats painted red and blue, and laughing when they capsized. A long row of *capanne* ran down the beach, with platforms, where people sat as on verandas, and there was social life, with bustle and indolent repose; visits were paid amid much chatter, punctilious morning toilettes hob-nobbed with comfortable and privileged dishabille.'[28]

If the new *borghesia* had a strong corporate identity, no unified architectural style evolved to express this. Architecture of the period was still feeling for a new language. Neoclassicism, once so radical and exciting an artistic movement, had become the style of the Establishment and then gradually faded out. Nineteenth-century designers such as Meduna, Cadorin and Fuin had experimented with Neo-Gothic and Neo-Lombardesque idioms, trying to find a means of expression which would blend into the rich architectural legacy of Venice. At the same time a distinctly romantic approach to design began to emerge. For example, in the Albergo Excelsior, the largest, most luxurious of the new Lido hotels, built between 1898 and 1908, the native Venetian architect Giovanni Sardi chose an ostensibly Neo-Byzantine style[29] (*Fig. 128*). Yet he deliberately avoided the symmetry and explicitness of true Veneto-Byzantine architecture. The long seafront façade, with its domes and turrets and its Moorish arches, has a picturesque, Oriental flavour more akin to Nash's Brighton Pavilion than to any Byzantine monument in Venice.

Probably the most successful of the Neo-Gothic buildings of the period was the striking 'Casa de Maria' on the island of Giudecca near the church of the Zitelle (*Fig. 129*). This house was designed for his own use by a painter from Bologna, Mario de Maria, and built between 1910 and 1913.[30] The plan is typically Venetian, with a long central hall opening on to smaller rooms on either side. But here Gothic forms are used not derivatively but in a completely original way. The three huge north-facing windows, looking across the Bacino towards the Salute and Piazza San Marco, admit the sunless light so important to painters. These windows are only superficially Gothic, for their sides are not straight, but continue the curves of the pointed arches to create unusually broad openings. Wrought-iron balconies in front of the *piano nobile* windows are unconventionally supported on elegant, outsized corbels. The diaper pattern in the brickwork, borrowed from the Doge's Palace, is the only example in Venice of the use of this form of decoration in a private house.

The most original style of the years leading up to the First World War was

the *Stile Liberty*, the Italian version of Art Nouveau, which, curiously, derives its name from the famous London shop. This movement combined simplified, almost abstract architectural forms with a graceful, flowing decorative language and pale, subtle colours. The most gifted exponent of the *Stile Liberty* in Venice was Guido Sullam, whose Villa Monplaisir on the Lido, built in 1904–5, was painted all over with flowers and undulating leafy stalks, and topped by a roof top *altana* in twisting wrought-iron work. This villa is now almost a ruin, but Sullam's abilities can still be seen in a palace which he erected at the end of the Bacino Orseolo, behind Piazza San Marco, between 1908 and 1910[31] (*Fig. 130*). Now that the art nouveau painted decoration has been lost, the essential simplicity of the forms is more obvious. The Ionic order of the *piano nobile* windows, with its exaggeratedly slim columns and protruding volutes, reveals the art nouveau predilection for slender, curving forms. This is the only reference in the façade to earlier decorative traditions. The rest of the detailing is reduced to basic geometrical shapes, seen for instance in the plain stone railings of the *piano nobile* balconies. Sullam was an imaginative, forward-looking architect, but he also managed to adapt his design to the scale and character of the older buildings around. The problem of how to integrate the abstract forms of contemporary architecture into the highly detailed texture of the urban fabric of Venice is one which has tested the skills of architects in Venice ever since.

ABOVE, LEFT
129 'Casa de Maria', Giudecca, by Mario de Maria, begun 1910 (*A.F.Kersting*)

ABOVE
130 Palace in the Bacino Orseolo, by Guido Sullam, begun 1908 (*Sarah Quill*)

The rise of Fascism: World War I to World War II

The two decades between the Wars saw further radical social and economic changes, which were to establish the city's rôle in the modern world. The gradual abandonment of large scale industry in Venice and Murano was accompanied by the development of Marghera on the nearby mainland as a major industrial centre, specializing in oil refining and the manufacture of chemicals. The new industrial zone had been established as early as 1903, but it was not until 1917 that modern port facilities were provided. A new residential area for the workers of Marghera was begun in 1920.[32] Without the major new source of income created by the industrialization of the lagoon, Venice would probably have become a ghost town, unable to support even a fraction of the present population. Yet, as well as bringing prosperity (above all, to the capitalist industrialists), this development has led to severe problems of air and water pollution, while the need to admit giant oil tankers has inhibited plans for flood-prevention schemes at the entrances to the lagoon.

While the new 'garden city' was under construction at Porto Marghera in the 1920s, modernization of the mainland town of Mestre was begun in earnest, in response to the town's new rôle as a Terraferma suburb of Venice.[33] The expansion of Mestre as a residential suburb was given a further boost by the construction in 1930–33 of the road link to Venice, alongside the nineteenth-century railway bridge. The new bridge, the Ponte della Libertà, with its long succession of low Istrian-stone arches at water level (reminiscent of the casemates of Sanmicheli's Fortezza di Sant'Andrea), was the work of the engineer Eugenio Miozzi, designer of the Ponte degli Scalzi and the Ponte dell'Accademia.[34] The new road bridge allowed the introduction of regular bus services for commuters between Mestre and Venice, supplementing the existing train connections. It also gave a new means of access for tourists, and led to the development of Piazzale Roma as the point of arrival for cars and buses. The first multi-storey car park on the site, erected in 1931–33 by the Ufficio Tecnico del Commune under Miozzi's direction, was not only a remarkable technical achievement, but also an extraordinarily advanced design, with its plain, functional geometrical forms.[35]

The large scale industrial and residential development of the nearby mainland necessitated parallel changes in the functions of Venice itself. The expansion of overseas shipping in the lagoon encouraged the city's marine insurance business, centred in the waterfront palaces at the western end of the Zattere. Tourism, already long-established in Venice, now became the chief source of income of the historic city centre, and ensured the survival of traditional crafts such as glass blowing, lace making and leather working. Meanwhile the city was beginning to establish itself as an international centre of scholarship and the arts. The Biennale, the bi-annual art exhibition, founded in 1895, not only promoted the city as a cultural centre, but also became the excuse for bold architectural experimentation in the little pavilions erected by different nations in the gardens at Castello, the home of the Biennale. An important series of technical and craft schools founded in the nineteenth century, together with the Accademia di Belle Arti and the nucleus of the present university at Ca' Foscari which dates back to 1829, provided an institutional framework for the development of Venice as an important educational centre.[36]

These very fundamental changes in the means of livelihood of the inhabitants of Venice were the background against which the architecture of the period evolved. Gradually, the nostalgic, retrospective mood faded, and a more adventurous, forward-looking approach to design set in. One of the last buildings in the city built in conscious imitation of an earlier style was the Casa Salviati, on the Grand Canal at San Vio (*Fig. 131*). This little palace, built by the engineer Dall'Olivo in 1924–26, belonged to an old-established glass manufacturing family, who used it as an excuse for blatant advertising. The façade, built in the style of the Early Renaissance, is incongruously decorated with mosaics – a medium not normally used in Venetian domestic architecture – in order to publicize the family's expertise in glass making.[37]

The arrival of the modern movement in architecture, in Venice as elsewhere in Italy, was linked with the growth of Fascism, which found a potent means of expression in the state-erected buildings of the 1930s. The speed and ruthlessness with which the tough, functional Fascist style imposed itself can be seen in the work of a talented local architect called Del Giudice. In the 1920s he designed two imaginative buildings on the Lido, the Villa Rossi on the Via Sandro Gallo and the neighbouring Casa del Farmacista[38] (*Fig. 132*).

BELOW, LEFT
131 Casa Salviati, by G. dall'Olivo, begun 1924 (*Sarah Quill*)

BELOW
132 Casa del Farmacista, Lido, by B. del Giudice, begun 1926 (*Sarah Quill*)

This enchanting little pharmacy, erected in 1926–7, shows how the architect took a vaguely Baroque style as his starting point, and imbued it with a pre-dilection for flowing curves and simplified forms inherited from the Stile Liberty, to creat something new and personal, well-suited to the elegant seaside atmosphere of the Lido. However, when he came to design the Fire Station on the Rio di Ca' Foscari in 1932–34, Del Giudice adopted a style dramatically different from the intimacy of his early work[39] (*Fig. 133*). This was the first attempt to introduce an uncompromisingly modern building into the ancient centre of Venice. Here Del Giudice exaggerated the severity of the plain round-headed and rectangular windows, which he had already used less conspicuously in the two Lido buildings, by means of their insistent repetition across the whole façade. Yet even in this imperious scheme, his innate sensibility revealed itself. Like Sullam in his palace in the Bacino Orseolo, Del Giudice tried to adjust the scale and the layout of his design to the older buildings around. The great waterfront arches, leading to the fireboat moorings, are enlivened by Baroque keystones, while the long *piano nobile* balustrade takes over a traditional Venetian feature.

On the Lido there was less need to tone down the brutal directness of the Fascist style in order to accommodate it to older buildings around. There was also more space for the huge scale and massive forms of Fascist public architecture. The most extreme manifestations of the style on the Lido were the Palazzo del Casinò and the adjoining Palazzo del Cinema, built in 1936–38 by Miozzi and a fellow engineer called Quagliata[40] (*Fig. 134*). The Palazzo del Casinò shows how far architecture had moved from the picturesque style of the nearby Albergo Excelsior, built less than half a century before (*Fig. 128*). Here the design is boldly symmetrical and aggressively functional. The pitched roofs are concealed by the clean shapes of the façade walls in order to simplify the skyline, and the huge shafts of the columns of the central 'portico' are conspicuously stripped of all classical reminiscences.

133 Fire Station on the Rio di Ca' Foscari, by Del Giudice, begun 1932 (*Sarah Quill*)

The post-War years

Since World War II the plight of Venice has become a cause for international concern.[41] The increasing severity of the flooding, known as *acqua alta*, which afflicts the city, has begun to make daily life more and more difficult. The floods occur whenever the equinoctal high tides coincide with south winds, which prevent the outgoing tide from flowing out of the lagoon. The chief cause of the worsening situation has been the steady draining of artesian water from the bedrock underneath the lagoon to satisfy the heavy demands of local industry, which has led to the progressive sinking of the terrain of Venice. Now that an aqueduct from the mountains has been installed to provide an alternative water supply for Marghera, further subsidence should be avoided, but serious damage has already been done. Every year more people, discouraged by life in such difficult conditions, emigrate to the mainland. While Mestre grows, its population swelled by disillusioned Venetians, the social structure of Venice itself continues to change. Working class housing in the city is well below twentieth-century standards, and there is a desperate shortage of amenities such as parks and children's playgrounds. Modernization of the more modest housing only raises the rents beyond the means of the original inhabitants, leading to further emigration.

The architectural heritage of the city suffers from similar ills to those which are gradually driving away the inhabitants. Repeated flooding, corrosion caused by atmospheric pollution, and erosion by waves stirred up by motor boats, are a constant threat to the survival of ancient buildings. The worst wave damage occurs in the narrower canals, such as the Rio di Ca' Foscari where the motor traffic is particularly heavy. In 1938 an extension to this *rio*, a newly excavated channel called the Rio Nuovo, was opened to provide an express route for motor boat services between Piazzale Roma and the *centro storico*.[42] And as the motor boat traffic grows, so the survival of the gondola is seriously threatened. One by one the *traghetti* (gondola ferries) are closing, for

134 Palazzo del Casinò, Lido, by Miozzi and Quagliata, begun 1936 (*Sarah Quill*)

231

the cost of building and maintaining the boats has become almost prohibitive.

At the same time there is a strong sense of the need to preserve the fabric of the city. In recent decades, fund-raising campaigns on an international scale have financed the restoration of a number of notable architectural monuments. Rigid planning controls now forbid visible alterations to historic buildings, and the authorities can even force owners to remove extra storeys added without permission.

However, in one conspicuous instance, planning restrictions prevented the erection of what might well have been the finest example of twentieth-century architecture in the city. In 1953 America's greatest architect, Frank Lloyd Wright, was commissioned to build the so-called 'Masieri Memorial House', a centre for foreign architectural students on the Grand Canal between the Palazzo Balbi and the mouth of the Rio di Ca' Foscari[43] (*Fig. 135*). Wright was by this time already in his eighties (he died in 1959 at the age of 92). He was chosen because the building was to be erected in memory of a young architecture student, Angelo Masieri, killed in an accident while on a pilgrimage to Wright's most famous building, 'Falling Water' in Pennsylvania. Never before had so distinguished an architect from outside Italy been awarded a commission in Venice. Wright's design shows how imaginatively traditional Venetian elements, such as tall windows with projecting balconies, could be incorporated into the personal style of a contemporary architect. With its informal arrangement of horizontal and vertical accents, and the casual build-up of shapes from the lower building on the left to the tall Palazzo Balbi on the right, Wright's house would have had none of the severity of Del Giudice's fascist-style Fire Station a few yards away in the Rio di Ca' Foscari (*Fig. 133*).

In the event the project was vigorously opposed, above all by the next-door neighbours, the wealthy owners of the Palazzo Balbi, who persuaded the authorities to reject the scheme. The final compromise solution, which insisted on the preservation of the façade of the existing building on the site, was a sad loss. In the course of the conversion, the old façade collapsed, and had to be largely rebuilt. The result is an exterior without character or distinction (*Fig. 92*). The interior was executed by the local architect, Carlo Scarpa, a devoted follower of Wright, who took over the project some 15 years later. Scarpa has a high reputation for his sensitive conversions of historic buildings, exemplified by his work in the Palazzo Querini-Stampalia in Venice and the Castello of Verona.

Only a year after Wright designed his Venetian house, the new railway station, a building of considerably less distinction, made its appearance in the urban scene of Venice (*Fig. 136*). In a national competition held 20 years earlier in 1934, 54 designs had been submitted, but all were rejected, and in the end the Amministrazione Ferroviario substituted its own less adventurous project.[44] Set back from the Grand Canal, and raised high on a broad flight of steps, the building makes no concessions to the scale, style or siting of those around it. However, with its clean lines and informal asymmetry the long white façade is not disagreeable, and the prospect which it offers to visitors to Venice from the

OPPOSITE
135 'Masieri Memorial House', unexecuted project by Frank Lloyd Wright, 1953. *Frank Lloyd Wright Memorial Foundation, Arizona)*

portico at the top of the steps is breathtaking and unforgettable (*Fig. 106*).

In the same year a new office block for the electricity company, the Società Adriatica di Elettricità, was begun on the banks of the Rio Nuovo[45] (*Fig. 137*). The architects of this building, Angelo Scattolin and Luigi Vetti, took over the approximate scale and rhythm of the bays from Venetian architectural convention, but otherwise the design makes few concessions to the environ-ment. Admittedly, the surroundings on the Rio Nuovo were neither historic nor architecturally distinguished. However, what one might call the 'international post-War office block style', even when reduced to three storeys, fits uneasily into the context of Venice as a whole.

The fate of contemporary architecture in Venice, as elsewhere, seems to indicate that public bodies, and those with wealth and influence, are less seriously restricted by planning controls than ordinary private individuals. (The exception is, of course, the Biennale, where architectural innovation has always been welcomed, even expected.) One of the most prominent recent instrusions into the Venetian *centro storico* is the new headquarters of the principal bank of Venice, the Cassa di Risparmio di Venezia, in Campo Manin (*Fig. 138*). The original appearance of this *campo*, formerly Campo San Paternian, is known from prints and old photographs.[46] These show the picturesque hexagonal campanile of San Paternian, which was demolished in 1871, together with the church of the same name, to make more space for a monument to Daniele Manin in the *campo*. In 1906 the Cassa di Risparmio erected their first building on the site, a discreet Neo-Lombardesque

136 Stazione di Santa Lucia, 1954 *(Sarah Quill)*

construction. Yet little over half a century later they decided to replace it. The new design produced in 1964 was the work of Italy's greatest twentieth-century architect, Pier Luigi Nervi, in collaboration with the Venetian architect Angelo Scattolin.[47] Nervi's brilliant use of concrete to create bold, dynamic spatial effects, seen for example in the two sports halls and the stadium which he built for the Rome Olympic Games in 1960, makes the interior of the new bank dramatic and imposing. The façade, based on a grid of horizontals and verticals like Scattolin's electricity company headquarters, is less daring, apart from the virtuosity of the remarkably slender elements which are made to appear to support the top two storeys.

The idea of employing a great non-Italian architect in Venice had not been forgotten since the rejection of Frank Lloyd Wright's project. In 1964, the year in which Nervi was employed by the Cassa di Risparmio, Le Corbusier produced his first sketches for a new civic hospital, to be erected in the *sestiere* of Cannaregio near San Giobbe, on the site of the nineteenth-century slaughterhouse[48] (*Fig. 139*). Seen from above, Le Corbusier's model looks like an abstract painting, with its rectangular blocks of different shapes and sizes, the ridges of the roofs arranged perpendicular to each other, fitted together in an informal but balanced composition. The side view of the model shows that Le Corbusier sensed the basic skeletal form of the typical Venetial building, with its strong horizontal elements supported on slimmer stilt-like verticals. Opposition from the residents of the quarter, and a general reluctance (shared by Corbusier himself) to demolish the solid nineteenth-century slaughter-house – not to mention the exorbitant cost of the scheme – have combined to delay the realization of this architectural showpiece. Although the project has had influential supporters in official circles, it is now becoming more and more doubtful that it will ever materialize.

It is not my place here to foretell what the future holds for Venice, nor to

137 Headquarters of the Società Adriatica di Elettricità, by Angelo Scattolin and Luigi Vetti, 1954 (*Sarah Quill*)

235

138 Cassa di Risparmio di Venezia, Campo Manin, by Pier Luigi Nervi and Angelo Scattolin, designed 1964 (*Sarah Quill*)

discuss the various schemes which have been put forward for rescuing the city from irreversible decline and physical decay.[49] The situation is not entirely a cause for pessimism. Despite its physical handicaps, Venice preserves a lively cultural identity as a centre for the visual arts, cinema, opera and academic study. Even the physical environment has utopian features which are the envy of architects and planners all over the world. Here pedestrians have their own complete street network, and virtually everyone uses public motor transport. The provision of car parking space on the outskirts, so desirable in other cities, is obviously indispensable in Venice. A huge area of reclaimed land on the

236

west of the city, called the Tronchetto, has been provided for this purpose, supplementing the garages of Piazzale Roma.

Despite the technical obstacles, the Venetian environment remains an exciting challenge to architects. The special quality of the light and the visual rôle of the water are an asset to any building, and the task of adapting contemporary ideas to the Venetian architectural tradition may continue to inspire designs of true distinction. Of course the conservation of the city's architectural heritage should be a long term aim, but this should not be allowed to stifle the creative energies of the architects of the future.

FINIS

139 Model for the still-unexecuted civic hospital at Cannaregio, by Le Corbusier, 1964 *(Lucien Hervé)*

Notes to Chapters I–IX

N.B. The *Bollettino CISA* is the *Bollettino del Centro Internazionale di Studi di Architettura 'Andrea Palladio'*.

I: Introduction

1   J.W. GOETHE, *Italian Journey 1786–1788*, trs. W.H. Auden and E. Mayer, Penguin Classics, 1970, p.77.
2   F. SANSOVINO, *Venetia città nobilissima et singolare*, ed. G. Martinioni, Venice, 1663 (hereafter SANSOVINO-MARTINIONI), p.5.
3   Recent accounts of the early history of Venice are to be found in F.C. LANE, *Venice: A Maritime Republic*, John Hopkins University Press, Baltimore, 1973; and J.J. NORWICH, *Venice: The Rise to Empire*, Allen Lane, London, 1977.
4   This translation is quoted from LANE (1973), pp.3–4. For the full text of the letter to the Venetians, see T. HODGKIN (ed.), *The Letters of Cassiodorus*, London, 1886, pp. 515–518.
5   T. OKEY, *The Old Venetian Palaces and Old Venetian Folk*, London, 1907, p.3.

II: Byzantine

1   E. HUBALA, *Venedig, Reclams Kunstführer Italien* II(i), Stuttgart, 1974, p.435.
2   ibid., pp.441–442.
3   ibid., p.429.
4   SANSOVINO-MARTINIONI, p.196.
5   HUBALA (1974), p.149.
6   SANSOVINO-MARTINIONI, p.197.
7   On the history of the Basilica of San Marco and the cult of Saint Mark in Venice, see O. DEMUS, *The Church of San Marco in Venice: History, Architecture, Sculpture*, Dumbarton Oaks Studies VI, Washington D.C., 1960, pp.3–60.
8   ibid., pp.64–69.
9   ibid., pp.69–75.
10 A. SCATTOLIN, 'The Surveyor of the Basilica', in *The Horses of San Marco*, Royal Academy exhibition catalogue, London, 1979, pp.7–12.
11 DEMUS (1960), p.74.
12 ibid., pp.83–87.
13 ibid., pp.88–100.
14 ibid., pp.103–104.
15 LANE (1973), pp.36–42.
16 DEMUS (1960), pp.101–103.
17 For a full account of the sculptural decoration of San Marco, see DEMUS (1960), pp.109–190.
18 E. ARSLAN, *Gothic Architecture in Venice*, trs. A. Engel, Phaidon Press, London, 1972, p.16.
19 F.C. LANE, 'Family Partnerships and Joint Ventures in the Venetian Republic', *Journal of Economic History*, IV, 1944, pp.178–196.
20 D. WALEY, *The Italian City Republics*, World University Library, London, 1969, pp.175–177.

21 ARSLAN (1972), pp.17–25; and G. SCATTOLIN, *Le case-fondaco sul Canal Grande*, Venice, 1961.
22 ARSLAN (1972), p.41, note 100.
23 For a recent account of the interior arrangement of Venetian palaces, see P. LAURITZEN & A. ZIELCKE, *Palaces of Venice*, Phaidon Press, Oxford, 1978, pp.23–34.
24 See J.S. ACKERMAN, 'Sources of the Renaissance Villa', *Studies in Western Art* II (Acts of the XXth International Congress of the History of Art), Princeton, 1963, pp.6–18.
25 E.R. TRINCANATO, *Venezia Minore*, Milan, 1948, pp.127 ff.
26 ARSLAN (1972), pp.26–38.

III: The Mediaeval City

1 LANE (1973), pp.18–19.
2 J. SCHULZ, 'The Printed Plans and Panoramic Views of Venice', *Saggi e Memorie di Storia dell'Arte*, VII, 1970, p.16.
3 On the history of the Rialto see R. CESSI & A. ALBERTI, *Rialto: l'isola – il ponte – il mercato*, Bologna, 1934.
4 T. CORYATE, *Crudities*, London, 1611, p.168.
5 See F. BRAUDEL, *The Mediterranean and the Mediterranean World in the Age of Philip II*, 2 vols., Collins, London, 1972–1973, I, pp.314–315.
6 H. JAMES, *Italian Hours*, London, 1909, p.16.
7 P. MOLMENTI, *La storia di Venezia nella vita privata*, 2nd edn., Turin, 1880, Part 1, p.145.
8 S. MURATORI, *Studi per una operante storia urbana di Venezia*, I, Rome, 1960. See also P. MARETTO, 'L'urbanistica veneziana del Trecento', *Bollettino del Centro Internazionale di Studi di Architettura 'Andrea Palladio'*, VII, 1965, pp.232 ff.; and E. TRINCANATO, 'Venezia nella storia urbana', *Urbanistica*, LII, 1968, pp.7–69.
9 GOETHE (1970 edn.), p.78.
10 Archivio di Stato di Venezia, Provveditori di Comun, *busta* 11, 'Atti 1541–1548', *carta* 16 (verso), 19 August 1548.
11 J. HOWELL, *A Survey of the Signorie of Venice*, London, 1651, p.35.
12 GOETHE (1970 edn.), p.98.
13 ibid., p.77.
14 SANSOVINO-MARTINIONI, p.290.
15 ibid., p.369.
16 A. SAGREDO, *Sulle consorterie delle arti edificative in Venezia*, Venice, 1856, pp.37–45; and M. PAVANINI, 'Traditional House Construction', *Architectural Review*, CXLIV, May 1971 (special issue devoted to Venice), pp.297–302.
17 On stone supplies in Venice see F. RODOLICO, *Le pietre delle città d'Italia*, Florence, 1953, pp.194–204.
18 See R. GALLO, 'Jacopo Sansovino a Pola', *Rivista di Venezia*, V, 1926, pp.255–286.
19 On timber supplies in Venice see F.C. LANE, *Venetian Ships and Shipbuilders of the Renaissance*, Baltimore, 1934, pp.217–233.
20 CORYATE (1611), p.165.
21 SAGREDO (1856), pp.44–45; and TRINCANATO (1948), p.110.
22 SANSOVINO-MARTINIONI, p.383.
23 See H. TAIT, *The Golden Age of Venetian Glass*, exhibition catalogue, British Museum, London, 1979.
24 SANSOVINO-MARTINIONI, p.384.
25 SAGREDO (1856); and A. WIROBISZ, 'L'attività edilizia a Venezia nel XIV e XV secolo', *Studi Veneziani*, VII, 1965, pp.307–343.

26 Information generously provided by Dr Susan Connell, whose doctoral thesis, *The Employment of Sculptors and Stone-Masons in Venice in the Fifteenth Century*, Warburg Institute, London, 1976, is a valuable source of information about fifteenth-century Venetian building practice.

27 M. LUTYENS (ed.), *Effie in Venice*, London, 1965, p.81.

28 SANSOVINO-MARTINIONI, pp.383–384.

29 ibid., p.382.

30 TRINCANATO (1948), pp.112–115.

31 Archivio di Stato di Venezia, Savi ed Esecutori alle Acque, *filza* 119, 'Relazioni Periti sopra la Laguna (1493–1579)', *carta* 189, 17 April 1550.

32 CORYATE (1611), p.262.

IV: Gothic

1 G. LUZZATTO, *Storia economica di Venezia dall'XI al XVI secolo*, Centro Internazionale delle Arti e del Costume, Venice, 1961, p.40.

2 LANE (1973), pp.151–2.

3 LUZZATTO (1961), p.130, in which the same statistics are given in 'money of account' rather than converted into suggested 'real' values.

4 H. DELLWING, *Studien zur Baukunst der Bettelorden im Veneto*, Deutscher Kunstverlag, Munich, 1970, pp.98–9. This book is the essential source of information for the study of Mendicant order churches in Venice and the Veneto.

5 ibid., pp.99 ff.

6 J. WHITE, *Art and Architecture in Italy 1250–1400*, Pelican History of Art, 1966, pp.7–8.

7 SANSOVINO-MARTINIONI, p.6.

8 R. GALLO, 'L'architettura di transizione dal gotico al rinascimento e Bartolomeo Bon', *Atti del istituto veneto di scienze, lettere ed arti*, 120, 1961–2, pp.201–2; and A.M. SCHULZ, 'The Sculpture of Giovanni and Bartolomeo Bon', *Transactions of the American Philosophical Society*, 68 (iii), 1978, pp.67 & 74.

9 DELLWING (1970), pp.117 ff.

10 For plan and description of Santa Croce see WHITE (1966), pp.8–11.

11 A. GUISCONI (i.e. F. SANSOVINO), *Tutte le cose notabili e belle che sono in Venetia*, Venice, 1556, p.16.

12 On the history of the church and its recent restoration, see A. CLARK & P. RYLANDS, *The Church of the Madonna dell'Orto*, Paul Elek, London, 1977, pp.9 ff. On the portal see GALLO (1961–2), pp.203–4; and A.M. SCHULZ (1978), pp.61, 67 & 74–5.

13 J. RUSKIN, *The Stones of Venice*, 1st edn., 3 vols., London, 1851–3, I, pp.21–2.

14 ibid., II, pp.209–10.

15 See M. LUTYENS (ed.), *Effie in Venice: Unpublished Letters of Mrs John Ruskin written from Venice between 1849 and 1852*, John Murray, London, 1965; and J.R. BRADLEY (ed.), *Ruskin's Letters from Venice 1851–2*, Yale University Press, New Haven, Conn., 1955.

16 RUSKIN (1851–3), I, p.17.

17 On the Palazzo Ducale see, for example, E. BASSI & E.R. TRINCANATO, *Il Palazzo Ducale nella storia e nell'arte di Venezia*, Milan, 1960; E. ARSLAN, *Gothic Architecture in Venice*, trs. Anne Engel, Phaidon, London, 1971, pp.36–7 & pp.141 f.; E.R. TRINCANATO, 'Il Palazzo Ducale', in G. SAMONA (ed.), *Piazza San Marco: l'architettura, la storia, le funzioni*, Marsilio, Padua, 1970, pp.111 ff. Many of the documents are published in G.B. LORENZI, *Monumenti per servire alla storia del Palazzo Ducale di Venezia*, Venice, 1868.

18 ARSLAN (1971), pp.141 ff. Arslan is among those who support the controversial theory, proposed in P. TOESCA, *Il Trecento*, Turin, 1950, pp.150 ff., that the new

Sala del Maggior Consiglio was built on top of Ziani's arcades, which were later renewed while the superstructure was supported by some kind of temporary scaffolding. The huge cost and technical difficulty involved in such a procedure would seem to me prohibitive, and I have therefore preferred to adhere to the more straightforward chronology – that the arcades and the Sala del Maggior Consiglio above were largely reconstructed in a single rebuilding programme between about 1340 and 1365.

19 For illustrations of these and other Italian communal palaces see WHITE (1966).

20 P. MARETTO, 'L'edilizia gotica veneziana', in *Studi per una operante storia urbana di Venezia*, Rome, 1960, II.

21 E.R. TRINCANATO, *Venezia minore*, Milan, 1948.

22 RUSKIN (1851–3), II, pp.249 ff; and A. WHITTICK (ed.), *Ruskin's Venice*, George Godwin, London, 1976, pp.190–2.

23 ARSLAN (1971), p.97.

24 G. LORENZETTI, *Venice and its Lagoon*, trs. J. Guthrie, Rome, 1961, p.324.

25 The documents are published in B. CECCHETTI, 'La facciata della Ca' d'Oro dello scalpello di Giovanni e Bartolomeo Buono', *Archivio Veneto*, XXXI, 1886, p.1 & pp.201 ff.; and P. PAOLETTI, *L'architettura e la scultura del Rinascimento in Venezia*, Venice, 1893, I, pp.20 ff. For summaries of their contents see ARSLAN (1971), pp.233 ff.; T. OKEY (1907), pp.62 ff.; & A.M. SCHULZ (1978), pp.68 ff.

26 ARSLAN (1971), p.240.

27 WHITTICK (ed.) (1976), p.57.

28 WHITE (1966), pp.336 ff.; and R. WITTKOWER, *Gothic vs. Classic*, Thames and Hudson, London, 1974, pp.21 ff.

29 WHITTICK (ed.) (1976), p.117.

30 OKEY (1907), p.52.

31 G. TASSINI, *Curiosità veneziane*, 5th edn., Venice, 1915, p.256.

32 SANSOVINO-MARTINIONI, p.388.

33 G. TASSINI, *Alcuni palazzi ed antichi edifici di Venezia*, Venice, 1879, p.182.

34 OKEY (1907), p.56.

35 For a full discussion of the Venetian Scuole Grandi see B. PULLAN, *Rich and Poor in Renaissance Venice*, Oxford University Press, 1971, pp.33 ff.

36 On the Venetian Scuole Piccole see LANE (1973), pp.104 ff. and pp.318 ff.

37 On the Scuola della Carità. see E. BASSI, *La Reale Accademia di Belle Arti di Venezia*, Florence, 1941; idem, *The Convento della Carità*, trs. C.W. Westfall, Pennsylvania State University Press, 1973, pp.13 ff.; PAOLETTI (1893), I, pp.56 f. & 91 f.; D. ROSAND, 'Titian's *Presentation of the Virgin in the Temple* and the Scuola della Carità', *Art Bulletin*, LVIII, 1976, pp.56 ff.; and LORENZETTI (1961), pp.665 ff. On the ceilings see W. WOLTERS, *Plastische Deckendekorationen des Cinquecento in Venedig und im Veneto*, Berlin, 1968, pp. 7 & 9; and J. SCHULZ, *Venetian Painted Ceilings of the Renaissance*, University of California Press, Berkeley and Los Angeles, 1968, pp.6–7.

38 On the Scuola Vecchia della Misericordia, see PAOLETTI (1893), I, p.55 and pp.90–91; and D. HOWARD, *Jacopo Sansovino: Architecture and Patronage in Renaissance Venice*, Yale University Press, New Haven and London, 1975, pp.98–9. The documentary evidence does not make it entirely clear whether or not the whole building was rebuilt in 1411/12. The decision to construct an *albergo* could refer either to the whole Scuola premises or merely to the separate small room for meetings of the Banca. On Bon's Madonna della Misericordia see also W. WOLTERS, *La scultura veneziana gotica 1300–1460*, Alfieri, Venice, 1976, I, pp.290–1, cat. no.250; and II, fig.831; and A.M. SCHULZ (1978), pp.14 ff.

39 C. RIDOLFI, *Le maraviglie dell'arte*, ed. D. von Hadeln, II, Berlin, 1924, p.61.

V: Early Renaissance

1   On the work of Tuscan sculptors in Venice and other visits from Florentine artists
    see W. WOLTERS, *La scultura veneziana gotica 1300–1460*, 2 vols, Alfieri, Venice,
    1976, especially vol. I, pp.82 ff., 109 and 116.

2   VASARI-MILANESI, II, p.434.

3   SANSOVINO-MARTINIONI, p.218.

4   F. SAXL, 'Petrarch in Venice' and 'Jacopo Bellini and Mantegna as Antiquarians',
    both lectures published in H. HONOUR & J. FLEMING (ed.), *A Heritage of Images:
    a Selection of Lectures by Fritz Saxl*, Penguin books, 1970.

5   For a recent discussion of Venice and humanism from a slightly different angle see D.
    CHAMBERS, *The Imperial Age of Venice 1380–1580*, Thames & Hudson, London,
    1970, especially pp.147 ff.

6   See the clear summary of the first Renaissance buildings in Venice by Heydenreich in
    L.H. HEYDENREICH & W. LOTZ, *Architecture in Italy 1400–1600*, trs. M.
    Hottinger, Pelican History of Art, 1974, pp. 86 ff.

7   See the recent monograph G. TRAVERSARI, *L'arco dei Sergi*, Padua, 1971.

8   On the history of the Ca' del Duca see L. BELTRAMI, *La Ca' del Duca sul Canal
    Grande*, Milan, 1900; and J.R. SPENCER, 'The Ca' del Duca in Venice and
    Benedetto Ferrini', *Journal of the Society of Architectural Historians*, XXIX, 1970, pp.3–8.

9   CONNELL (1976), pp.19–21 and p.131.

10 SPENCER (1970), p.7.

11 J.R. SPENCER (ed.), *Filarete's Treatise on Architecture*, 2 vols., Yale University Press,
    New Haven, Conn., 1965, I, p.xviii; and F. FRANCO, 'L'interpolazione del Filarete
    trattatista fra gli artefici del Rinascimento architettonico a Venezia', *Atti del IV
    Convegno Nazionale di Storia dell'Architettura*, Milan, 1939, pp.269–270.

12 FRANCO (1939), pp.270 ff.

13 H. BURNS, 'Quattrocento Architecture and the Antique', in R. BOLGAR (ed.),
    Classical Influences on European Culture, A.D. *500–1500*, Cambridge, 1971, pp.269–287.

14 E.R. TRINCANATO, 'Il Palazzo Ducale', in G. SAMONÀ et al., *Piazza San
    Marco* (1970), pp.122 ff.

15 M. MURARO, 'La Scala senza Giganti', in M. MEISS (ed.), *De artibus opuscula XL:
    Essays in Honor of Erwin Panofsky*, N.Y. University Press, 1961, pp.350–370.

16 SANSOVINO-MARTINIONI, p.320.

17 MURARO (1961), pp.351–352.

18 SAXL, 'Jacopo Bellini . . .' (1970); and V. MOSCHINI, *Disegni di Jacopo Bellini*,
    Bergamo, 1953, especially plates 14 & 18.

19 MURARO (1961), pp.353–354.

20 C.A. ZEVI, *Le collezioni veneziane d'arte e d'antichità dal secolo XIV ai nostri giorni*,
    Venice, 1900.

21 F. CORNER, *Notizie storiche delle chiese e monasteri di Venezia*, Padua, 1758,
    pp.283–288.

22 PAOLETTI (1893), I, pp.190 ff; HUBALA (1974), pp.281–282; and G.
    MARIACHER, 'P.Lombardo a Venezia', *Arte Veneta*, IX, 1955, pp.39 f.

23 HEYDENREICH & LOTZ (1974), p.87.

24 Catholic Encyclopaedia, New York, 1913 edn., II, pp.505–507.

25 P. SANPAOLESI, 'Aspetti dell'architettura del '400 a Siena e Francesco di Giorgio',
    Studi artistici urbinati, I, Urbino, 1949, p.166.

26 See R.E. LIEBERMAN, *The Church of Santa Maria dei Miracoli in Venice*,
    unpublished Ph.D. dissertation, New York University, 1972.

27 ibid., pp.99 ff.

28 PAOLETTI (1893), I, part II, pp.163–190 and II, pp.109–114.

29 SANSOVINO-MARTINIONI, p.154.

30 T. TEMANZA, *Vite dei più celebri architetti e scultori veneziani*, Venice, 1778,
    pp.93–97.

31 L. OLIVATO PUPPI & L. PUPPI, *Mauro Codussi e l'architettura veneziana del Primo Rinascimento*, Electa Milan, 1977, pp.18–45, and cat. no. 1. Before the publication of this brilliant monograph, which is both searching and informative, the only available monograph was L. ANGELINI, *Le opere in Venezia di Mauro Codussi*, Milan, 1945, which is still useful for the measured drawings and plans of the buildings.

32 PUPPI & PUPPI (1977), pp.18 ff. There is no direct evidence that the monks themselves possessed a copy of Alberti's treatise *De re aedificatoria*, but the work was certainly known among the Venetian nobility. (Bernardo Bembo had a manuscript copy made for his own personal library.) On the possible links between Alberti and the Camaldolese order in Florence see PUPPI & PUPPI (1977), p.22, and p.42 note, 99.

33 The contract is published in PUPPI & PUPPI (1977), p.257.

34 ibid., pp.110–122 and cat. no. 9.

35 See W. TIMOFIEWITSCH, 'Genesi e struttura della chiesa del Rinascimento veneziano', *Bollettino CISA*, VI, 1964, pp.271–282.

36 SANSOVINO-MARTINIONI, p.39.

37 PUPPI & PUPPI (1977), pp.206–209; and R. LIEBERMAN, 'Venetian church architecture around 1500'; *Bollettino CISA*, XIX (1977), p.42.

38 SANSOVINO-MARTINIONI, pp.493–495.

39 PUPPI & PUPPI (1977), pp.122–135 and cat. no.11.

40 See J. McANDREW, 'Sant'Andrea della Certosa', *Art Bulletin*, LI, pp.15–28.

41 PUPPI & PUPPI (1977), p.61, pp.73–89, and cat. no.7.

42 P.L. SOHM, 'The Staircases of the Venetian Scuole Grandi and Mauro Coducci', *Architectura*, VIII, 1978, p.128.

43 ibid., pp.130–132.

44 ibid., pp.135 ff; and PUPPI & PUPPI (1977), pp.93–110 and cat. no. 12.

45 SOHM (1978), p.140.

46 PUPPI & PUPPI (1977), pp.140 ff., and cat. no.14.

47 SANSOVINO-MARTINIONI, p.387.

48 PUPPI & PUPPI (1977), pp.165–171, and cat. no. 10.

49 L.B. ALBERTI, *Ten Books on Architecture*, trs. J. Leoni, ed. J. Rykwert, London, 1955, pp.170–171.

50 ibid., p.174.

51 On the political position of Venice at this time, see F. GILBERT, 'Venice in the Crisis of the League of Cambrai', in the J.R. HALE (ed.), *Renaissance Venice*, Faber & Faber, London, 1973, pp.274–292.

52 M. SANUDO, *I Diarii*, ed. R. Fulin, 58 vols., Venice 1879–1903, XV, col.541.

53 E. VIO, 'Le Procuratie Vecchie', in G. SAMONÀ (ed.), (1970), pp.143 ff. On Bon's career, see also L. ANGELINI, *Bartolomeo Bono, Guglielmo d'Alzano: architetti bergamaschi in Venezia*, Bergamo, 1961.

54 SANSOVINO-MARTINIONI, p.293.

55 ASV, *Procuratia de Supra*, *busta* 33, *processo* 68, 'Proprietà in Campo Rusolo', *fascicolo* 2.

56 HOWARD (1975), pp.50 ff.

57 ibid., pp.74–77.

58 HUBALA (1974), pp.334 ff.

59 See LIEBERMAN (1977), pp.41–46.

60 PULLAN (1971), pp.146 ff.

61 ibid., pp.146 and 159.

62 ibid., p.158.

63 SANSOVINO-MARTINIONI, p.288.

VI: 'Roman' Renaissance

1   LORENZI (1868), p.169.

2   CHAMBERS (1970), especially Chapter I 'Another New Rome' (pp.12–31).

3   S. SERLIO, *Tutte l'opere d'architettura et prospettiva*, Venice, 1619, p.123 (verso). On Serlio in Venice see also D. HOWARD, 'Sebastiano Serlio's Venetian Copyrights', *Burlington Magazine*, CXV, 1973, pp.512–516; and W.B. DINSMOOR, 'The Literary Remains of Sebastiano Serlio', *Art Bulletin*, XXIV, 1942, pp.55–91, 115–54.

4   L. CHIODI (ed.), *Lettere inedite di Lorenzo Lotto su le tarsie di Santa Maria Maggiore in Bergamo*, Bergamo, 1962, p.47. On Sansovino's career in Venice see especially G. VASARI (ed. G. MILANESI), *Le vite de' più eccellenti architetti, pittori, et scultori italiani*, 9 vols., Milan, 1878–1885 (henceforth called VASARI-MILANESI), VII, pp.499–513; M. TAFURI, *Jacopo Sansovino e l'architettura del '500 a Venezia*, Marsilio, Padua, 1969, revised paperback edn. 1972; and HOWARD (1975).

5   On Sanmicheli in the Veneto see especially VASARI-MILANESI, VI, pp.341–375; P. GAZZOLA, *Michele Sanmicheli*, exhibition catalogue, Venice, 1960; G. FIOCCO et al., *Michele Sanmicheli 1784–1859: Studi raccolti dall'Accademia di Agricoltura, Scienze e Lettere di Verona*, Verona, 1960; and L. PUPPI, *Michele Sanmicheli: architetto di Verona*, Marsilio, Padua, 1971.

6   See J.R. HALE, *Renaissance Fortification: Art or Engineering?*, Thames & Hudson, London, 1977.

7   See R. GALLO, 'Michele Sanmicheli a Venezia', in FIOCCO et al. (1960), pp.97–112.

8   VASARI-MILANESI, VI, p.349.

9   ibid., VI, p.348.

10 ibid., VI, p.348.

11 HOWARD (1975), pp.38–47.

12 SERLIO (1619), p.133 (verso).

13 VASARI-MILANESI, VII, p.504.

14 F. SANSOVINO, *Delle cose notabili che sono in Venetia*, Venice, 1561, p.24.

15 A. PALLADIO, *I quattro libri dell'architettura*, Venice, 1570, Book I, p.5.

16 For my own view of the controversy over Sansovino's intentions for this end of the Library, see D. HOWARD, 'Two Notes on Jacopo Sansovino', *Architectura*, II, 1974, pp.137–146. On the building of the Library and Sansovino's improvements to Piazza San Marco, see HOWARD (1975), pp.8–28.

17 See J.S. ACKERMAN, *The Architecture of Michelangelo*, Pelican Books, 1970, pp.139 173 and pp.321–325.

18 On the Loggetta, see HOWARD (1975), pp.28–35. On the Fabbriche Nuove di Rialto, see ibid., pp.54–61.

19 D. LEWIS, 'Un disegno autografo del Sanmicheli . . .', *Bollettino dei musei civici veneziani*, XVII-3/4, 1972, pp.7–36.

20 HOWARD (1975), pp.126–132.

21 ibid., pp.132–146.

22 GALLO (1960), pp.120–125.

23 F.C. LANE, 'Naval actions and fleet organization', in HALE (ed.), (1973), pp.148 ff.

24 SANSOVINO-MARTINIONI, p.387.

25 O. LOGAN, *Culture and Society in Venice 1470–1790*, Batsford, London, 1972, pp.176–181.

26 HOWARD (1975), pp.64–74.

27 R. WITTKOWER, *Architectural Principles in the Age of Humanism*, 3rd edn., Tiranti, London, 1962, pp.102–107 and 155–157.

28 HOWARD (1975), pp.88–94.

29 On the Salt Office's election of *proto* in 1554 see LORENZI (1868), pp.281–282. On the Scala d'Oro project see LORENZI (1868), pp.287–288; and G.G. ZORZI, *Le*

opere pubbliche e i palazzi privati di Andrea Palladio, Neri Pozza, Venice, 1964, p.137. On Palladio's Rialto Bridge designs see H. BURNS, B. BOUCHER & L. FAIRBAIRN, *Andrea Palladio 1508–1580: The Portico and the Farmyard*, catalogue of Arts Council exhibition, Hayward Gallery, London, 1975, pp.124 ff.

30 Palladio had submitted a design for the façade of San Pietro di Castello in 1558, but this was probably not the model adopted when the present façade was eventually begun by Francesco Smeraldi in 1594 (L. PUPPI, *Andrea Palladio*, 2 vols., Electa, Milan, 1973, Ii, pp.321–323).

31 See E. BASSI, *The Convento della Carità*, University of Pennsylvania Press, University Park and London, 1973.

32 PUPPI (1973), II, pp.345–357.

33 WITTKOWER (1962), pp.89–90, suggested that Palladio intended to imply two temple fronts, one superimposed upon the other, but according to this idea the smaller temple front would be excessively broad and squat.

34 On the church of San Giorgio Maggiore see G.G. ZORZI, *Le chiese e i ponti di Andrea Palladio*, Neri Pozza, Venice, 1966, pp.42–77; and W. TIMOFIEWITSCH, *Die sakrale Architektur des Palladios*, Fink Verlag, Munich, 1968, pp.13–53.

35 A. PALLADIO, *The Four Books of Architecture*, trs. I. Ware, London, 1738, Dover paperback facsimile edn., New York, 1965, pp.81–82.

36 ibid., p.82.

37 LIEBERMAN (1977), p.46.

38 P. MURRAY, 'Palladio's churches', from *Arte in Europa: scritti in onore di E. Arslan*, Milan, 1966, pp.603–604.

39 D. HOWARD, 'Le chiese del Sansovino a Venezia', *Bollettino CISA*, XIX, (1977), p. 55.

40 BURNS et al. (1975), pp.143–145.

41 W. TIMOFIEWITSCH, *The Chiesa del Redentore*, Pennsylvania State University Press, University Park and London, 1971.

42 ibid., pp.36–38.

43 PALLADIO (1570), Book IV, p.5.

44 ibid., Book IV, p.7.

45 BURNS et al. (1975), pp.155–160.

VII: Baroque

1 E. BASSI, *Architettura del Sei e Settecento a Venezia*, Naples, 1962, p.84.

2 See H. POTTERTON, *Venetian Seventeenth-Century Painting*, catalogue of National Gallery exhibition, London, 1979.

3 See D. ARNOLD, *Monteverdi*, London, 1963; and J. GLOVER, *Cavalli*, Batsford, London, 1978.

4 On Venetian history of the period see especially B. PULLAN (ed.), *Crisis and Change in the Venetian Economy*, University Paperbacks, London, 1968; and LANE (1973), pp.297 ff.

5 For a complete chronology of Longhena's career see D. LEWIS, 'Baldassare Longhena', *Arte Veneta*, XXVII, 1973, pp.328–330. Lewis publishes here what is probably Longhena's baptismal record in January 1599.

6 BASSI (1962), p.83.

7 On Santa Maria della Salute see especially R. WITTKOWER, 'S. Maria della Salute', *Saggi e Memorie di Storia dell'Arte*, III, 1963, pp.33–54; and M. MURARO, 'Il Tempio votivo di Santa Maria della Salute in un poema del Seicento', *Ateneo Veneto*, XI, 1973, pp.87–119. See also the review of Wittkower's 1963 article by J. SCHULZ in the *Journal of Aesthetics and Art Criticism*, XXIV, 1965/6, pp.458–459, in which it is suggested that the presbytery of the Salute was re-designed in about 1656. This date coincides with the time when, according to Muraro, the iconography was also altered.

8 MURARO (1973), p.104.

9 WITTKOWER (1963), p.35, note 10.

10 BASSI (1962), pp.85–89.

11 MURARO (1973), pp.113–114.

12 Longo's poem was discovered by Dott. Giorgio Ferrari, Director of the Marciana Library in Venice. The section which relates to the Salute is published in MURARO (1973), pp.98–104. Muraro's article gives a full discussion of the poem and its implications for the iconography of the church in the context of the political climate of the time.

13 MURARO (1973), figs.10–12.

14 Translation from WITTKOWER (1963), p.43.

15 See B. BOUCHER, 'Baroque Architecture in Venice', *Apollo*, CX, 1979, p.389.

16 MURARO (1973), fig.10.

17 M. LEVI D'ANCONA, *The Iconography of the Immaculate Conception in the Middle Ages and Early Renaissance*, New York, 1957, p.20.

18 WITTKOWER (1963), p.43.

19 ibid., pp.35, 39–40, & 48–50.

20 ibid., pp.46–47.

21 For an outline of the work of Longhena's Roman contemporaries see R. WITTKOWER, *Art and Architecture in Italy 1600–1750*, Pelican History of Art, revised paperback edn., 1973.

22 BASSI (1962), pp.109–110. It is generally assumed that Longhena had some knowledge of an engraving in LABACCO's *Libro di architettura*, published in 1558, showing a project for San Giovanni dei Fiorentini in Rome by Antonio da Sangallo. In this project similar huge scrolls surround the base of the dome (illustrated in WITTKOWER (1963), fig.35).

23 BASSI (1962), p.112.

24 ibid., pp.112–113.

25 ibid., pp.112–113; and E. BASSI, 'Episodi dell'architettura veneta nell'opera di Antonio Gaspari', *Saggi e Memorie di Storia dell'Arte*, III, 1963, pp.88–93.

26 BASSI (1962), pp.146–154.

27 GILBERT (1973), p.277.

28 BASSI (1962), pp.185–188.

29 ibid., p.190.

30 ibid., pp.192–194.

31 ibid., pp.196–198; and F. HASKELL, *Patrons and Painters*, Icon Edition, Harper & Row, New York, 1971, pp.248–249.

32 BASSI (1962), pp.233–234.

VIII: Palladianism and Neoclassicism

1 LANE (1973), p.43. See also M. BERENGO, *La società veneta alla fine del Settecento*, Florence, 1956.

2 HASKELL (1971), pp.245–75, especially pp.268 ff.

3 For a stimulating discussion of Neo-Palladianism in Venice see W. BARCHAM, 'Canaletto and a Commission from Consul Smith', *Art Bulletin*, LIX, 1977, pp.383–393.

4 N. MANGINI, *I teatri di Venezia*, Milan, 1974.

5 BASSI (1962), pp.207 & 269.

6 G. D. ROMANELLI, 'Ca' Corner della Regina a San Cassiano', in *L'Archivio storico delle arti contemporanee: Contributi*, 4, Venice, 1976, pp.35 ff.; and E. BASSI: *Palazzi di Venezia: 'Admiranda Urbis Venetae'*, Venice, 1976, pp.166–73.

7 BASSI (1962), p.207.

8 ibid., pp.269 ff.

9 ibid., pp.335 ff.

10 ibid., pp.295 ff.; and A. MASSARI, *Giorgio Massari, architetto veneziano del Settecento*, Vicenza, 1971.

11 BASSI (1976).

12 BASSI (1962), pp.359 ff.; and BARCHAM (1977), pp.388–9 & 392.

13 HOWARD (1975), p.58.

14 E. BASSI, *Giannantonio Selva, architetto veneziano*, Padua, 1936.

15 For a concise account of the whole European movement see H. HONOUR, *Neo-classicism*, Penguin Books, 1968.

16 HASKELL (1971), pp.300 & 320–3.

17 MANGINI (1974), pp.165 ff.

IX: Venice since the Fall of the Republic

1 LANE (1973), pp.423–427.

2 For a complete account of demolitions and the loss of works of art in the Napoleonic period see A. ZORZI, *Venezia scomparsa*, 2 vols., 2nd edn., Electa, Milan, 1977, I, pp.70–137, and II, catalogue of monuments destroyed, altered or converted to other use.

3 On the work of the Commissione all'Ornato and Selva's rôle, see G. ROMANELLI, *Venezia Ottocento: Materiali per una storia architettonica e urbanistica della città nel secolo XIX*, Officina, Rome, 1977, pp.38–70 and 96–103.

4 On Napoleonic changes to Piazza San Marco see ibid., pp.71–95.

5 On San Geminiano see HOWARD (1975), pp.82–84. Sansovino's remains were finally given a solemn burial in the Baptistery of the Basilica of San Marco in 1929, the 400th anniversary of his appointment to the office of *proto* to the Procuratia de Supra.

6 *The Age of Neoclassicism*, Arts Council exhibition catalogue, London, 1972, pp.624–625.

7 ROMANELLI (1977), p.102.

8 ibid., pp.140–162.

9 ibid., pp.200–201.

10 ibid., p.314.

11 Recent accounts of the events of 1848–1849 can be found in A. BERNARDELLO, P. BRUNELLO and P. GINSBORG, *Venezia 1848–49: La rivoluzione e la difesa*, Comune di Venezia, Venice 1979 (with useful accompanying booklet *Guida alla Venezia del Quarantotto*); and P. GINSBORG, *Daniele Manin and the Venetian Revolution of 1848–49*, Cambridge University Press, 1979.

12 On Santi's activities in Venice see ROMANELLI (1977), pp.185–193.

13 ROMANELLI (1977), pp.195–212.

14 ibid., pp.226–229.

15 T. MANN, *Death in Venice, Tristan, Tonio Kröger*, trs. H.T. Lowe-Porter, Penguin Classics, 1955 edn., p.24; and ROMANELLI (1977), pp.212–213.

16 ZORZI (1977), I, pp.165–170.

17 ROMANELLI (1977), pp.215–225 and 281–283.

18 The demolitions of the period are described in ZORZI (1977), I, pp.138–191.

19 ROMANELLI (1977), pp.363–411; and ZORZI (1977), I, pp.192–197.

20 ROMANELLI (1977), pp.422–426.

21 ibid., pp.430–431.

22 ibid., pp.432–440.

23 ibid., pp.440–445 and 448.

24 Illustrated in BERNARDELLO et al. (1979), p.135.

25 See J. JULIER, *Il Mulino Stucky a Venezia*, Centro Tedesco di Studi Veneziani, Quaderni 7, Venice, 1978.

26 GOETHE (1970 edn.), pp.96–97.

27 ROMANELLI (1977), p.447.

28 MANN (1955 edn.), p.35.

29 P. MARETTO, *Venezia, Architettura del XX secolo in Italia* I, Vitali e Ghianda, Genoa, 1969, p.61.

30 ibid., pp.72–73.

31 ibid., pp.62–63.

32 E. TRINCANATO and U. FRANZOI, *Venise au fil du temps*, Paris, 1971, section XV 'Venise, une ville de l'Italie 1891–1940'; and ZORZI (1977), I, pp.242–244.

33 MARETTO (1969), pp.144–146.

34 ibid., p.92.

35 ibid., p.100; and ZORZI (1977), I, plates 200–202. The engineers who executed the project were Gino Cipriani and Alberto Magrini (TRINCANATO and FRANZOI (1971), section XV).

36 ROMANELLI (1977), p.202 and pp.445–447.

37 MARETTO (1969), p.87.

38 ibid., p.88.

39 ibid., p.91.

40 ibid., p.102.

41 See A. ROGATNIK, 'Venice in perplexity', *Architectural Review*, CXLIX, 1971, pp.261–273.

42 ZORZI (1977), I, p.250.

43 MARETTO (1969), pp.116–117; and ANON, 'Three projects', *Architectural Review*, CXLIX, 1971, pp.317–318.

44 MARETTO (1969), pp.97–99.

45 ibid., p.126.

46 ZORZI (1977), I, pp.200–201, and II, pp.380–381.

47 MARETTO (1969), p.129.

48 ibid., pp.130–131; and ANON (1971), pp.318–319.

49 See for example P. NICHOLS, 'The Politics of Rescue', *Architectural Review*, 1971, p.309; and S. FAY and P. KNIGHTLEY, *The Death of Venice*, Andre Deutsch, London, 1976.

Bibliography

Bibliography I: Some suggestions for further reading

Historical background

Useful general works in English include:

F.C. LANE, *Venice: a Maritime Republic*, Johns Hopkins University Press, Baltimore, 1973.

J.J. NORWICH, *Venice: the Rise to Empire*, Allen Lane, London, 1977.

D. CHAMBERS, *The Imperial Age of Venice 1380–1580*, Thames and Hudson, London, 1970.

O. LOGAN, *Culture and Society in Venice 1470–1790*, Batsford, London, 1972.

Guidebooks

The first true guidebook to Venice was:

F. SANSOVINO, *Venetia città nobilissima et singolare*, Venice, 1581. The edition quoted in this book is the 3rd edition, of 1663, revised by G. MARTINIONI.

The most stimulating guidebook for a first visit to Venice is:

H. HONOUR, *The Companion Guide to Venice*, Collins, London, 1965.

The best modern guidebook is:

G. LORENZETTI, *Venezia e la sua laguna*, Istituto Poligrafico dello Stato, Rome, 1956, and English translation by J. GUTHRIE, Rome, 1961.

Useful material on the city's architecture is to be found in:

E. HUBALA, *Venedig, Reclams Kunstführer: Italien*, II, i, Stüttgart, 1974.

Studies of Venetian architecture

A valuable historical and photographic survey of architecture and urban development in Venice is:

E. TRINCANATO and U. FRANZOI, *Venise au fil du temps*, Éditions Joël Cuenot, Paris, 1971.

Individual periods

Origins of the city

S. BETTINI, *Venezia, nascita di una città*, Electa, Milan, 1978.

Byzantine

O. DEMUS, *The Church of San Marco in Venice, History, Architecture, Sculpture*, Dumbarton Oaks Studies VI, Washington D.C., 1960.

Gothic

H. DELLWING, *Studien zur Baukunst der Bettelorden im Veneto*, Deutsche Kunstverlag, Munich, 1970.

E. ARSLAN, *Gothic Architecture in Venice*, trs. A. ENGEL, Phaidon, London, 1971.

Early Renaissance

P. PAOLETTI, *L'architettura e la scultura del Rinascimento in Venezia*, 3 vols, Venice, 1893.

L. HEYDENREICH and W. LOTZ, *Architecture in Italy 1400–1600*, Pelican History of Art, Harmondsworth, 1974.

High Renaissance

D. HOWARD, *Jacopo Sansovino: Architecture and Patronage in Renaissance Venice*, Yale University Press, New Haven and London, 1975.

H. BURNS, B. BOUCHER and L. FAIRBAIRN, *Andrea Palladio 1508–1580: The Portico and the Farmyard*, Arts Council exhibition catalogue, London, 1975, especially section on Venice.

Baroque to Neoclassicism

E. BASSI, *Architettura del Sei e Settecento a Venezia*, Edizioni Scientifiche Italiane, Naples, 1962.

Nineteenth century

G. ROMANELLI, *Venezia Ottocento: Materiali per una storia architettonica e urbanistica della città nel secolo XIX*, Officina, Rome, 1977.

Twentieth century

P. MARETTO, *Venezia, Architettura del XX secolo in Italia* I, Vitali e Ghianda, Genoa, 1969.

Bibliography II: List of sources cited

ACKERMAN, J.S., 'Sources of the Renaissance Villa', *Studies in Western Art*, II (Acts of the XXth International Congress of the History of Art), Princeton, 1963, pp.6–18.

ACKERMAN, J.S., *The Architecture of Michelangelo*, Pelican Books, 1970.

The Age of Neoclassicism, Arts Council exhibition catalogue, London, 1972.

ALBERTI, L.B., *Ten Books on Architecture*, trs. J.Leoni, ed. J. Rykwert, London, 1955.

ANGELINI, L., *Le opere in Venezia di Mauro Codussi*, Milan, 1945.

ANGELINI, L., *Bartolomeo Bono, Guglielmo d'Alzano: architetti bergamaschi in Venezia*, Bergamo, 1961.

ANON., 'Three Projects', *Architectural Review*, CXLIX, May 1971, pp.317–319.

ARNOLD, D., *Monteverdi*, London, 1963.

ARSLAN, E., *Gothic Architecture in Venice*, trs. A. Engel, Phaidon Press, London, 1972.

BARCHAM, W., 'Canaletto and a commission from Consul Smith', *Art Bulletin*, LIX, 1977, pp.383–393.

BASSI, E., *Giannantonio Selva, architetto veneziano*, Padua, 1936.

BASSI, E., *La Reale Accademia di Belle Arti di Venezia*, Florence, 1941.

BASSI, E., and TRINCANATO, E.R., *Il Palazzo Ducale nella storia e nell'arte di Venezia*, Milan, 1960.

BASSI, E., *Architettura del Sei e Settecento a Venezia*, Edizioni Scientifiche Italiane, Naples, 1962.

BASSI, E., 'Episodi dell'architettura veneta nell'opera di Antonio Gaspari', *Saggi e Memorie di Storia dell'Arte*, III, 1963, pp.57–108.

BASSI, E., *The Convento della Carità*, trs. C.W. Westfall, Pennsylvania State University Press, University Park & London, 1973.

BASSI, E., *Palazzi di Venezia: 'Admiranda Urbis Venetae'*, Venice, 1976.

BELTRAMI, L., *La Ca' del Duca sul Canal Grande*, Milan, 1900.

BERENGO, M., *La società veneta alla fine del Settecento*, Florence, 1956.

BERNARDELLO, A., BRUNELLO, P., and GINSBORG, P., *Venezia 1848–49: La rivoluzione e la difesa*, Commune di Venezia, Venice, 1979 (with accompanying booklet *Guida alla Venezia del Quarantotto*).

BOUCHER, B., 'Baroque Architecture in Venice', *Apollo*, CX, 1979, pp.388–395.

BRADLEY, J.R., ed., *Ruskin's Letters from Venice 1851–2*, Yale University Press, New Haven, Conn., 1955.

BRAUDEL, F., *The Mediterranean and the Mediterranean World in the Age of Philip II*, 2 vols., Collins, London, 1972–1973.

BURNS, H., 'Quattrocento Architecture and the Antique', in R. BOLGAR (ed.), *Classical Influences on European Culture, A.D. 500–1500*, Cambridge, 1971, pp.269–287.

BURNS, H., BOUCHER, B., & FAIRBAIRN, L., *Andrea Palladio 1508–1580: The Portico and the Farmyard*, catalogue of Arts Council exhibition, Hayward Gallery, London, 1975.

CASSIODORUS, see HODGKIN.

CECCHETTI, B., 'La facciata della Ca' d'Oro dello scalpello di Giovanni e Bartolomeo Buono', *Archivio Veneto*, XXXI, 1886, pp.201 ff.

CESSI, R., & ALBERTI, A., *Rialto: l'isola – il ponte – il mercato*, Bologna, 1934.

CHAMBERS, D., *The Imperial Age of Venice 1380–1580*, Thames and Hudson, London, 1970.

CHIODI, L., ed., *Lettere inedite di Lorenzo Lotto su le tarsie di Santa Maria Maggiore in Bergamo*, Bergamo, 1962.

CLARK, A., and RYLANDS, P., *The Church of the Madonna dell'Orto*, Paul Elek, London, 1977.

CONNELL, S.M., *The Employment of Sculptors and Stone-Masons in Venice in the Fifteenth Century*, unpublished Ph.D. thesis, Warburg Institute, London, 1976.

CORNER, F., *Notizie storiche delle chiese e monasteri di Venezia*, Padua, 1758.

CORYATE, T., *Crudities*, London, 1611.

DELLWING, H., *Studien zur Baukunst der Bettelorden im Veneto*, Deutscher Kunstverlag, Munich, 1970.

DEMUS, O., *The Church of San Marco in Venice: History, Architecture, Sculpture*, Dumbarton Oaks Studies VI, Washington D.C., 1960.

DINSMOOR, W.B., 'The Literary Remains of Sebastiano Serlio', *Art Bulletin*, XXIV, 1942, pp.55–91, 115–154.

FAY, S., and KNIGHTLEY, P., *The Death of Venice*, André Deutsch, London, 1976.

FILARETE (Antonio Averlino called 'Il Filarete'), see SPENCER.

FIOCCO, G., et al., *Michele Sanmicheli 1484–1559: Studi raccolti dall'Accademia di Agricoltura, Scienze e Lettere di Verona*, Verona, 1960.

FRANCO, F., 'L'interpolazione del Filarete trattista fra gli artefici del Rinascimento architettonico a Venezia', in *Atti del IV Convegno Nazionale di Storia dell'Architettura*, Milan, 1939.

GAZZOLA, P., *Michele Sanmicheli*, exhibition catalogue, Venice, 1960.

GALLO, R., 'Jacopo Sansovino a Pola', *Rivista di Venezia*, V, 1926, pp.255–286.

GALLO, R., 'Michele Sanmicheli a Venezia', in FIOCCO, G., et al., *Michele Sanmicheli 1484–1559*, Verona, 1960.

GALLO, R., 'L'architettura di transizione dal gotico al rinascimento e Bartolomeo Bon', *Atti del Istituto Veneto di Scienze, Lettere ed Arti*, CXX, 1961–1962, pp.187–204.

GILBERT, F., 'Venice in the Crisis of the League of Cambrai', in HALE, J.R., ed., *Renaissance Venice*, Faber and Faber, London, 1973, pp.274–292.

GINSBORG, P., *Daniele Manin and the Venetian Revolution of 1848–49*, Cambridge University Press, 1979.

GLOVER, J., *Cavalli*, Batsford, London, 1978.

GOETHE, J.W., *Italian Journey 1786–1788*, trs. W.H. Auden and E. Mayer, Penguin Classics, 1970.

GUISCONI, A., (i.e. SANSOVINO, F.), *Tutte le cose notabili e belle che sono in Venetia*, Venice, 1556.

HALE, J.R., ed., *Renaissance Venice*, Faber & Faber, London, 1973.

HALE, J.R., *Renaissance Fortification: Art or Engineering?*, Thames and Hudson, London, 1977.

HASKELL, F., *Patrons and Painters*, Icon Edition, Harper & Row, New York, 1971.

HEYDENREICH, L.H., and LOTZ, W., *Architecture in Italy 1400–1600*, trs. M. Hottinger, Pelican History of Art, 1974.

HODGKIN, T., ed., *The Letters of Cassiodorus*, London, 1886.

HONOUR, H., *Neo-classicism*, Penguin Books, 1968.

HOWARD, D., 'Sebastiano Serlio's Venetian Copyrights', *Burlington Magazine*, CXV, 1973, pp.512–516.

HOWARD, D., 'Two Notes on Jacopo Sansovino', *Architectura*, 1974, pp.132–146.

HOWARD, D., *Jacopo Sansovino: Architecture and Patronage in Renaissance Venice*, Yale University Press, New Haven and London, 1975.

HOWARD, D., 'Le chiese del Sansovino a Venezia', *Bollettino del Centro Internazionale di Studi di Architettura 'Andrea Palladio'*, XIX (1977), pp. 49–67.

HOWELL, J., *A Survey of the Signorie of Venice*, London, 1651.

HUBALA, E., *Venedig, Reclams Kunstführer Italien* II(i), Stüttgart, 1974.

JAMES, H., *Italian Hours*, London, 1909.

JULIER, J., *Il Mulino Stucky a Venezia*, Quaderni VII, Centro Tedesco di Studi Veneziani, Venice, 1978.

LANE, F.C., *Venetian Ships and Shipbuilders of the Renaissance*, Baltimore, 1934.

LANE, F.C., 'Family Partnerships and Joint Ventures in the Venetian Republic', *Journal of Economic History*, IV, 1944, pp.178–196.

LANE, F.C., *Venice: A Maritime Republic*, Johns Hopkins University Press, Baltimore, 1973. (This book is always the 'LANE (1973)' referred to in the notes. *D.H.*)

LANE, F.C., 'Naval actions and fleet organization', in HALE, J.R., ed., *Renaissance Venice*, Faber & Faber, London, 1973, pp.146–173.

LAURITZEN, P., and ZIELCKE, A., *Palaces of Venice*, Phaidon Press, Oxford, 1978.

LEVI D'ANCONA, M., *The Iconography of the Immaculate Conception in the Middle Ages and Early Renaissance*, New York, 1957.

LEWIS, D., 'Un disegno autografo del Sanmicheli e la notizia del committente del Sansovino per S. Francesco della Vigna', *Bollettino dei Musei Civici veneziani*, XVII, 3–4, 1972, pp.7–36.

LEWIS, D., 'Baldassare Longhena' (review of CRISTINELLI, G., *Baldassare Longhena architetto del '600 a Venezia*, Padua, 1962), *Arte Veneta*, XXVII, 1973, pp. 328–330.

LEWIS, D., 'Sansovino and Venetian Architecture' (review of HOWARD, D., *Jacopo Sansovino: Architecture and Patronage in Renaissance Venice*, New Haven & London, 1975), *Burlington Magazine*, CXXI, 1979, pp.38–41.

LIEBERMAN, R.E., *The Church of Santa Maria dei Miracoli in Venice*, unpublished Ph.D. dissertation, New York University, 1972.

LIEBERMAN, R.E., Venetian church architecture around 1500', *Bollettino del Centro Internazionale di Studi di Architettura 'Andrea Palladio'*, XIX (1977), pp. 35–48.

LOGAN, O., *Culture and Society in Venice 1470–1790*, Batsford, London, 1972.

LORENZETTI, G., *Venice and its Lagoon*, 1956 edn., trs. J. Guthrie, Istituto Poligrafico dello Stato, Rome, 1961.

LORENZI, G.B., *Monumenti per servire alla storia del Palazzo Ducale di Venezia*, Venice, 1868.

LOTTO, see CHIODI.

LUTYENS, M., ed., *Effie in Venice: Unpublished Letters of Mrs John Ruskin written from Venice between 1849 and 1852*, John Murray, London, 1965.

LUZZATTO, G., *Storia economica di venezia dall' XI al XVI secolo*, Centro Internazionale delle Arti e del Costume, Venice, 1961.

MANN, T., *Death in Venice, Tristan, Tonio Kröger*, trs. H.T. Lowe-Porter, Penguin Classics, 1955 edn.

MANGINI, N., *I Teatri di Venezia*, Milan, 1974.

MARETTO, P., 'L'edilizia gotica veneziana', *Studi per una operante storia urbana di Venezia*, II, Rome, 1960.

MARETTO, P., 'L'urbanistica veneziana del Trecento', *Bollettino del Centro Internazionale di Studi di Architettura 'Andrea Palladio'*, VII, 1965, pp.232 ff.

MARETTO, P., *Venezia, Architettura del XX secolo in Italia*, I, Vitali e Ghianda, Genoa, 1969.

MARIACHER, G., 'P. Lombardo a Venezia', *Arte Veneta*, IX, 1955, pp.36 ff.

MASSARI, A., *Giorgio Massari, architetto veneziano del Settecento*, Neri Pozza, Vicenza, 1971.

MOLMENTI, P., *La Storia di Venezia nella vita privata*, 2nd edn., Turin, 1880 (re-published with illustrations, 3 vols., Bergamo, 1905–1908).

MOSCHINI, V., *Disegni di Jacopo Bellini*, Bergamo, 1953.

MURARO, M., 'La Scala senza Giganti', in MEISS, M., ed., *De artibus opuscula XL: Essays in Honor of Erwin Panofsky*, New York University Press, 1961, pp.350–370.

MURARO, M., 'Il Tempio votivo di Santa Maria della Salute in un poema del Seicento', *Ateneo Veneto*, XI, 1973, pp.87–119.

MURATORI, S., *Studi per una operante storia urbana di Venezia*, I, Rome, 1960.

MURRAY, P., 'Palladio's churches', in *Arte in Europa: scritti in onore di E. Arslan*, Milan, 1966, pp.597–608.

NICHOLS, P., 'The Politics of Rescue', *Architectural Review*, CXLIX, 1971, p.309.

NORWICH, J.J., *Venice: The Rise to Empire*, Allen Lane, London, 1977.

OKEY, T., *The Old Venetian Palaces and Old Venetian Folk*, London, 1907.

PALLADIO, A., *I quattro libri dell'architettura*, Venice, 1570.

PALLADIO, A, *The Four Books of Architecture*, trs. I. Ware, London, 1738, Dover paperback facsimile edn., New York, 1965.

PAOLETTI, P., *L'architettura e la scultura del Rinascimento in Venezia*, 3 vols., Venice, 1893.

PAVANINI, M., 'Traditional House Construction', *Architectural Review*, CXLIX, 1971, pp.297–302.

POTTERTON, H., *Venetian Seventeenth-Century Painting*, catalogue of National Gallery exhibition, London, 1979.

PULLAN, B., ed., *Crisis and Change in the Venetian Economy*, University Paperbacks, London, 1968.

PULLAN, B., *Rich and Poor in Renaissance Venice*, Oxford University Press, Oxford, 1971.

PUPPI, L., *Michele Sanmicheli: architetto di Verona*, Marsilio, Padua, 1971.

PUPPI, L., *Andrea Palladio*, 2 vols., Electa, Milan, 1973 (English translation by P. Sanders, Phaidon Press, London, 1975).

PUPPI, L. OLIVATO, and PUPPI, L., *Mauro Codussi e l'architettura veneziana del Primo Rinascimento*, Electa, Milan, 1977.

RIDOLFI, C., *Le maraviglie dell'arte*, ed. D.von Hadeln, 2 vols., Berlin, 1914–1924.

RODOLICO, F., *Le pietre delle città d'Italia*, Florence, 1953.

ROGATNIK, A., 'Venice in Perplexity', *Architectural Review*, CXLIX, 1971, pp.261–273.

ROMANELLI, G.D., 'Ca' Corner della Regina a San Cassiano', in *L'Archivio storico delle arti contemporanee: Contributi*, IV, Venice, 1976.

ROMANELLI, G.D., *Venezia Ottocento: Materiali per una storia architettonica e urbanistica della città nel secolo XIX*, Officina, Rome, 1977.

ROSAND, D., 'Titian's "Presentation of the Virgin in the Temple" and the Scuola della Carità', *Art Bulletin*, LVIII, 1976, pp.55–84.

RUSKIN, E., see LUTYENS.

RUSKIN, J., *The Stones of Venice*, 1st edn., 3 vols., London, 1851–1853.

RUSKIN, J., see also BRADLEY.

RUSKIN, J., see also WHITTICK.

SAGREDO, A., *Sulle consorterie delle arti edificative in Venezia*, Venice, 1856.

SAMONÀ, G., et al., *Piazza San Marco: l'architettura, la storia, le funzioni*, Marsilio, Padua, 1970.

SANPAOLESI, P., 'Aspetti dell'architettura del '400 a Siena e Francesco di Giorgio', *Studi artistici urbinati*, I, Urbino, 1949.

SANSOVINO, F., *Delle cose notabili che sono in Venetia*, Venice, 1561.

SANSOVINO, F., *Venetia città nobilissima et singolare*, Venice, 1581, all references here taken from 3rd edn., ed. G. Martinioni, Venice, 1663 (called SANSOVINO-MARTINIONI in the notes).

SANSOVINO, F., see also GUISCONI.

SANUDO, M., *I Diarii*, ed. R. Fulin, 58 vols., Venice, 1879–1903.

SAXL, F., 'Petrarch in Venice' and 'Jacopo Bellini and Mantegna as Antiquarians', both lectures published in HONOUR, H., and FLEMING, J., ed., *A Heritage of Images: A Selection of Lectures by Fritz Saxl*, Penguin Books, 1970.

SCATTOLIN, A., 'The Surveyor of the Basilica', in *The Horses of San Marco*, Royal Academy exhibition catalogue, London, 1979, pp.7–12.

SCATTOLIN, G., *Le case-fondaco sul Canal Grande*, Venice, 1961.

SCHULZ, A.M., 'The Sculpture of Giovanni and Bartolomeo Bon', *Transactions of the American Philosophical Society*, LXVIII (3), 1978.

SCHULZ, J., review of WITTKOWER, R., 'S.Maria della Salute' (*Saggi e Memorie di Storia dell'Arte*, III, 1963), in the *Journal of Aesthetics and Art Criticism*, XXIV, 1965/6, pp.458–459.

SCHULZ, J., *Venetian Painted Ceilings of the Renaissance*, University of California Press, Berkeley and Los Angeles, 1968.

SCHULZ, J., 'The Printed Plans and Panoramic Views of Venice', *Saggi e Memorie di Storia dell'Arte*, VII, 1970.

SERLIO, S., *Tutte l'opere d'architettura et prospettiva*, Venice, 1619.

SOHM, P.L., 'The Staircases of the Venetian Scuole Grandi and Mauro Coducci', *Architectura*, VIII, 1978, pp.125–149.

SPENCER, J.R., ed., *Filarete's Treatise on Architecture*, 2 vols., Yale University Press, New Haven, Conn., 1965.

SPENCER, J.R., 'The Ca' del Duca in Venice and Benedetto Ferrini', *Journal of the Society of Architectural Historians*, XXIX, 1970, pp.3–8.

TAFURI, M., *Jacopo Sansovino e l'architettura del '500 a Venezia*, Marsilio, Padua, 1969, revised paperback edn., 1972.

TAIT, H., *The Golden Age of Venetian Glass*, exhibition catalogue, British Museum, London, 1979.

TASSINI, G., *Alcuni palazzi ed antichi edifici di Venezia*, Venice, 1879.

TASSINI, G., *Curiosità veneziane*, 5th edn., Venice, 1915.

TEMANZA, T., *Vite dei più celebri architetti e scultori veneziani*, Venice, 1778.

TIMOFIEWITSCH, W., 'Genesi e struttura della chiesa del Rinascimento veneziano', *Bollettino del Centro Internazionale di Studi di Architettura 'Andrea Palladio'*, VI, 1964, pp.271–282.

TIMOFIEWITSCH, W., *Die sakrale Architektur des Palladios*, Fink Verlag, Munich, 1968.

TIMOFIEWITSCH, W., *The Chiesa del Redentore*, Pennsylvania State University Press, University Park and London, 1971.

TOESCA, P., *Il Trecento*, Turin, 1950.

TRAVERSARI, G., *L'arco dei Sergi*, Cedam, Padua, 1971.

TRINCANATO, E.R., *Venezia Minore*, Milan, 1948.

TRINCANATO, E.R., 'Venezia nella storia urbana', *Urbanistica*, LII, 1968, pp.7–69.

TRINCANATO, E.R., 'Il Palazzo Ducale', in SAMONÀ, G., et al., *Piazza San Marco*, Padua, 1970, pp.110–137.

TRINCANATO, E.R., and FRANZOI, U., *Venise au fil du temps*, Joël Guenot, Paris, 1971.

VASARI, G., *Le vite de' più eccellenti architetti, pittori, et scultori italiani*, ed. G. Milanesi, 9 vols., Milan, 1878–1885 (called VASARI-MILANESI in the notes).

VIO, E., 'Le Procuratie Vecchie', in SAMONÀ, G., et al., *Piazza San Marco*, Padua, 1970, pp.142–149.

WALEY, D., *The Italian City Republics*, World University Library, London, 1969.

WHITE, J., *Art and Architecture in Italy 1250–1400*, Pelican History of Art, 1966.

WHITTICK, A., ed., *Ruskin's Venice*, George Godwin, London, 1976.

WIROBISZ, A., 'L'attività edilizia a Venezia nel XIV e XV secolo', *Studi Veneziani*, VII, 1965, pp.307–343.

WITTKOWER, R., *Architectural Principles in the Age of Humanism*, 3rd edn., Alec Tiranti, London, 1962.

WITTKOWER, R., 'S.Maria della Salute', *Saggi e Memorie di Storia dell'Arte*, III, 1963, pp.33–54.

WITTKOWER, R., *Art and Architecture in Italy 1600–1750*, Pelican History of Art, revised paperback edn., 1973.

WITTKOWER, R., *Gothic vs. Classic*, Thames and Hudson, London, 1974.

WOLTERS, W., Plastiche Deckendekorationen des Cinquecento in Venedig und in Veneto, Berlin 1968.

WOLTERS, W., *La scultura veneziana gotica 1300–1460*, 2 vols., Alfieri, Venice, 1976.

ZEVI, C.A., *Le collezioni veneziane d'arte e d'antichità dal secolo XIV ai nostri giorni*, Venice, 1900.

ZORZI, A., *Venezia scomparsa*, 2 vols., 2nd edn., Electa, Milan, 1977.

ZORZI, G.G., *Le opere pubbliche e i palazzi privati di Andrea Palladio*, Neri Pozza, Venice, 1964.

ZORZI, G.G., *Le chiese e i ponti di Andrea Palladio*, Neri Pozza, Venice, 1966.

Index

Ackerman, James, 172
Adam, Robert, 210
Agnadello, Battle of, 127, 133, 136
Alberti, Leon Battista, 103, 104, 116, 118,
    121, 124, 125, 136, 157, 171, 243, n.32
Aldine Press, 121, 182
Alessi, Galeazzo, 172
Altinum, 15
Antiquity, attitudes to, 104, 108, 111, 114,
    116, 127, 136, 140, 151, 173, 210, 216
Aquileia, 15, 19, 76
Architect, the role of the, 15, 60
Athens, Tower of the Winds, 125, 184
Augustinian order, 70, 76, 131, 161
Austrian rule in Venice, 122, 213, 216,
    218–21, 222, 223

Barbari, Jacopo de', 46, 50, 51, 54, 71, 118,
    122, 123, 125, *Figs. 1, 21, 24, 63, 66*
Barbarian invasions, 15, 16, 18, 19, 41, 136
Barbarigo, Doge Agostino, 110
    Doge Marco, 110
Barbaro family, 166
    Antonio, 190
    Daniele, 161, 172
    Marc'Antonio, 172
Bastiani, Lazzaro, 147, 152
Bellini, Gentile, 35, 36, 80, 82, 150, *Fig. 10*
    Giovanni, 121, 129
    Jacopo, 110, 125
Bellini, Vincenzo, 212
Benedictine order, 69, 103, 115, 160,
    163–5, 169, 185, 225
Bergamo, 67, 114, 129
Bernardino, San, 112–3
Bernini, Gian Lorenzo, 178, 183, 184, 192
Bessarion of Trebizond, Cardinal, 104, 121,
    146
Bianchi, Pietro, 209–10
Biennale, 214, 228, 234
Black Death, 55, 67, 81; *see also* plague
Bologna, 38, 53, 226
    Peace of, 128
    San Petronio, 102
Bon, Bartolomeo, the elder, 72, 77, 100,
    107, 108, 129; the younger, 129,
    133–5, 139
    Filippo, 187
    Giovanni, 92, 108, 129
Borghesia, 225–6; *see also* citizen class
Borromini, Francesco, 178, 183, 189, 192
Boschini, Marco, 179–81
Bramante, Donato, 65, 138, 139, 155, 157,

169, 172
Bregno, Antonio, 108
Brescia, 67
Brick, use of, 37, 56
Bridges, 47–50, 219, 220, 221
Brighton Pavilion, 226
Brunelleschi, Filippo, 102, 104, 112, 113,
    118, 157
Buon, *see* Bon
Buora, Giovanni, 121
Burlington, Lord, 198
Byzantine Empire, 15, 16, 19, 20, 22, 27,
    41, 121, 210
Byzantium, *see* Constantinople

Cadorin, Lodovico, 219
Calergi family 123
Camaldolese order, 115, 122, 127, 158
Cambrai, Wars of the League of, 122,
    127–37, 140
Canal, Matino da, 32
Canaletto, Antonio da Canal, called il, 57,
    63, 161, 194, 197, 205, *Fig. 25*
Canova, Antonio, 208, 216
Cappello, Procurator Antonio, 140, 141
Capuchins, *see* Franciscan order, Capuchin
    branch
Carmelite order, 70, 193
Carpaccio, Vittore, 48, 59, 63, 65, 72, 125,
    152, *Figs. 19, 26, 29*
Casoni, Giovanni, 219, 220
Cassiodorus, 17
Castagno, Andrea del, 103
Caterina, Queen of Cyprus, 154, 196
Cavalli, Francesco, 176
Cavazza, Gerolamo, 189
Celestro, il, 129–30
Cesariano, Cesare, 136
Chambers, David, 136
Charlemagne, 16, 19
Charles V, Emperor, 137
Chimneys, 63
Chioggia, 67, 202
    Cathedral, 179
    War of, 67, 68
Cicognara, Leopoldo, 93
Cimarosa, Domenico, 212
Cistercian order, 69
Citizen class, 98
Clement VII, Pope, 140
Clement XIII, Pope, 188
Clergy, Venetian, 27, 98, 118
Codussi, Mauro, 114–27, 131, 145, 150,

158, 163, 165, 184, 185
Colonna, Francesco, 111, 182
Cominelli, Andrea, 188
Commissione all'Ornato, 214, 219, 224
Constantine, Emperor, 19
Constantinople 15, 19, 30, 32, 35, 40,
  136–7
  Church of Hagia Sophia, 23
  Church of the Holy Apostles
   (Apostoleion), 29, 30, 31, 32
Contarini family, 63
  Doge Domenico, 29
  Marino, 57, 89–94
  Doge Niccolo, 179
Corbusier, Le, 235–6
Corfu, 141
Corner family (Cornaro), 38, 106, 154,
  157, 196
  Andrea, 106
  Federico, 68
  Procurator Zorzi, 154
Coronelli, Vincenzo, 196
Cortona, Pietro da, 192
Coryate, Thomas, 49, 66
Council of Ten, 98, 133, 141–2, 144, 152
Council of Trent, 167, 172
Counter Reformation, 75, 133, 167, 172,
  180, 192, 194, 198
Cozzarelli, Giacomo, 113
Craftsmen, 60, 97; see also Scuole
Crete, 123, 141, 176
Crusades, 20, 32, 33, 35, 37, 43, 67, 95
Cyprus, 141, 144, 155, 173, 176

Dalmatia, 32, 67, 104, 190
Dandolo, Doge Enrico, 32, 38
Dario, Giovanni, 108
Defence, 67–8; see also fortification
Delfino, Pietro, 115–6
Dellwing, Herbert, 71
Diedo, Antonio, 216
Doge, office of (Dogado), 27, 38, 110, 215
Dolomites, 58
Dominican order, 70–2, 193, 199, 202
Dolfin, Zuanne, 139; see also Delfino
Donà, Doge Leonardo, 165
  Doge Pietro, Abbot, 115
Donatello, 102
Donizetti, Gaetano, 212

England, 194, 208, 225
Enlightenment, 194, 208
Ephesus, Church of St John, 29

Falconetto, Giovanmaria, 105, 140, 150,
  153
Falier, Doge Vitale, 29
Ferrini, Benedetto, 106–7, 108
Filarete, Antonio Averlino, called il, 106–7,
  108, Fig. 50
Fini, Vincenzo, 192
Florence, 17, 38, 46, 65, 72, 97–8, 102, 103,
  108, 110
  Baptistery, 114, 127
  Duomo, 118
  Laurentian Library, 148

Palazzo Medici, 124
Palazzo Rucellai, 116, 124
Palazzo Vecchio, 85
Piazza del Duomo, 49
Ponte Vecchio, 48
Sta. Croce, 74
S. Lorenzo, Old Sacristy, 113
S. Marco, library, 103
Sta. Maria Novella, 71
S. Miniato, 113
S. Salvatore al Monte, 158
Foresti, Padre Pietro, 201
Fortification, 140–4
Foscari, Doge Francesco, 81, 94–5, 102,
  104, 108
Foundations, 56, 181
Franciscan order (Frati Minori), 70, 74,
  133, 158
  Capuchin branch, 170, 172
  Conventual branch, 158
  Observant branch, 112–3, 157–8, 169,
   172
French Revolution, 209
Franchetti, Baron, 93
Fuin, Giovanni, 226

Gallo, Jacopo, 189, 190
Gambello, Antonio, 105, 112, 121, 127
Gaspari, Antonio, 186, 188, 199, 200
  Giacomo, Fig. 102
Genoa, 38, 176
Genoese, Wars against the, 33, 37, 67
Gentile da Fabriano, 103, 110
Gerardo, Maffei, Patriarch of Venice, 117
Ghiberti, Lorenzo, 102, 114
Giocondo, Fra, 105, 131, 136, 139, 140
Giordano, Luca, 176
Giorgio, Francesco di, 113
Giorgione, 56
Giovanni di Martino da Fiesole, 102
Giudice, B. del, 229–30, 233
Giustiniani family, 95
Glass industry, 34, 58–9, 176, 223
Goethe, Johann Wolfgang, 14, 51, 52, 53,
  225–6
Goldoni, Carlo, 87
Grado, 21, 22
  Patriarch of, 27
Grassi family, 202–3
  Giovanni, 196
Great Council (Maggior Consiglio), 68,
  80–1, 83, 110, 213
Greece, architecture of, 30, 138, 161, 206,
  210, 219
Grigi, GianGiacomo de', 155
  Guglielmo de', 129
Grimani family, 155–7, 163
  Doge Antonio, 155–6
  Procurator Gerolamo, 155
  Procurator Vettor, 140, 142, 153
Gritti, Doge Andrea, 140, 152, 157
Guariento, 81
Guberni, Pietro de', 160–1
Guilds, see Scuole

Hapsburgs, see Austrian rule

Heating, 62
Heraclius, Emperor, 21
Hospitals, 158–9, 174–5, 200–2
Howell, James, 52
Humanism, 103–4

Innocent VIII, Pope, 120
Inquisition, 208
Interdict, Papal, 176–8, 179
Iron, use of, 59
Istria, 57, 116
Istrian stone, use of, 57, 117, 150, 165, 167, 184

James, Henry, 50
Jesuit order, 180, 192, 193
Jews, 38, 53, 225
Jones, Inigo, 198, 210
Julius II, Pope, 127, 128, 138
Justinian, Emperor of Byzantium, 23, 29
Juvarra, Filippo, 194

Labacco, Antonio, 246 n.22
Labia family, 188
Lamberti, Niccolò di Pietro, 102
   Pietro di Niccolò, 102
Legnago, 139
Leo X, Pope, 138
Lepanto, Battle of, 105, 173
Lieberman, Ralph, 114
Lippi, Filippo, 103
Liss, Johann, 176
Lodoli, Carlo, 201, 208
Lombard invasions, see Barbarian invasions
Lombard stonemasons in Venice, 34, 35, 43, 92–3, 102, 112, 114
Lombardi workshop, 101, 112, 114, 127
Lombardo, Pietro Solari, called il, 110, 112–4, 121, 127
   Tullio, 121, 131
London, 46, 49
   British Museum, 110
   Fire of, 131
   National Gallery, 57, 197
   Victoria and Albert Museum, 100
Longhena, Baldassare, 65, 103, 129, 176–89, 192, 195, 196, 197, 199, 203, 245 n.5
Longo, Lorenzo, 179, 181, 246, n.12
Loredan, Andrea, 122
   Doge Leonardo, 188
Loreto, Holy House (Santa Casa), 179
Loth, Johann Carl, 176
Lotto, Lorenzo, 138
Lucca, 113
Lugano, Lake of, 178, 195

Maccaruzzi, Bernardino, 212
Maderno, Carlo, 189
Maggior Consiglio, see Great Council
Malamocco, 16, 80
Malcontenta, Villa, 217
Malipiero, Domenico, 118
   Doge Pasquale, 104, 112
Manin, Daniele, 219
Manin family, 195
   Doge Ludovico, 154, 213

Mann, Thomas, 221, 226
Manufacturing industry, 176, 223–5, 228–9
Mantua, 104, 145
Manuzio, Aldo, see Aldine Press
Marble, use of, 57
Maretto, Paolo, 85
Marghera, Porto, 225, 228, 231
Mark, Saint, 19, 27–8, 32, 121, 238 n.7
Marino da Pisa, 74
Maria, Mario de, 226
Martini family, 113
Mary the Virgin, Saint, 21, 22, 24, 113, 119, 120–1, 178, 179, 180, 181, 184
Masaccio, 102
Masegne Pier Paolo dalle, 81, 83
Maser, Tempietto, 166, 198, 199
Masieri, Angelo, 233
Massari, Giorgio, 188, 199–204, 205, 206, 224
Medici, Cosimo dei, il Vecchio, 103
Meduna, Giambattista, 226
Memmo, Andrea, 208
Mendicant orders, 44, 69–77, 113, 131, 240 n.26
Mestre, 54, 67, 228, 231
   Teatro Balbi, 212
Mezzani, Giuseppe, 217
Michelangelo, 48, 65, 138, 139, 148, 151–2
Michelozzo, 103, 104, 112, 185
Milan, 46, 49, 67, 102, 104, 214, 221
   Cathedral, 93
   S.Ambrogio, 29
   S.Barnaba, 172
Miozzi, Eugenio, 221, 228, 230
Mocenigo, Doge Alvise II, 196
Monteverdi, Claudio, 176
Moro, Doge Cristoforo, 108, 112–3
Mosaics, 22, 24, 25, 26, 27, 30, 32–5, 72, 103, 229
Moschini, Abbot, 216
Mosto, Alvise da, 197
Murano, 19, 20, 34, 35, 59, 115, 223, 228
   Sta. Chiara, 113
   Sti. Maria e Donato, 24–5, 33, 72, Fig. 4
Muratori, Saverio, 51
Music, 158–9, 169, 176, 194, 201, 212

Nanni di Bartolo, called il Rosso, 102
Naples, 46, 67, 104, 176, 178, 209
Napoleon, 212, 213, 214, 216, 217, 222
Napoleonic rule in Venice, 129, 131, 185, 213–8, 222, 225
Nash, John, 226
Nervi, Pier Luigi, 235
Neville, Alfred, 221
Nobile Società 209–12
Nobility, Venetian, 37–8, 68, 98, 103, 157, 176, 188, 193, 202–3, 213, 225
Northern Europe, contacts with, 104, 176, 194, 208, 224–5

Observant Franciscans, see Franciscan order, Observant branch
Olivo, G. dall', 229
Olivolo-Castello, Bishopric of, see Rialto, Bishopric of

Oratorian order, 199
Orphanages, *see* hospitals
Orseolo, Doge Orso, 21
  Doge Pietro, 29
Osservanti, *see* Franciscan order, Observant
  branch
Ottoman Empire, *see* Turks

Padua, 42, 53, 57, 67, 103, 111, 127, 140,
    150, 153, 160
  Arena chapel, 114
  Eremitani, church of the, 72
  Palazzo della Ragione, 83
  Scrovegni chapel, 103
  Sta. Giustina, 165, 167, 169
Paisiello, Giovanni, 209
Palaces, interior planning of, 40–1, 63,
    85–7, 186, 239 n.23
Palermo, 46
Palladio, Andrea, 48, 105, 117, 140, 146,
    153, 158, 160–73, 174, 176, 178, 179,
    181–6, 189, 190, 194, 196, 197, 198,
    199, 200, 206, 208, 210, 211, 217, 245
    n.29 and n.33
Palma Vecchio, 91
Paris, 46, 214
Parish churches, 26–7, 76, 118
Parma, 140
Partecipazio, Doge Angelo, 80
Pasti, Matteo dei, 116
Patriarch of Venice, 27, 218
Patriciate, Venetian, *see* nobility, Venetian
Pellegrini, Giovanni Antonio, 194, 205, 206
Pépin, 16
Perugia, 38
Peruzzi, Baldassare, 137
Pesaro family, 186–7
  Doge Giovanni, 186
Petrarch, 41, 103
Pharos, Tower of Ptolemy, 125
Piacenza, 140
Piranesi, Giovanni Battista, 206, 207
Pisa, 38, 49
Pisanello, 103
Pisano, Giovanni, 103
Plague, 55, 170, 176, 178, 184; *see also*
    Black Death
Plato, 158
Pola, 57, 104, 116
  Arco dei Sergi, 104–5, 127
Polo, Marco, 36, 40
Ponte, Antonio da, 48
Population, 46, 55, 67, 68, 193, 223
Pozzo, Andrea, 206
Priuli, Girolamo, 94, 123, 128
Procurators of Saint Mark's, 28, 36, 129,
    133, 139, 144–8, 152, 184, 196–7
Protestantism, 179, 192, 225
Puccini, Giacomo, 212
Puppi, Lionello and Loredana Olivato, 127

Quercia, Jacopo della, 102
Quarenghi, Giacomo, 208

Railways, 221, 222
Raphael, 138, 139

Ravenna, 15, 16, 19, 21, 115–6, 127
  Mausoleum of Galla Placida, 22
  S. Apollinare in Classe, 22
  S. Apollinare Nuovo, 22, 116
  S. Vitale, 23, 182
Raverti, Matteo, 92–3
Religious orders, 69–77, 131, 214
Rezzonico family, 187
  Carlo, Pope Clement XIII, 188
Rialto, Bishopric of, 16, 27
Ricci, Marco and Sebastiano, 194
Rimini, 104
  Tempio Malatestiano, 116
Rivo Alto, 15, 17, 19, 80; *see also* Venice,
    Rialto
Rizzo, Antonio, 108, 110
Roman Empire, 15, 19, 41, 136
Rome, 17, 46, 104, 116, 121, 136–8, 140,
    145, 151, 191, 192, 194, 199, 207, 208,
    220
  Baths, 167, 172
  Capitoline Palaces, 151–2
  Colosseum 151
  Cortile del Belvedere, 128, 138
  Gesù, 169, 172
  House of Raphael, 65, 155
  Lateran Baptistery, 20
  Olympic Stadia, 235
  Palazzo Gaddi, 138, 155
  Pantheon, 172, 199, 206
  Piazza di S. Pietro, 183
  Porta Maggiore, 145
  S. Andrea al Quirinale, 183–4
  Sta. Costanza, 182
  S. Giovanni dei Fiorentini, 246 n.22
  Sta. Maria del Popolo, 169
  St. Peter's, 128, 136, 138
  Spanish Steps, 194
  Teatro Argentina, 212
  Tempietto at S. Pietro in Montorio, 138,
    172
  Theatre of Marcellus, 151
  Villa Madama, 138
Rome, Sack of, 137, 138
Rossellino, Antonio, 113
Rossi, Domenico, 195–6, 197, 198, 199,
    200, 203
Rossini, Gioacchino, 212
Rosso, Zuan Antonio, 160
Rusconi, Giovanni Antonio, 145, 206
Ruskin, Effie, 62, 78
Ruskin, John, 44, 77–8, 79, 87–9, 93, 94,
    95, *Fig. 38*

Salt Office (Proveditori al Sal), 140, 160
Sangallo family 139
  Antonio da, the younger, 246 n.22
  Giuliano da, 138
Sanmicheli, Michele, 65, 137, 138–57, 173,
    180, 210, 228
  Polo, 139
  Giangirolamo, 139
Sansovino, Andrea, 138
  Francesco, 15, 25, 27, 54, 58, 59, 62, 72,
    76, 94, 103, 110, 114, 118, 123, 129,
    134, 145, 157, 164, 169

Jacopo, 30, 35, 48, 57, 65, 103, 110, 129, 131, 137, 138–59, 160, 161, 162–3, 165, 173, 174, 175, 176, 184, 186, 188, 189–90, 196, 197, 201, 203, 206, 210, 216, 247 n.5

Santi, Lorenzo, 216, 219–20

Sanudo, Marin, 128–9

Sardi, Giovanni, 226
    Giuseppe, 188–92, 195, 200, 201

Sarpi, Fra Paolo, 179

Saxl, Fritz, 103

Scalfarotto, Giovanni, 198–9, 206

Scamozzi, Vincenzo, 129, 147, 174–5, 176, 178, 179, 184–5, 197, 210

Scarpa, Carlo, 233

Scarpagnino, Antonio, 110, 131, 133–5, 136, 140

Scattolin, Angelo, 234–5

Selva, Giannantonio, 154, 205, 206, 207–12, 214–5, 216, 217, 218, 219

Senate, 112, 121, 137, 164, 170, 172, 178, 181, 188

Serlio, Sebastiano, 105, 137–8, 140, 145, 173, Fig. 69

Servite order, 70

Sforza, Duke Francesco, of Milan, 94, 106, 141

Shakespeare, William, 145

Shipping, see trade

Sicily, 194

Siena, 38, 127
    Osservanza, church of the, 113, 158
    Palazzó Pubblico, 85

Smeraldi, Antonio, called 'il Fracao', 178–9
    Francesco, 178

Smith, Consul Joseph, 205, 208

Soli, Giuseppe Maria, 216

Somascan order, 179–80, 216

Sorella, Simon, 175–6

Spalato, 104, 116

Spavento, Giorgio, 131–2

Steno, Doge Michele, 141

Streets, 49–51, 219, 220, 222, 228, 236–7

Strozzi, Bernardo, 176

Stuart and Revett, 206

Stucky, Giovanni, 224–5

Sullam, Guido, 227–230

Taglioni Mademoiselle, 92–3

Temanza, Tomaso, 114, 178, 195, 196, 199, 206–7, 208, 211

Terraferma, Venetian, 17, 67, 94, 128, 141, 160, 164, 176, 199, 203, 228

Terrazzo flooring, 58

Theatine order, 174, 197

Theodore, Saint, 19, 27, 112

Tiepolo, Giambattista, 199, 200, 202
    Doge Jacopo, 70

Timofiewitsch, Wladimir, 170

Tintoretto, Jacopo, 101, 134

Tirali, Andrea, 195–8, 199, 201

Titian, 56, 75, 100, 148

Torcello, island of, 18, 19, 20–24, 28, 35, 48
    Baptistery, 18, 20, plan p. 21
    Cathedral, 18, 20–22, 25, 33–4, Figs. 2–3, plan p. 21

Sta. Fosca, 22–4, 25, 29, Fig. 2, plan p. 23

Trade and Shipping, 37, 38, 103, 104, 176, 181, 193, 213–4, 217, 218, 228

Traghetti, 48–9, 231–2

Tremignon, Andrea, 192, 195

Treviso, 58, 67, 140, 224
    Palazzo dei Trecento, 122
    S. Francesco, 71
    S. Nicolo, 74

Trieste, 214, 217, 219

Turks, 20, 67, 105, 108, 127, 172, 176, 180, 193, 194

Tuscany, architecture of, 112–4, 115, 118, 127

Uccello, Paolo, 35, 103

Udine, 195

Umiliati order, 77

Urbino, 104

Vasari, Giorgio, 103, 131, 140, 142, 144, 145, 147, 161, 206

Vendramin family, 154

Venetia, Roman Province of, 15

Venetian Republic, Fall of, 14, 38, 66, 209, 212, 213–4

Venetian State Archives, 163–4, 166

Veneto, 42, 112, 137–40, 157, 160, 176, 207, 213, 222

Venice, founding of the city, 15, 25

Venice, Accademia di Belle Arti, 48, 56, 59, 72, 99, 161, 205, 206, 208, 216, 217, 218

    Ala Napoleonica, 216, Fig. 118

    Albergo Excelsior, Lido, 226, Fig. 128

    Archivio di Stato, see Venetian State Archives

    Arco Foscari, 108, 117, 125, 127

    Arsenal, 46, 141, 142, 219; gateway, 104–6, 108, 112, 127, Fig. 48

    Bacino Orseolo, 227, 230, Fig. 130

    Bacino di S. Marco, 181, 226

    Biblioteca Marciana, see Venice Library of St. Mark's

    Ca' del Duca, 106–7, 116, 145, 187, Fig. 48

    Ca' Foscari, 86, 94–5, 102, 106, 229, Fig. 43, plan p. 86

    Ca' da Mosto (Osteria del Leon Bianco), 44, 53, 85, Fig. 17

    Ca' d'Oro, 57, 86, 89, 91–4, 95, 101, 108, Fig. 42

    Ca' Pesaro, see Venice, Palazzo Pesaro

    Ca' Rezzonico, formerly Bon, 62, 187–8, 196, Fig. 97, plan p. 187

    Caffè Florian, 219, Fig. 122

    Caffè Quadri, 219

    Calle del Paradiso, 53, 87, 125, Fig. 23

    Campanile of S. Marco, 37, 54, 57, 110, 147, 150, 152, Fig. 75

    Campo Manin, 234, Fig. 138

    Campo S. Fantin, 210–11

    Campo S. Polo, 50, Fig. 21

    Cannaregio, civic hospital planned for, 235–6, Fig. 139

Venice, *contd*

Casa del Farmacista, Lido, 229–30, *Fig. 132*

Casa de Maria, 226, *Fig. 129*

Casa Salviati, 229, *Fig. 131*

Cassa di Risparmio, 234–5, *Fig. 138*

Clock Tower, *see* Venice, Torre dell'Orologio

coffee house in Giardini Reali, 220, *Fig. 123*

Convento della Carità, 161–3, 196, 218, 220, *Figs. 84–5*

Corpo di Guardia, Arsenal, 219, 220, *Fig. 121*

Corte seconda del Milion, 36, *Fig. 11*

Dogana, 181

Doge's Palace, *see* Venice, Palazzo Ducale

Fabbriche Nuove di Rialto, 152–3, 206, *Fig. 78*

Fabbriche Vecchie di Rialto, 122

Fenice Theatre, *see* Venice, Teatro la Fenice

Fire station, 230, *Fig. 133*

Fondaco dei Tedeschi, 56, 130

Fondaco dei Turchi, 38, 40, 43, *Figs. 13–4*

Fortezza di S. Andrea, 141–5, 150, 228, *Fig. 70*, plan p. 142

Frari, *see* Venice, Sta. Maria Gloriosa dei Frari

Gesuati (Sta. Maria del Rosario), 199–200, *Figs 107–8*

Ghetto, 38, 53, *Fig. 22*

Giardini at Castello, 214, 228

Giardini Reali, 215, 220

Giudecca, 54, 170, 183, 226, *Fig. 24*
Canal, 113, 170, 181, 199, 223

Grand Canal, 46, 52, 108, 154, 174, 181, 184, 199, 202, 203, 205, 220, 221, 223, 229, 233

Incurabili hospital and church, 158–9, 169, 175, 201, *Fig. 83*, plan p. 160

Library of St. Mark's (Biblioteca Marciana), 57, 103, 140, 146–52, 163, 165, 184–5, 216, 244 n.16, *Figs. 72–4 and 76*, plan p. 147

Lido, 55, 225–6, 227, 229–30

Loggetta, 57, 152–3, 163

Loggia Zenobio, *see* Venice, Palazzo Zenobio

Maddalena, 206–7, *Fig. 114*

Madonna dell'Orto, 77, *Fig. 36*

Masieri Memorial House, 233, *Fig. 135*

Mendicanti hospital and church, 169, 174–5, 190–1, 196, 200, 201, plan p. 175

Merceria, 50, 70, 125, 131

Mint, *see* Venice, Zecca

Mulino Stucky, 223–5, *Fig. 127*

Museo Correr, 147, 186, 201, 216

Museo del Settecento, *see* Venice, Ca' Rezzonico

Natural History Museum, 17, 38

Ospedaletto, 189, 190, 191, 201

Osteria del Leon Bianco, *see* Venice, Ca' da Mosto

Venice, *contd*

Palazzi Giustiniani, 58, 86, 95, 101, *Fig. 43*, plan p.86

Palazzao Balbi, 174, 233, *Fig. 92*

Palazzo Bembo, 154

Palazzo Bon, *see* Venice, Ca' Rezzonico

Palazzo del Casinò, Lido, 230, *Fig. 134*

Palazzo Cavalli, 96

Palazzo Centani, 87, *Fig. 28*

Palazzo del Cinema, Lido, 230

Palazzo Civran, 205, *Fig. 113*

Palazzo Centani (house of Carlo Goldoni), 87, *Fig. 28*

Palazzo Contarini-Fasan ('House of Desdemona'), 65, 95–6, *Fig. 44*

Palazzo Corner at S. Maurizio, 154–7, 186, 188, 196, 203, *Fig. 80*

Palazzo Corner della Regina, 196, 203, *Fig. 104*, plan p. 197

Palazzo Dario, 108, 117, *Fig. 51*

Palazzo Dolfin (later Manin), 154–5, 157, *Fig. 79 (frontispiece)*

Palazzo Donà, 43–4, 88, *Fig. 16*

Palazzo Ducale (Doge's Palace), 17, 30, 68, 76, 79–85, 89, 91, 95, 96, 99, 101, 103, 108–12, 125, 140, 145, 146, 150, 152, 160, 161, 172–3, 213, 216, 226, 240–1 n.18, *Figs. 37, 39, 52–3*, plan p. 80

Palazzo Farsetti, 38, 40, *Fig. 12*, plan p.41

Palazzo Foscari, *see* Venice, Ca' Foscari

Palazzo Giovanelli, 96

Palazzo Grassi, 202–3, 224, *Figs. 111–2*

Palazzo Grimani at S. Luca, 155–7, *Fig. 81*, plan p.156

Palazzo Labia, 188

Palazzo Leon, Corte del Remer, 44

Palazzo Loredan (Municipio), 38–40, 43, 85, *Fig. 12*, plan p.41; *see also* Venice, Palazzo Vendramin-Calergi, formerly Loredan

Palazzo Patriarcale, 219–20

Palazzo Pesaro, 41, 65, 186–7, 188, 196, *Fig. 96*

Palazzo Pisani-Moretta, 96, *Fig. 45*

Palazzo Priuli at S. Severo, 89, *Fig. 41*

Palazzo Priuli-Bon at S. Stae, 53, 88–9, *Fig. 40*

Palazzo Querini-Stampalia, 233

Palazzo Vendramin-Calergi, formerly Loredan, 57, 122–4, 156, 157, *Fig. 62*

Palazzo Zenobio, gardener's house, 206–7, 211, *Fig. 115*

Palazzo Zorzi at S. Severo, 89–90

Piazza San Marco, 36, 46, 50, 52, 53, 55–6, 80, 110, 125, 128–30, 139, 150, 165, 184–5, 197, 215–7, 219, 226, 227, *Figs. 10, 63, 75*, plan p. 148

Piazzale Roma, 228, 231, 237

Piazzetta, 80, 125, 146, 147, 150, *Fig. 9*, plan p.148

Piazzetta dei Leoncini, 57, 220

Pietà hospital and church, 169, 200–2, *Figs. 109–10*, plan p. 202

Ponte dell'Accademia, 48, 221, 228

Ponte di Ghetto Nuovo, 221, *Fig. 125*

Venice, *contd*

Ponte della Libertà, 228

Ponte di Rialto, *see* Venice, Rialto Bridge

Ponte degli Scalzi, 48, 221, 228

Porta della Carta, 108, 110, 125

Prisons, 110, 145

Procuratie Nuove, 129, 184–5, 215–6

Procuratie Vecchie, 43, 129–30, 131, 152, 216, *Figs. 63, 65,* 119

Redentore, 117, 158, 169–73, 178, 179, 181, 182, 199, *Figs. 89–91,* plan p. 171

Rialto, 15, 49, 51, 52, 55, 70, 125, 129, 130–1, 222, 223; *see also* Rivo Alto; Bridge, 46–8, 49, 50, 154, 161; market, 26, 52, 53, 130–1, 136, *Fig. 66*

Rio di Ca'Foscari, 230, 231, 233, *Fig. 133*

Rio Nuovo, 231, 234

Rio dell'Osmarin, 91

Rio di S. Anna, 214

Rio di S. Barnaba, 187–8

Rio Terà di S. Agnese, 220, *Fig. 124*

Riva degli Schiavoni, 40

Salizzada S. Lio, 42, 51, 53, *Fig. 15*

Salute, *see* Venice, Sta. Maria della Salute

S. Fantin, 209

S. Felice, 48, 222

S. Francesco del Deserto, 74

S. Francesco della Vigna, 74, 157–9, 163, 166, 167, 169, 170, 172, 197, 214, *Figs. 82 and 86,* plan p.159

S. Geminiano, 150, 163, 185, 189, 215–6

S. Giacomo all'Orio, 76, 83

S. Giacomo di Rialto (S. Giacometto), 25–7, 30, 31, 118, *Fig. 5,* plan p. 26

S. Giobbe, 112–3, 118, 127, 157–8, 169, 172, *Fig. 54*

S. Giorgio Maggiore, 69, 103, 117, 158, 163–9, 170, 171, 181, 182, 183, 185, 197, 199, 217, *Figs. 87–8,* plan p.166; library, 103, 104, 185, 188; lighthouse towers, 217, *Fig. 120;* monastery staircase, 185–6, 188, 203, *Fig. 95,* refectory, 160, 164, 185

S. Giovanni in Bragora, 76, *Fig. 35*

S. Giovanni Crisostomo, 36, 51, 114, 118, 119–20, *Fig. 60*

S. Giovanni di Malta, 159

Sti. Giovanni e Paolo, 70–74, 75, 89, 96, 99, 107, 163, *Figs. 30–1,* plan p.71

S. Girolamo, 195, 224

S. Giuliano, 140, 163

S. Lazzaro dei Mendicanti, *see* Venice, Mendicanti hospital and church

S. Lorenzo, 175–6

Sta. Lucia, 221

S. Marco, Basilica di, 17, 20, 25, 27–35, 44, 72, 76, 77, 79, 83, 103, 108, 114, 116, 118, 121, 127, 136, 139, 140, 150, 152, 157, 159, 163, 165, 169, 170, 181, 182, 184, 197, 215, 216, 220, *Figs. 6–10 and* 75, plan p.28

S. Marco, island of, 49, 70

Sta. Maria della Fava, 199–200

Sta. Maria Formosa, 115, 118–9, 120,

Venice, *contd*

Figs. 58–9, plan p.119

Sta. Maria del Giglio, 190–2, 194, 222, *Fig. 100*

Sta. Maria Gloriosa dei Frari, 74–76, 89, 99, 133, 158, 163, 214, *Figs. 32–3*

Sta. Maria dei Miracoli, 113–4, 117, 118, 127, 163, *Fig. 55*

Sta. Maria della Pietà, *see* Venice, Pietà hospital and church

Sta. Maria della Salute, 178–184, 188, 189, 192, 199, 216, 226, 245 n.7, *Figs. 93–4,* plan p. 183

Sta. Maria degli Scalzi, 189–90, *Fig. 99*

Sta. Marta, 223, 225

S. Maurizio, 216, *Fig. 119*

S. Michele in Isola, 115–7, 120, 121, 122, 127, 145, 158, 163, 165, 216, *Fig. 56*

S. Moisè, 191–2, 194, 222, *Fig. 101*

S. Nicolò di Lido, 31, 141, 225

S. Nicolò da Tolentino, 174, 197–8, 199, 206, *Fig. 105*

S. Pietro di Castello, 27–8, 49, 72, 115, 117–8, 178, 214, 245 n.29, *Fig. 57*

S. Salvatore, 17, 131–3, 163, 167, 189, *Fig. 98,* plan p.130

S. Simeon Piccolo, 198–9, 206, *Fig. 106*

S. Stae (S. Eustachio), 195–6, 200, *Figs. 102–3*

Sto. Stefano, 76, 83, 163, *Fig. 34*

Sto. Spirito in Isola, 131

S. Tomà, 36

S. Vidal, 57, 197

S. Zaccaria, 103, 121, 182

Scala del Bovolo, Palazzo Contarini, 63, *Fig. 27*

Scala dei Giganti, Palazzo Ducale, 110

Scala d'Oro, Palazzo Ducale, 161

Scuole (guilds), 69, 97–101, 214 Piccole, 97–8, 101, 133; Grandi, 97, 98–101

Scuola dei Calegheri at S. Tomà, 101, *Fig. 47*

Scuola Grande della Carità, 97, 99–100, 161, 218

Scuola Grande di S. Giovanni Evangelista, 97, 114, 122, 185, *Fig. 61*

Scuola Grande di San Marco, 97, 114, 115, 121–2, 185, *Fig. 30*

Scuola Grande della Misericordia, 97, 100–101, 241 n.38, *Fig. 46*

Scuola Grande di S. Rocco, 97, 133–5, 150, 165, 178, *Figs. 67–8,* plan p.135

Scuola Grande di S. Teodoro, 97, 187, *Fig. 98*

Scuola di S. Orsola, 72

Società Adriatica di Elettricità, headquarters, 234, *Fig. 137*

Slaughterhouse at S. Giobbe, 221, 235–6

Stazione Marittima, 223

Stazione di Sta. Lucia (rail terminal), 48, 221, 222, 224, 233–4, *Fig. 136*

Strada Nova, 222

Teatro la Fenice, 209–12, *Figs. 116–7,* plan p.210

Teatro S. Benedetto, 209

Venice, *contd*
  Terra Nova granaries, 215, 225
  Torre dell'Orologio, 124–5, *Figs. 63–4*
  Tronchetto, 237
  Via Eugenia, now Via Garibaldi, 214
  Via Sandro Gallo, Lido, 215
  Via 22 Marzo, 222, *Fig. 126*
  Via Vittore Emmanuele II, *see* Venice, Strada Nova
  Villa Monplaisir, Lido, 227
  Villa Rossi, Lido, 229
  University, *see* Venice, Ca' Foscari
  Zattere, 159, 170, 216, 220, 223
  Zecca 144–5, 146, 147, 150, 151, 154, *Figs. 71–4*
  Zitelle, 183, 226
Verdi, Giuseppe, 15, 212
Verona, 57, 67, 104, 116, 131, 135, 137, 138, 139, 153, 157, 213
  Castello, 233
  Madonna di Campagna, 180
  Palazzo Canossa, 154
  Palazzo del Podestà, 139
  S. Fermo, 76
  S. Zeno, 76
Veronese, Paolo, 148
Verrocchio, Andrea, 106
Vetti, Luigi, 234

Vicenza, 67, 153, 160
  Basilica, 83, 210
  Monte Berico, 181
  S. Lorenzo, 72
  Sta. Corona, 71
Victor Emmanuel II, King of Italy, 222
Vienna, 208, 213, 219
Vignola, Giacomo Barozzi da, 48, 169, 172
Visentini, Antonio, 205–6, 208
Vitruvius, 136, 147, 157, 161, 171, 184, 206
Vittoria, Alessandro, 174, 176
Vivaldi, Antonio, 201

Wagner, Richard, 123, 212
Water supply, 63, 231
Waterways authority, 140, 196
Wittkower, Rudolf, 181, 182, 183
Wood, Robert, 206
Wood, use of, 37, 58
Wren, Sir Christopher, 131
Wright, Frank Lloyd, 233
Wullekopf, Ernst, 224–5

Zeno, Soramador, 92
Ziani, Doge Sebastiano, 36, 43, 80, 81, 129
Zorzi, Fra Francesco, 158
  Marco, 122
Zuan di Franza, 92